Dear Justin,
Here's to allowing the light
that you are to shine very

LIGHTING THE WAY:

Metaphysical Perspectives on

Navigating the Human Experience

by

Rev. Rosanne Bonomo Crago

brightly, illuminating your
path for your highest + best
good.

Love,
Rosanne

ACKNOWLEDGEMENTS

The reading I had done by Jo'Ann Ruhl opened the flood-gates for me to begin to understand my own spiritual journey. Jo'Ann recommended Alan Cohen's book, "A Deep Breath of Life – Daily Inspirations for Heart Centered Living." I have been reading a page from this book daily since April 2002, and these pages have become the inspiration for so many of the talks in this book. Oprah and Deepak Chopra's 21 Day Meditation Series' have provided tremendous guidance and insight. The classes I took from Rev. David Miller and a number of other teachers at United Fellowship Chapel in Tucson, Arizona, helped to guide me on my path. I continue to be inspired by my co-founders at Community of Light. Our talks and meditations are recorded and available on our website. (www.thecommunityoflight.org)

My former partner, Clyde M. Feldman, Ph.D., listened to each of these talks, and helped me edit them to bring them to their best form.

My dad, Ralph Bonomo, taught me more than I will ever know. His comment after hearing each of my talks was, "It was very good. Could you make it a little shorter."

DEDICATION

To Marie, who kept telling me, "They're SO good. When are you going to put them in a book?" This is for you with love.

INTRODUCTION

Lighting the Way – Metaphysical Perspectives on Navigating the Human Experience is a series of 75 talks that use wisdom, insight, and humor to look at many of life's experiences that each of us deals with on a daily basis. As a metaphysical minister for the last ten years, writing what is true for me seems to have a wide range of appeal. Covering topics that include Life, Love, Hope, Changes, Patience, Integrity, the Twelve Mind Powers and beyond, each talk reflects a journey of spiritual exploration. Even though some have similar titles, each one is unique. Incorporating personal experience to illustrate metaphysical principles, these thought-provoking talks support you on your own personal journey. The talks are presented in chronological order of when they were written. Read one a time. Read them all. Choose whichever one you are guided to choose. Consider me your Inner Light Coach, guiding you on your own path of exploration, as you choose whichever topic speaks to you on any given day.

CONTENTS

UNDERSTANDING AND IMAGINATION

12/14/08

I UNDERSTAND. Think about how powerful it is to either say or hear those words. It's a point of connection for people. I feel comforted when someone says it to me. It washes over me like warm water. When I say it to someone else, it means I reach into experiences I have had or thoughts and have a feeling wash over me of connection. I remember reading the book, Stranger in a Strange Land by Robert Heinlein when I was a teenager – the expression used in that book was to "grok" something – that was to understand it completely – physically, psychologically, emotionally, experientially – as fully as a human being could comprehend something. In order to say I understand, we must either have had a similar kind of experience or be able to imagine what the other person is going through. Understanding comes upon us in different levels. We can say, "I see," and understand in our heads, on some level. Or we can really "get it." Fully and deeply. Sometimes understanding grows with us. When I was growing up, there was a sign we passed often on the side of the highway that said, "Mom, if we lived here, we'd be home now." At age 6, I didn't understand what that meant at all. It took me years to figure out what it meant, and now it seems funny that I didn't get it the first time around. In the thesaurus, understand can also mean appreciate, know, recognize, comprehend, realize, be aware of, value, identify with, empathize, grasp, get it. Those are some words to ponder as we think about understanding. Physically, understanding is represented by the feet. Think about taking a step back so that you can see something more clearly, see the bigger picture. When you only look at one piece of a puzzle, you can only see that piece. When you step back, you can see the whole picture and then the single piece makes sense in a whole different way. Understanding, as all aspects of development, evolves continually. When we are young, we learn about everything and our understanding develops as we grow. As babies, we learn that when we cry, mom comes and picks us up and takes care of us. Eventually, we understand the concept of "mother" in many different ways. When I was learning to dance, my understanding developed gradually. I learned how to move my body. I already understood how to listen to music. I learned the steps. Eventually, I understood about connection and following. That continues to grow all the time. When I was learning to do Reiki and healing, I learned to open myself up to the energy, learned how and where to place my hands on the person I was working on. I felt the flow of energy and it kind of unnerved me at first. As soon as I felt it, I would move my hands to another part of the person's body. Now, I understand much better about energy flow and what happens in my body and in the other person's body. I feel comfortable. I allow energy to flow easily and freely. I understand about getting out of the way and allowing the process to work. I understand the messages that come up for me on some level. As I share them with the person I'm working on, they understand them for themselves. Two of the things I've come to understand better and better since studying metaphysics are gratitude and forgiveness. They are both important components of every day for me. I am so grateful for so many things in my life. I give thanks every day for so many things. I can't IMAGINE my life without gratitude. I find ways to be grateful for everything. Even if I experience physical sensations that are less than pleasant, I am grateful for the things I am releasing and the ways in which I am moving forward on my path. Several months ago, a good friend of mine gave me a gratitude journal. I held on to it for a while, then finally opened it one day. It said a lot about the power of gratitude to transform our lives. It's easy to be grateful when our lives "hum", more challenging to be grateful when the road gets rocky. The suggestion is to use the journal to write down five things you're grateful for each day. I started doing that last summer, and it has made such a difference in my life. I notice that some days it's really hard to think about what I'm grateful for. Once I start, though – the energy starts flowing and I realize how many things I'm grateful for in the course of a day. Some days, I even write down more than five things. As I look back at the entries over time, some themes emerge. I'm always grateful for my amazing friends, who get me through the good times and the bad and who understand me even when I don't understand myself so well. Forgiveness is one of the most powerful things in my life. It is especially important to remember to forgive myself, always for everything. "I forgive you" are three very powerful words to use and remember. The mind powers are all connected. Wisdom and order come into play in understanding. You have to be wise enough to accept your understanding of a concept or situation. You have to understand that things unfold in divine order – in their own time and in the proper sequence. If you put your shoes on before you put your socks on, that's not going to work out very well for you. Understanding involves paying attention – noticing when things come out and how they affect the way that you "get" things. Allowing is important in understanding also. Letting information come to you and allowing and accepting it is a gift to be appreciated. Understanding comes to us in many different ways. Sometimes the way someone says something just makes sense. Sometimes we have to be ready to hear and/or receive the information. Sometimes understanding is reflected back to us by people in our lives. A good friend of mine was talking about something she had bought in a Hallmark store, and I sarcastically remarked, "Oh, I don't go into Hallmark stores, they're too schmaltzy and sappy." She is my friend because she sees through to the center of me and she said – Oh, you mean it's really romantic and seeing those things reminds you of how much you want romance in your life. I really appreciate the ways in which she understands me and sees through the outer shell to the soft center. It's important to pay attention to the people and things in our lives that cause us challenge, irritation, frustration – what are we learning about ourselves in this process? If I'm constantly coming into contact with stupid, careless or inconsiderate drivers – what do I need to be looking at in my own choices and behaviors. What am I creating? Another thing that helps with understanding is talking about what you learn. When you explain something to someone else, you acquire a much deeper understanding of it yourself. If someone asks you to define a word, even though it's a word you're accustomed to hearing – you have to think about it in a different way in order to explain it well to someone else. It's a growth process. Change is something I've come to understand and appreciate. It used to be really hard for me to accept changes and sometimes hard for me to make changes. Today, I embrace and appreciate the opportunities that are presented to me to do things differently. Sometimes, I experiment with trying something new. I love to go out dancing and I want to dance a lot when I'm there. So, I often ask guys to dance. Some nights, I sit more quietly and wait to see who might ask me and what the experience is like. Some nights, I sit anxiously. Some nights, I'm able to sit and feel inviting. It's interesting to examine the results and increase my understanding. As I grow in understanding, sometimes I'm able to look back at situations and experiences in the past and understand them in a different way. As I gain knowledge, sometimes I can look back and say – That's why I created that EFFECT. This behavior of mine was the CAUSE. I didn't make room for that person to give me anything – that's why I didn't get much from him. If you can see it, you can be it. Our imagination is at work all the time, constantly. Every thought, every idea that comes into our minds

uses our imagination. When we're getting ready to go out or go to work or do anything, we imagine the situation. When I think of my ideal partner, I am using my imagination. When I want to try something new, I imagine it ahead of time. I've been working on a stand up comedy routine, so I imagine myself on stage, saying funny things and making people laugh. When I dance in a competition, I imagine connecting with my partner, really hearing and feeling the nuances in the music, and having lots of fun. Something that is hard for me to imagine is what life will be like without my parents. I'm so lucky – my dad is 100 and my mom is 86. I really can't imagine what it's going to be like when I can't pick up the phone and talk to them every day and can't visit them frequently. I can only imagine that it will be very different. And I understand that it will open up new and different doorways that will bring different things into my life. When I think about my dad and the things he's seen change in his lifetime, it's hard to imagine. He was born in 1908. So, I called him and asked him to tell me about some of the things he couldn't have imagined when he was young. Here are some of the things he shared with me. TV, computers, atomic bombs, a country like Israel coming out of nowhere in 1948 - I never thought it was possible. Social security and unemployment insurance were things no one ever thought of. All the different types of automobiles – there were hardly any in my youth, and I knew all the names of all the makes and models – now, there are all kinds of beautiful vehicles, and there are no more horses or horse shit in the street. Coming out of the service (in WWII), and getting
the right to get an education. Jet engines, going to the moon – that was unthought of, unheard of, unimaginable in those days. The growth in population, the amount of homes that have been built, the number of people getting an education and the cost of getting an education – it's out of sight. Gambling and casinos. The world of clothing and fashion – the people who wear the type of clothing they do today. They are better groomed than they were in those days – the apparel, the

shoes, everything connected with a person was unimaginable in my youth. Who would have thought that a transcontinental road from east to west and north to south would be built – those are real achievements. The prison system – they allow people - husband and wife - to meet and have a love feast. There are so many changes in the type of warfare today – they don't use people, they use robots and they use missiles. The strides they have made in medicine – in WWI, more people died of disease than any other war. Today, it's different, someone gets wounded and they fly them to a hospital a thousand miles away to get treated. The jet age – no one knew what it was to ride in an airplane, now there's hardly a person who hasn't been in an airplane. The roads and people who travel – there are hotels everywhere. Who ever thought of a United Nations – nations getting together once a year to discuss the problems of the world. Nations now talk to one another – in my day they went to war. How many people died from health reasons, not from ammunition – malaria was discovered during WWI. Those are some of the things that were unimaginable in the last 50 to 100 years. Imagine what may happen in our lifetimes that we haven't even thought of yet. Let's let our consciousness be full and expansive. Entertain thoughts and ideas even if they seem preposterous at this moment. You can't imagine what might occur.

BEING WHOLE

2/1/09

At the beginning of each service, we affirm enthusiastically: I am that I am the light of the living God and therefore I am free and all knowing. Ignite my soul with thy spirit, oh God I pray. Are you willing to live that statement? I am the light of the living God. I AM. This is an acknowledgment of the god within us. God is in all things and all people. I am God, you are God and we are the light. Having faith in yourself as all knowing ignites the light within you and radiates it out to shine on everyone you come into contact with. I am free and all knowing. I encourage you to live this proudly. Trust in your own inner knowing. Have faith in yourself.

Recently, I was reading a newsletter put out by Scott Kalechstein, who is a pretty amazing character. He describes himself as a full time inspirational speaker, musician, writer, traveling reverend and transformational humorist. I've heard him perform several times and own some of his CD's. I often find that what he has to say is just what is perfect for me to hear at that moment. He speaks from the heart and his words often resonate deeply with me.

Scott was talking about being a seeker, a student of truth, wisdom, and healing. He said that he began to question his status of seeker-hood some years ago, while attending a Course in Miracles conference. He said he had gone to his room to take a nap, then was awakened about ten minutes later by a strong urge to go to a specific workshop. When he arrived at the workshop, where the leader was fielding questions, he raised his hand, told the leader about being awakened, and asked: "Do you have a message for me?"

The answer rocked his world: "Why do you assume that you were guided to come here because you had something to receive? Perhaps you were awakened from sleep because you had something valuable to give."

It is time for each of us to take a giant step - to give up this business of seeking and trust our inner knowing instead.

Seeking can lead to all kinds of teachers, methods, practices, books and workshops. They can all have a positive impact on us, and broaden our horizons. The value in these experiences is the igniting of knowledge within ourselves. We can acknowledge that we are not learning anything new, but more accurately being reminded of what we know – what we came in with. We affirm that we are not broken, but whole and complete and ready to extend our love and gifts to others.

When you are a seeker, no authority figure comes up to you and says – "OK, you're done. You are now a powerful being, whole and complete, with permission to share your gifts and uplift the world." We recognize this and are the ones to tell ourselves that we have everything that is beneficial already inside of us and it is time to share and shine.

If our message to ourselves is that we must become perfect or close to it before we can offer ourselves to God or the world, we may never think that we have arrived at that place. We have the choice to say – I am not perfect, and I choose to give of myself anyway. We may find that in sharing our gifts wholeheartedly, complete with imperfections, that we inspire others to share their gifts as well. We may also choose to understand that we ARE perfect, right now, in this moment, just as we are.

Does it seem outrageous and maybe even a little arrogant to

behold yourself as whole, capable and good enough just as you are? I say go ahead and be outrageous. Believe in yourself. It is time to rise up and give of yourself with all of your heart and soul. If you are waiting till you think you are perfect, you might put it off forever. If you dare to start living as if there is nothing wrong with you, life will meet your dare and put you to work. And in doing God's work, you will be far too busy and happy to spend another moment trying to fix yourself.

Scott says, "We have been napping, you and I, and we have been dreaming a frightening dream. In our nightmare it seemed that we were broken and guilty, and now we are waking up to the truth that we are quite whole and holy beings, warts and all. This is the quantum leap, the end of the illusion of original sin and the opening of the gates to heaven on earth. Please do not wait another moment for permission to enter. It's your own consent you have been waiting for."

I really like Scott's words. As I learn and grow and teach others, I am a very strong proponent of the notion of seeking your own inner guidance. When I give someone a message and they ask me what it means, the first thing I always ask in return is, "It is your message. What does it mean for you?" It is very empowering to know that you have all the answers within yourself. And we do. Lots of times, the messages, readings, or whatever other kinds of guidance we receive are only reminders of what we already know.

In the film Willow, a young man wants to become an apprentice to the village shaman. The wizard says, "If you can answer this question correctly, I will teach you the ancient magic." The wizard extends his hand and asks, "In which finger does the power lie?" Willow makes his choice, and it is incorrect. He then goes off to live his life of adventure and romance and grows over time. Eventually, Willow returns to the village, and the wizard asks him, "What did you want to answer when I gave you the test?"

"I wanted to say, 'The power lies in my own hand.'"

"That was the correct answer," the wizard affirms. "Why did you not say it?"

"I guess I just didn't believe in myself enough," Willow admits.

I encourage you to believe in yourself. To believe you are free and all-knowing.

We are whole and perfect, just as we are, right now, in this moment. Here in my spiritual community, I have learned that messages or guidance from Spirit do not necessarily come with fanfare, but may be only an image, a whisper, a fleeting thought, a notion, a small feeling. I have been learning to pay attention to the little clues. Sometimes, when I'm thinking about calling someone, I take a moment to check in with myself. Sometimes the answer is yes, and sometimes the guidance is to wait for a more opportune time. I encourage you to pay attention to your hunches, even when they don't make sense – follow them and see what transpires.

It may come as a surprise to those of you who only know me in the context of the Chapel, but in the past, I had a tendency to be a little hot-headed and could fly off the handle with small provocation. (When I practiced this talk with my parents yesterday, my mom said – what do you mean the past? It's not nice to lie in church.) One of the ways in which I've grown is to not react instantly and without thinking. I use those hot-headed thoughts as a beacon or guide that I can take a breath, slow down and wait. In the last couple of months, I've had several situations come up where I felt very strongly reactive to something someone said or did. I find that when I wait a while and let it sit and percolate, I'm able to frame my response in a much more positive and constructive way. I'm able to accomplish much more than I would have if I'd just gone with my initial response. I also find that as I let things sit, my thoughts gather in a different way and I come up with different ways to connect with people and communicate far more effectively than I have done in the past. I have learned to trust my inner guidance more and more and it really serves me well.

Breathing is always a good idea. When in doubt, breathe! I find that when I am contemplating whether or not to do something, if I take a breath and wait a moment, the answer becomes very clear to me. I've learned to pay attention to those small clues – a word, a phrase, a sentence. An inner nod or an inner head shake. The more I trust in that inner guidance the better off I am. The all-knowing within you lets you know whether you're in the right place and doing the right thing if you allow yourself to trust yourself.

Another way that I've been allowing my guidance to work is in the way I listen to others. In the past, my tendency has been to argue and be invested in being right. Now, I'm more likely to stop and breathe and listen. Sometimes the answer is not what I wanted to hear or not what I wanted to do, but when I open myself up to these new experiences, I go beyond what I have done before and I grow in my development. I'm not always able to do this right away. Sometimes my old habit of arguing pops up for a minute. As I get more familiar with my new way of listening, it gets easier to stop and breathe and listen and take in the new information and see things in a different light. This talk is the perfect example. When I first wrote it, I just copied Scott's words, then added a few of my own. I asked my teacher if that would be OK and he said he really preferred for people to speak their own words and thoughts. He said that the words that inspired me might not be the words that inspire someone else. I insisted that it felt right, and argued for a little while. Then I stopped and just let it sit. I came home and completely rewrote this talk. I still used Scott's words as the basis and inspiration, but I did a lot more thinking and going beyond for myself. I know that I grew and developed much more by listening to my teacher and using my own thoughts and words to tell you things today. I thank my teacher for reminding me to believe in myself.

Now I encourage you to think about the phrase: It takes one to know one.

I would like you to take a moment to think of someone you admire.

It takes one to know one.

We often use that phrase in a derogatory way, but it works in a positive way too. As you think about someone you admire, affirm for yourself – it takes one to know one and see the qualities in yourself that you admire also. It's another way to affirm your all-knowing and the guidance within you.

In giving up "seeker-hood", faith also comes into play. What do you believe? What and whom do you trust? Do you have faith in God and in the God within you? Do you have faith in yourself as all knowing?

This is illustrated beautifully in one of my favorite movies, The Wizard of Oz. Towards the end of the movie, Dorothy asks Glinda, the Good Witch of the North, if she can help her get home.

Glinda says,"You don't need to be helped any longer. You've always had the power to go back to Kansas."

Dorothy says: "I have?"

The Scarecrow asks: "Then why didn't you tell her?"

And Glinda answers: "Because she wouldn't have believed me. She had to learn it for herself."

We have to learn this for ourselves. We are strong, powerful, competent beings. We are meant to stride forward with ease, shining with light, making a positive impact on those around us.

I encourage you to see yourself as whole and perfect, and keep breathing.

FAITH, HOPE & LOVE

3/22/09

In order to feel like my talk is inspiring – I have to feel inspired by what I say. I would like to share a quote with you that I love:

"When you come to the edge of all the light you know

And are about to step off into the darkness of the unknown

Faith is knowing that one of two things will happen:

There will be something solid to stand on

Or you will be taught to fly."

That inspires me to have faith. It makes me smile and believe all things are possible. And I thought I would be talking to you about Faith today. In thinking about Faith, I looked it up in the Bible. The verse that kept coming up for me is: There are three things that endure: Faith, Hope and Love. So, that's what I'm going to be speaking about today.

When I turn on the light switch, I have faith that the light will come on.

When I put the key in the ignition, I have faith that the car will start and take me where I want to go.

When I dial the phone, I have faith that I will be connected with someone across town, across the country, or across the world.

When I lay my hands on someone, I have faith that divine

unconditional love channels through me to help them heal themselves.

When I stand in front of you, I know I'm saying things that are useful for me to hear, and I have faith that I am guided to say words that are inspiring to you, also.

Some of these are solid steps, and some feel like learning to fly. Some are small steps and some are giant leaps of faith.

When I affirm enthusiastically: I am FREE and ALL-KNOWING – I am igniting the mind power of Faith – Faith is knowing, and knowing is very powerful. When I affirm enthusiastically: I am FREE and ALL-KNOWING – I am igniting light within myself that radiates out and shines brightly – igniting the light in others, also.

As I walk on the path of unfoldment and think about faith, questions arise for me. What do I believe? What and whom do I trust? And why? Do I have faith in God and in the God within me? Do I have faith in myself as all-knowing? Am I good enough?

Having doubts and questions can serve to make us think about things in a different way . . . can motivate us to mine the depths instead of just skimming the surface . . . can stimulate us to go beyond what we have thought or known. Having questions can take us on a journey that brings us to treasures beyond our current imagination. Answering our own questions strengthens our faith.

I choose to trust in what makes the most sense for me at any given moment. If you had asked me seven years ago whether I would be standing here in this position at this time, I would have laughed out loud and said, "I don't think so. You must have me confused with someone else." Yet, here I am, trusting in my knowing that I am in the right place and this is the right time for me and for you. Here I am, trusting in my own divinity. Here I am, trusting in the guidance that comes from Spirit. Here I am having Faith.

When I looked in the thesaurus, I thought it was interesting that trust is a synonym for both faith and hope. Some other synonyms for faith are confidence, reliance, assurance, conviction, and belief. When I hear these words, they feel strong and powerful. It takes strength and power to have faith and believe. We have to be wise in what we believe and what we trust. We rely on Divine Order to know that things unfold in the proper sequence and time. And we infuse all our beliefs with love, the most powerful light of all.

When I was thinking about what to say today, I had a conversation with my friend Andy. I told him I wanted to talk about faith, hope, and love. He talked to me about the connection for him between faith and hope – and his trust or faith that hope is what remains. He then related the story of Pandora's Box. I knew about Pandora opening the box and releasing all kinds of evils, but I didn't know about Hope - which is what remained. He said that was his favorite part of the story – in the midst of pestilence and worry and ills, that Hope remains – sometimes small, but ever present and stalwart – a beacon for us to use as a guide.

When I looked up hope, I read that Hope is a combination of the desire for something and the expectation of receiving it. How I am using the word Hope today is optimistic knowing. It is knowing that all things operate perfectly in Divine Order. And that means – everything, all the time. Order operates perfectly in our lives every moment of every day. It's not some nebulous concept that exists in the stratosphere – it's how the world works – perfectly, even when it doesn't seem that way to our impatient selves. It is knowing that things unfold for our highest and best good. It is knowing that the effects that we experience in our life are caused by our thoughts, words, and actions. The cause is the effect and the effect is the cause.

It seems to me that this is a perfect time to be talking about Optimistic Knowing. If you watch the news or read the newspaper, you may be confronted with thoughts of fear and lack. I use these thoughts as triggers to remind me to hold abundance consciousness, now more than ever.

The universe is perfectly abundant. There is plenty for everyone. This is a YES universe. If you hold thoughts of lack, you draw lack to you. Are those the seeds you want to plant? Is that what you want to harvest? I say dig up that soil, and plant new seeds. If you hold thoughts of prosperity, you draw happiness, health and wealth to you. That is what I choose to plant. That is how abundance works. If you are experiencing feelings of lack, the best thing to do is to start giving something to others. It may not always be money – it may be time, energy, love, words – whatever fits for you in that moment. The important thing is to open the flow by giving. And keep optimistically knowing that everything works out for the best.

If you are wanting more of something in your life, notice where it already exists. If you are wanting more prosperity and abundance, notice where it already exists. Notice how much air there is to breathe. Notice how many birds are singing. Notice how much sunshine we have to enjoy, especially here in Tucson. Notice how many times you smile in the course of a day. Abundance is all around you. The key is allowing it to flow easily to you, and not getting in your own way. I have a good friend who says what he wants in one breath, and in the next breath says why he can't have it. Allow your good to flow to you. You deserve it.

There are three things that endure: Faith, Hope and Love. And the greatest of these is Love. I saved the best for last.

Love ... breathe in and think about love.

It feels so good. There are so many different kinds of love. As

29

you walk through your day, you may enjoy paying attention to the moments when love shows up in your life. If you are wanting more love in your life, notice where it already exists. Notice loving friendships, children, pets – love is all around you.

I LOVE that outfit you're wearing.

I LOVE CHOCOLATE.

I love my little kitty cat.

I have a number of friends that I say "I love you" to on a very regular basis.

I tell my parents that I love them every day.

I tell my daughters that I love them every time I talk to them.

And there is the special someone who looks into your eyes and tells you that he or she loves you.

When I do healing or Reiki, I believe I am a channel for Divine Unconditional Love.

And as I was writing this talk, Whitney Houston's song, "The Greatest Love of All" kept running through my mind. It says, "Learning to love yourself – it is the greatest love of all." I think this is where love proceeds from. As I learn to love myself, everything else falls into place.

Recently, I looked for some guidance in Louise Hay's book, "Heal Your Body." The suggested affirmation was: I release anything unlike love.

These are the words I'd like to leave you with today... Release anything unlike love in your life and move forward gracefully with faith, optimistic knowing, love and ease.

BEGINNING
THROUGH ETERNITY

5/3/09

In the movie, The Sound of Music, Julie Andrews sings – Let's start at the very beginning, a very good place to start. When you read, you begin with A, B, C, when you sing you begin with Do, Re, Mi. It would be nice if everything was that simple. Where do we begin? Some beginnings are concrete. There was a day we began our existence on the earth plane. We had a first day of school. I know the day I became a mother for the first time. I remember the first day I came to this spiritual community. I woke up at a certain time this morning. And let's think about beginnings in broader terms. As metaphysicians, we begin with I am that I am. Every breath we take is a new beginning. Every thought we have is a new beginning. Every change we make is a new beginning. We are changing, growing and reinventing ourselves in each moment.

Our cycle of life consists of forming things from the invisible to the visible, then back to the invisible to begin the cycle again. Birth is the perfect and most powerful example. As our consciousness forms, we come into physical being. We move from the invisible to the visible as we take on a physical form. Our spiritual being and our physical being are points on the same continuum. Our physical being is manifested by our spiritual being. Both are constantly changing. Initially, our physical being is formed by past life experiences. As we grow in this existence on the earth plane, our physical being changes in harmony with our spiritual being. As we change, we release things through our physical being. It is a reflection of our spiritual being. We come into contact with people, places and things, and then make choices based on our spiritual growth.

Everything happens in stages. The egg and sperm come together and then change into something more than just the sum of the two parts. The fetus develops and gradually changes into a viable human being. The baby is born and knows how to breathe, eat, sleep and eliminate. The baby then gradually learns to communicate – not all at once or overnight, but through a process of growth and change. The baby cries and someone takes care of its needs. The baby hears sounds, then imitates them and gets results. It is a process of absorbing what goes on around itself – trying new things, seeing what works.

The baby later learns to sit and crawl and walk – in an orderly fashion – a perfect demonstration of Divine Order – unfolding in just the right time and just the right sequence. And this is different for each person. It is development. And spiritual growth happens in this way, also – in just the right time and just the right sequence that is perfect for each person. I remember one of my first meditations in a class at my spiritual community. I think I fell asleep and I didn't really remember anything. The person next to me (who was ordained later that year) had this whole past life experience with a husband and family and career – and I wondered what was wrong with me. Nothing was wrong with me, I was just at a different place on my path of unfoldment. I encourage you to be gentle, easy and loving with yourself wherever you are on YOUR path – because it is the perfect path for YOU.

Consciousness is the physical world. It is the manifestation of creation, the manifestation from the invisible to the visible. We come into physical existence with all the wisdom of the universe inside us. Through our experiences, that wisdom is ignited. We remember more clearly who and what we are. We remember more clearly who and what we are capable of being and becoming. We remember our purpose for being on the earth plane.

The first Superman movie shows a powerful metaphor for the way we learn our purpose on Earth. Baby Superman is placed in a space capsule by his parents to escape the destruction of their planet. As the infant is hurtling through space, he listens to tapes, preprogrammed by his parents, teaching him about himself and his purpose. The tapes remind him of his origin, his strengths, and his mission on Earth. When he arrives, he is clear about his identity, and he goes about the business of being Superman.

We also arrive on Earth with great innate wisdom, seeded with the knowledge of our purpose. Before our coming into this physical being, we consciously chose, in co-creatorship with Spirit, who we would be and what we would accomplish while we are here.

Unlike Superman, sometimes when we arrive, we forget what we know. We may become distracted by the limits that our physical body imposes on us and the negative messages that may be around us in the world. We wonder what we are supposed to be doing. And as we begin to ask questions, we begin our spiritual journey of remembering who we truly are. We regain the sense of purpose we came to live. We take steps along our path.

The more we connect with Spirit, the more we are able to change in ways that are for our highest and best good. What is your ultimate goal? Mine is to be the best human being I can be while I'm on the earth plane. I want to continue learning and changing and growing all the time. I want to develop physically, mentally, emotionally, and spiritually to the best of my abilities. And then I want to continue learning and growing and developing after I make a transition to the spiritual plane. I want to be able to say with confidence and conviction: I am that I am the light of the living God and therefore I am FREE and ALL-KNOWING. I want to remember who I truly am.

For me, true prayer is communication between myself and Spirit. It is a conversation with God. It starts with gratitude. I thank you for everything and I have no complaint whatsoever. It can consist of sharing, asking for guidance and help, asking for healing for self or others, a sense of joy, a plea for forgiveness – just about anything. True prayer is offered with the intention of love, an expression of love for God and for others and for self. It is offering myself to be connected with Spirit, perfectly.

It is opening myself up to whatever God and the god-self within me has to offer and allowing it to come in.

It is the ultimate connection.

One of the most important things that we pay attention to as metaphysicians is natural law. Natural law is a process of change. What you think, what you say, and what you do is what you draw more of to you. As metaphysicians, we continually go beyond – beyond what we have thought, what we have known, what we have learned. One of the ways this operates for me is really paying attention to my thoughts, words and actions. As I write my talks, I listen to what I'm saying. Is this what I really mean to say? Is this what I want to draw more of into my life? As I have conversations with friends and family, I listen carefully. Lately, I hear a lot of fear and lack in things people are saying. I find myself reminding people frequently of who they truly are. I choose not to read newspapers or listen to the news on radio and TV. If they said anything positive on a consistent basis, I would be happy to give that my attention. I choose to think abundantly.

I was talking to my sister recently and she said she was feeling "down" and worried. In my experience, she is someone who has always lived abundantly and freely. I reminded her of something that happened many years ago involving a pair of very expensive shoes. It made her laugh and reminded her of who she is. I encouraged her to be the kind of person that she wants to attract to her – to be the one who has fun and thinks abundantly. The next day when I talked to her, she thanked me for turning her world around and reminding her of who she truly is.

Another thing I choose to pay a lot of attention to is gratitude. I keep a gratitude journal every night. I write down at least five things that I am grateful for that day. I spend time and really think about my day and what I am grateful for. Sometimes I have a hard time getting started, but once I think of one thing – other things usually flow freely and easily. I look for opportunities to be grateful all the time. Whenever someone does something that I appreciate, I make a point of thanking them. I like to eat in restaurants and enjoy services, and I know that management receives their share of complaints when things go wrong. I do my best to "catch people in the act of doing something right." Whenever a server does a good job, I take the time to tell the manager and express my appreciation. I was really happy with my haircut this month, so I called my hairdresser (who I've been going to for years) to thank her for doing such a good job. Recently, I had a situation of getting some repair work done, and I felt like the company and the technician went out of their way to make everything work out well. I made sure to call and thank them the next morning. It was actually how I started my day and I thought – what a perfect way to start the day – by saying, "Thank you."

I am incredibly grateful for being on the path that I find myself on at this time. I am happy, healthy, and wealthy. I make better and better choices all the time. I am loving and kind and gentle with myself and with others. I am learning and growing and changing and appreciating so much.

We have all the time in the world – literally. Our existence has been forever and goes on forever. We learn at exactly the right pace in exactly the right way. The more we remember that, the easier life is. And that's the way it can be – all about ease.

SPIRITUAL GARDENING – THOUGHTS ON LIFE, DEATH & LOVE

5/31/09

It's springtime and I've been doing some gardening lately – not literally – I actually hate getting dirt under my fingernails – but metaphysically. I've been looking at my thoughts, words, and actions, and the people, places and things in my life. I'm checking in with what's growing strong and healthy, and what needs weeding and pruning. As the Byrds and the Bible say, to everything there is a season. So, here are my thoughts on life, death, and love.

In the last couple of months, I have been aware of quite a few people who have made their transition out of the earth plane. These people have been in varying degrees of proximity to me, and I notice that my response has varied accordingly. There have been people that I've heard about, through friends, and I can nod sagely and say – It was their time. In one case, the transition was made by a four month old baby, and I thought – well, his time on the earth plane was complete very quickly – he was finished with what he needed to do. I felt sorry for the loss that his parents and family experienced, and believe that everything happens in divine order. In one case, the transition was made by the mother of one of my closest friends. I actually knew this woman and had spent time with her when she was healthy, and also near the end of her life when she was in hospice care. She was in her mid-80's and was very ill, and it seemed like her transition was a release and a relief for her. I comforted my friend in her time of loss, and again believe that everything happens in divine order.

In one case, however – the transition was made by someone very close to me. This was a man I had been romantically involved with for about a year and loved. This transition affected me very personally. I think of him often and sometimes feel a stabbing pain when a thought catches me off guard. At other times, I think of him and smile. I think of the things we got to do together, and I think of the things we'll never have the chance to do. He was a very special man. He was the same age as I am, and his "cause of death" was a heart attack.

So, I started thinking about what that means. What happens when the love center of your being comes under attack?

I would like you to point to yourself.

Look around and notice how many of us pointed to our hearts.

In ancient Egypt, when mummifying bodies, the heart was left intact because the Egyptians believed the heart was where the essence of a person resided. Since the Egyptians considered the brain unimportant, it was thrown away.

In the book, The Little Prince (by Antoine de St. Exupery), it says: "It is only with the heart that one can see rightly; what is essential is invisible to the eye."

In Proverbs 3:27, it says, "As a man thinketh in his heart, so is he." This is the basic truth and essence of everything we learn in metaphysics. What you think is what you manifest. If you plant seeds of unhappiness and dis-ease, that is what you harvest. If you plant seeds of prosperity, you are happy, healthy and wealthy. For me, my heart is the foundation of all I am and all I do. My heart guides my thoughts and my actions. Thoughts and actions without heart are empty and meaningless. My heart supports me. It is large and full of love. I let love inspire me on a daily basis.

We are instructed by our doctors and the media on ways to take care of our physical heart. Pay attention to your diet. Do cardiovascular exercise. Avoid excesses like smoking and drinking.

How do we take care of our "heart center?"

In the last seven years, one of the things that I've been doing in that regard is learning to love myself. Just like forming any new habit, learning to love myself requires attention and daily practice. When I took my first Reiki class, my teacher gave us a handout called "Learning to Love Yourself." Here's what it says:

I love and accept myself as I am.

I love my physical body as it is in this moment.

I honor my emotional body and
allow my feelings freedom to flow.

I open to my creative body and
allow my life to flow in bliss and abundance
of happiness, health, wealth, wholeness and love.

I am full of happiness, health,
wealth, wholeness and love.

I allow my Divine Core Essence to surround
and support my being with every breath.

I deserve the best in life.

I have the best in life.

I deserve love.

I have love

And I love myself.

I completely love and accept myself.

I have been saying this out loud every day for the last seven years. It has helped me to develop the habit of loving myself. Now, when thoughts that are unlike love come up for me, I stop and release them, then replace them with thoughts that are kind and loving and gentle and supportive. I feel a lot better these days.

A Course in Miracles affirms that love and fear cannot exist in the same space. Each thought, word, and action comes down to a choice between love and fear. Which do you choose? Choosing love on a consistent basis is another way to take care of our heart center. Sometimes when I'm walking down a steep flight of stairs, I get scared that I'm going to trip and fall. As soon as I notice those kinds of thoughts creeping in, I stop and cancel them out. Then I say, "I am safe. I am protected. I am secure."

My daughter lived in Africa twice in the last several years. People often asked if I was worried about her. I said that when I thought of her, I always thought of her being safe, secure, and protected. I would wrap her in love with my thoughts and send that out to her. She had great experiences while she was there.

We are inundated with love in songs, poems, movies and books. When I put the word "love" in the library search box, 15,808 entries popped up instantly. "Love is a many-splendoured thing," "Love makes the world go 'round," "All you need is love," "The power of love", "Love is letting go of fear" "What I did for love", "Stop in the name of love", "The greatest love of all." I could go on for days.

There is a book that came to my attention in the last year called, "The Five Love Languages" (by Gary Chapman). The premise is that people express and receive love in different ways. It is useful to recognize the ways in which you express love and the ways in which the significant people in your life express love in order to communicate more effectively, and in order to express love and feel loved. The author believes that there are five primary ways that people express love:

Words of Affirmation
Quality Time
Receiving Gifts
Acts of Service
Physical Touch

Words of Affirmation are simple, straightforward compliments and words of appreciation that are specific to the person involved.

Quality Time means giving someone your undivided attention and doing something that has meaning for them.

Receiving Gifts: Gifts are visual symbols of love, and are more important to some people than to others. A gift is something you can hold in your hand and know that someone was both thinking of you, and actually implemented the thought by getting the gift and giving it to you.

Acts of Service involve doing things the other person would like you to do, and expressing your love by doing those things.

Physical Touch is a powerful vehicle for expressing love. Human and animal babies need touch in order to thrive. When we arrive and leave and stand and greet each other here our spiritual community, we hug each other.

These are things you can think about as you interact with

people in your life. If someone is complaining about not feeling loved, perhaps you are speaking different languages. You may need to learn each other's primary "love language" to communicate more effectively.

So, I find my spiritual garden in pretty good shape these days. I like the amount of love that I have in my life. I affirm that divine order is operating perfectly. I weed out those thoughts, words, and actions that no longer serve me, and "tiptoe through the tulips" as gracefully as I possibly can.

CHANGE AND EASE

8/2/09

It's interesting to notice how the metaphysical principles are demonstrated in popular culture. Songwriter John Mayer talks about "waiting on the world to change." Michael Jackson takes a completely different approach. He says:

"I'm starting with the man in the mirror
I'm asking him to change his ways
And no message could have been any clearer
If you want to make the world a better place
Take a look at yourself, and then make a change."

Is there anything you've been wanting to change – either in the world or in your own life?

The way to effect change in your life and in the world is to start with "the man (or woman) in the mirror." We see bumper stickers that advise: Visualize world peace. If you want the world to be a more peaceful place, notice how you talk to the people in your life and how you choose to resolve personal conflicts. Notice how you respond to other drivers in traffic. Notice your ability to quiet your thoughts in order to fall asleep easily and sleep well. Notice your thoughts as you watch television or read the newspaper. If you don't appreciate what you're seeing or hearing, turn the page or turn it off.

As I thought about the way individual actions can change the world, the "butterfly effect" came to mind. When I looked it up online, I read that small variations of the initial condition of a dynamical system may produce large variations in the long term behavior of the system. What this means is that in the same way that a flapping wing can alter the path of a tornado, each of us has the ability to change the world – one breath at a time. In the 12 Step programs, people are encouraged to take things "one day at a time." I always amend that to one BREATH at a time. Sometimes getting through a whole day can seem impossibly daunting. Almost everyone feels able to get through one breath at a time.

The only way to make changes in the universe is to make changes in yourself. And, as you make changes in yourself - you may not be able to do everything at once - start with small incremental steps, then give yourself credit for the small successes. The first time you cook something, it does not necessarily turn out the way it does for Emeril on TV. When I was first learning to dance, I felt awkward and unsure. Now, I feel comfortable and confident to dance with even the most experienced professionals. Spiritual muscles develop in much the same way. As we form new habits, changes occur in our lives. When I first started meditating, I didn't necessarily see or experience much in a conscious way. This has changed gradually over time.

This is the way things happen in our lives. We start with a small change in ourselves - that changes our vibration, then we attract people, places and things of our new vibration to us, and that initiates a chain reaction that allows us to change things in our lives. I was talking to my sister recently, and she was commenting on the fact that she's had to "let go" of a lot of people in her life in the last few years. She questioned whether that reflected a flaw in her ability to judge people's characters. I told her that I thought it was much more of a reflection of the changes that she's made in herself. As she grows and changes and develops, the people around her change. Instead of seeing it as a loss, I encouraged her to see it as a marker of the tremendous growth that she's been experiencing.

It's useful to check in with yourself on a regular basis. Your body is a very reliable indicator of what's going on and what's beneficial for you. Your stomach area and solar plexus chakra area represent wisdom and discernment. When you have a decision or choice to make, check in with your body first and see what your "gut reaction" tells you. If the thought of doing something makes you nauseous, it's a pretty good indicator that it's not the ideal choice for you at that moment. Use your imagination to visualize how your actions will play out. Visualize the situation making first one choice, then another, and see which one plays out in a way that works best for you. See how your body reacts to each scenario, and let that help guide your choice. It's okay to take your time. When someone asks you to do something, it's okay to take your time to either take a breath before answering or to tell them that you need to think about it, and you'll get back to them.

One of my favorite authors is Jill Conner Browne, the Sweet Potato Queen from Jackson, Mississippi. Her wit and wisdom have served me well for years. Her consistent advice is: Be Particular. This applies to any and all situations. It's always a good idea to be particular – in who you associate with, in where you go, in what you do, and even in what you think. Pay attention to your surroundings and the way the people, places and things in your life make you feel. If it's not working for you, change it.

In her most recent book, Jill Conner Browne talks about therapy. She distills it down to this. The patient says, "It hurts when I do this." And the therapist responds, "Don't do that." She says that you can spend thousands of dollars over decades of your life talking to a therapist, but if you actually want to GET BETTER, you have to STOP doing what's making you miserable and START doing something else instead. My spiritual teacher says the same thing – Recognize, release, and replace.

Many of us do a credible job at recognizing what's going on in our lives, and recognizing things that we might want to change. The next step is releasing, and sometimes that presents more of a challenge. The third step is essential – that is replacing. If we don't replace what we've been doing with something different, we just get better at doing what we've already been doing. If we don't form new habits, we just strengthen our old habits.

There is a book I read on a daily basis called, "A Deep Breath of Life – Daily Inspirations for Heart Centered Living" by Alan Cohen. Alan talks about ease. Life is not meant to be a struggle. Think of the power of the affirmation: My life is about ease. This doesn't mean sitting back, being lazy and expecting other people to do everything for you. It means being alive, acting from a place that has meaning for you, and proceeding from joy rather than obligation. Ask yourself, "How would I be doing this differently if I were willing to let it be easy?" As you live this way, you free yourself to have much more creative energy and health. You develop your power to manifest the life you choose, and interestingly enough, serve others much better in the process.

My life is about ease. Take a moment and breathe and think about your life being about ease. One of the things we learn about at our spiritual community is Natural Law. In the book, "The Astonishing Power of Emotions," Esther & Jerry Hicks share some of the teachings of Abraham related to the Law of Attraction, the Law of Creation, and the Law of Allowing. The premise is that we are vibrational beings moving in the Stream of Life. Think about the energy involved in paddling with all your might against the current. Now, imagine turning your canoe downstream and going with the current in the Stream of Well-Being. This is our natural state of being. Allowing yourself to think downstream thoughts keeps you in harmony and balance with who you really are and what you really want. When you flow with the current, your life is about ease.

So:

Start with the person in the mirror
Ask him to change his ways
And no message could have been any clearer
If you want to make the world a better place
Take a look at yourself, and then make a change.

WHICH WOLF DO YOU FEED?

10/04/09

There is a Cherokee legend about a man teaching his grandson about life. "A fight is going on inside me," he said to the boy.

"It is a terrible fight and it is between two wolves. One is anger, envy, sorrow, regret, greed, arrogance, self-pity, guilt, resentment, inferiority, lies, false pride, superiority, and ego." He continued, "The other is joy, peace, love, hope, serenity, humility, kindness, benevolence, empathy, generosity, truth, compassion, and faith. The same fight is going on inside you - and inside every other person, too."

The grandson thought about it for a minute and then asked his grandfather, "Which wolf will win?"

The old Cherokee simply replied, "The one you feed."

Which wolf do you feed? We have a choice in each moment about which wolf we feed. One of the ways this comes up for me is in thinking about what is enough. Do I choose to feed the negative polarity or the positive polarity...the wolf of lack or the wolf of abundance?

I was at lunch at Applebee's the other day, where they have an unlimited soup & salad combo that I enjoy. I ordered what I usually order. As the waiter was clearing the plate, I told him that I just couldn't finish it all. He said something about how they serve you enough to gorge yourself in America and I told him that was what I was going to talk about on Sunday – what is enough?

48

Do you feel like you have enough? Do you feel like you are enough? Do you believe that you have enough time, enough food, enough money, enough love? Am I good enough? How much is enough? As I have said before (I'm pretty consistent as I read back through my talks), the answer lies inside each one of us. If you are not enough, nothing is ever enough.

How do you develop this sense of sufficiency? It can only happen from the inside, and then move outward. Having a bigger house or more money or more clothes or more jewelry or more boyfriends or girlfriends or more of anything external may seem like it will help. I believe the only way to truly fill yourself is with love and from the inside.

I was talking to a friend about her work and she said she thought she'd been passed over for a management position. She said she had helped a friend get another job with the same company, and then that friend had applied for the same management position, without even checking with her first. She said this friend lives in a multi-million dollar house and she probably doesn't "need" this job. As we talked, I realized: if you are not enough, nothing is ever enough.

This same friend was talking about feeling like people were not seeing her worth. This reminded me of a quote one of the other ministers used in her talk a few weeks ago: "We see people and things not as THEY are, but as WE are." How are you seeing things these days?

I told my friend that I thought that if other people were not seeing her worth, it might reflect the fact that they were not seeing their own worth. She recognized the importance of seeing her own worth and valuing herself very highly, because then that would be reflected back to her.

A couple of months ago, I referenced the song, "Man in the Mirror" in my talk. I'm going there again, in a little different way.

What we see in others is a reflection of who we are and who we think we are. If you feel like someone is not seeing your worth accurately or sufficiently, what are you seeing in yourself that is being reflected back to you. What are you seeing in them? What are they seeing in themselves? Do you need to make someone else feel smaller in order to make yourself feel larger?

In thinking about what is enough, I realized that it represents thoughts and feelings of lack. In thinking of recognizing, releasing, and replacing, I realized that I desire to replace these thoughts with thoughts of abundance. One of the ways I do this is through gratitude. One of the affirmations that I say each day is, "I thank you for everything, I have no complaint whatsoever." I also keep a gratitude journal. Each night, I write down at least five things that I am grateful for that day. It's amazing what comes up for me. It's amazing how once I start thinking about what I'm grateful for, other things come pouring out. I sometimes find myself writing all over the page to make room for all the things I'm grateful for. It's very difficult to experience thoughts of lack when you are expressing gratitude.

How are you seeing things these days? Are you seeing your life as full of lack or full of abundance? Are you seeing your life as full of loss or are you acknowledging that you are going through lots of transitions and changes? Are you seeing yourself as lonely or as exquisitely connected to everyone and everything? Are you seeing yourself as enough?

One of my friends has been talking to me about all the losses she has experienced in the last year. She has experienced the transition of her mother, a couple of very significant close relationships, one of her horses, and a very close friend. Another way to frame this is to recognize how much she is changing and that as she releases people and things from her life, she creates opportunities and space for new and better things to come in. She has had some challenges in the past in her relationship with one of her daughters. Since her mother made her transition, her relationship with her daughter has really changed. It has grown and deepened in ways that didn't seem possible once. In order to bring something new into our lives, it is necessary to release something else to make space for the new person, thing, or event to come to us.

As metaphysicians, we are taught to go beyond. I went to a memorial service recently and I loved the way the person's transition was presented. The minister talked about this person's "graduation." I thought that was such a perfect way to think about transitioning from the earth plane to the spiritual plane. In our seminary, one of our assignments has been to create services that go from the cradle to the grave. I am definitely incorporating the notion of graduation into the service I think of as a "Celebration of Life." I spent some time looking up quotes and readings for this type of service. My favorite is: "What the caterpillar perceives is the end, to the butterfly is just the beginning."

How do you think about transitions? When babies come into the world, we generally see this as cause for celebration and joy. When we get a promotion or make money on a beneficial business deal, we see this as cause for celebration and joy. When we or those close to us graduate from each level of school or training, we see this as a cause for celebration and joy. When someone makes a transition to the spiritual plane, it can also be seen as a cause for celebration and joy – even though as the ones still here on the earth plane, we also experience feelings of loss, sadness, and grief. It is important to keep perspective on what this transition means for the person experiencing it. I really like thinking about transition in that way – as a graduation to a new level – a new level of thinking, a new level of being, a new level of developing.

I notice that my father is changing. He is frustrated with not being able to do the things he was once able to do. He doesn't see as well as he once did. He doesn't feel as strong as he once did. He can't walk as far or as fast as he once did. He is, of course, 101 years old. I keep encouraging him to recognize the things that he IS doing, rather than the things he is not able to do. I also recognize that the changes that he is making are preparing him for graduation at some point.

What are you creating? What are you reflecting?

We see things not as they are, but as we are. We are constantly changing, growing and evolving. We do not stay the same – sometimes we just get better at being who we have been. Sometimes we change and are no longer the people we once were.

It's all in how you look at something. You can see the glass as half empty, or you can see the glass as half full, or you can see the glass as full – full of liquid, air, dust, whatever molecules are flying around in there – it's always full, just as we are always full. The question is, what do we choose to fill ourselves with?

I like to think of myself as full of joy and love and life – full of happiness, health and wealth, full of promise and potential, full of spirit.

What is enough? How much is enough? If you fill the space with love from the inside, you will always feel as though you are enough. If you fill the space from the inside, no one can take anything away from you. If you fill yourself with love and spirit, you cannot feel empty. If you fill yourself with love and spirit, you feel like enough, and no one else's perception can affect or change that. If you do not feel like you are enough, nothing can ever be enough.

So, in closing I ask you, which wolf do you feed?

RETHINKING MISTAKES AND PERFECTION

9/13/09

In the last few weeks, some of our speakers have been bringing our attention to words that we often use and helping us think about them in different ways. Today, I want to continue that theme and look a little more closely at "mistakes" and "perfection."

When I looked up "famous mistakes" online, I came up with some interesting examples:

"This 'telephone' has too many shortcomings to be seriously considered as a means of communication. The device is inherently of no value to us." (Western Union internal memo, 1876)

"I think there is a world market for maybe five computers." (The chairman of IBM, 1943)

"There is no reason anyone would want a computer in their home."
(The founder of Digital Equipment Corp. 1977)

"The concept is interesting and well-formed, but in order to earn better than a 'C,' the idea must be feasible."
(Yale professor in response to a paper proposing reliable overnight delivery written by the man who later founded FedEx.)

"If I had thought about it, I wouldn't have done the experiment. The literature was full of examples that said you can't do this."
(written about the development of the unique adhesives for "Post-Its")
Henry Ford forgot to put a reverse gear on his first automobile.
Albert Einstein's parents were told he might be mentally retarded.
Napoleon finished near the bottom of his military school class.
The Beatles were turned down for a recording contract by Decca Records.
One of the other ministers talked about how we learn to define words, and the way that words can trigger emotions in us. Mistakes and perfection definitely fall into that category for me.

The other day in class, my teacher said something that really caught my attention. He said that when you read something and there's a "typo," it causes you to think about the words much more carefully than you might have if it was all typed correctly. He had done the newsletter for the spiritual community and had written Know THE Self, instead of Know Thy Self, as the name of one of the classes being offered. This "mistake" made others pay closer attention to what was written and made him think about what he was actually going to teach during that class. It was no "mistake."

I started thinking about the way this impacts me. I definitely notice "mistakes," especially when I'm reading. In the past, I would hear a very critical voice in my head saying – what's wrong with people, don't they have editors, don't they use spell check, don't they read their own writing. I'm now thinking about this as an opportunity to think about things more fully and deeply and in new ways. I still notice the "typos," I've just given myself permission to think about them differently.

I can be really handy with a red pen. Whenever anyone needed something edited, I would be the first one they'd call. I lived with two different men while they got their Ph.D.'s, and edited everything they wrote. I've been really good at finding mistakes. I've been really good at finding fault. I've been really good at picking things apart. Some might say I'm a "perfectionist." And where did I learn this?

When I was growing up, it was not okay to make mistakes in my family. I took piano lessons and practiced, and then when my dad came home from work, I would be so excited to show him what I'd learned. I'd play my little piece and his response was: "Do you know how many mistakes you made?" I always felt crushed when he said that. Even now, when I talk to him, he sometimes interrupts me to tell me how many times I've used the phrase, "you know" in my sentence. I believe that his intentions were to teach me, but the effect was not particularly positive for me.

I notice that often my first reaction to something or someone is to immediately find all the faults. It's definitely been my first reaction to myself. I've gotten a lot better at encouraging other people to be gentle and loving and easier with themselves. I'm working on putting that into practice when I look into the mirror and when I think about and talk to myself.

As a parent, I decided that I would teach my kids a different way of thinking about things. I told them that mistakes are your friends because you learn from them. I told them it was OK to try things and that if at first you didn't succeed, it was OK to keep at it. I encourage my children and my friends to give themselves credit for small, incremental steps on the way to learning new things and making changes.

I recently ran into a man that headed the department that my then-husband worked for at the University. These two men did not see eye to eye on almost anything. My husband's experience was that this man was very obstinate and refused to consider any of the possibilities that my husband wanted to put into practice. It made life difficult for him at the time. Because of this opposition, my husband moved his career in an entirely different direction that ultimately benefited him so much more than his original path might have done. Mu husband said he'd always wanted to write the man a thank-you note because his obstructions ended up being the best thing that could have happened. It was no "mistake."

I also thought about the story of Joseph in the Bible. Joseph's brothers resented him so much that they thought about killing him or leaving him in the bottom of a well. Instead, they ended up selling him to a caravan of travelers. Ultimately, Joseph became one of the most powerful men in Egypt and was able to save his family during a time of famine. Did Joseph's brothers make a "mistake" in what they did? Or was their choice perfect in moving Joseph forward on his path.

I have a couple of friends who've had babies in the last several years, that they describe as "accidents," or at the very least, unplanned. Are there ever really any accidents? In both cases, the children have enriched their lives in ways that they couldn't have imagined.

Coming to the chapel and learning about metaphysics has really changed my views about words like mistakes and perfection. We were talking about the word perfect in class one day. Traditionally, perfect means that no more change is needed. However, we know that change is constant and conditions don't exist where no more change ever occurs.

People often say to me, "Nothing's perfect." And I always reply, "Everything's perfect." We are constantly creating our lives, perfectly. We reap what we sow. Our thoughts, words, and actions create our experiences. We have spiritual, emotional, mental, and physical bodies. We process our experiences at each of these levels. If they do not get resolved, they are expressed physically. When we express things physically, it means that we have gone through an experience and are releasing it. We are changing and growing and moving forward. I always encourage people to thank their illness or injury and move on.

Earlier, I mentioned the notion that I might be considered a "perfectionist." This often means that one constantly finds flaws and errors that other people have overlooked. If there are many aspects of a job that are well done, and one that isn't, they will focus on that one. In truth, they are "imperfectionists." If they were "perfectionists," they would find perfection everywhere, instead of finding the "mistakes."

What does the word "perfect" mean to you? Before studying metaphysics, I might have thought that perfect meant that nothing needed to be changed and that the food or the art or the moment could not possibly be improved on in any way and should stay exactly the way it was. I think a little differently about the word perfect now. I think everything is perfect – we create perfectly in our lives, according to our thoughts, words, actions, and experiences. What we give our attention to is what we draw more of into our lives.

And it's all in our perception anyway. If you like onions and your food has an abundance of them, you might think, "This is perfect." But if you don't like onions, and your food has an abundance of them, you might wonder what people were thinking putting in all those onions, and ruining a perfectly good meal.

Sometimes, our "mistakes" are the parts of our experiences that make us most truly and uniquely who we are. The important thing is not whatever "mistakes" you make, but how you look at them and what you do with the knowledge that

Rev. Rosanne Bonomo Crago

they ignite in you.

REALIGNING

1/10/10

I went to the chiropractor this week and got an adjustment. It had been about six months since my last adjustment, and my alignment was definitely out of whack. After the adjustment, I felt kind of sore for a little while. It took some time for my body to feel comfortable with being realigned correctly, even though, in the long run, being aligned correctly feels better and is healthier for me. I notice that in the process of getting adjusted, sometimes I tense up a little bit more and have to remind myself to just relax and breathe, and then everything falls into place more easily. I still have all the same parts – muscles, bones, nerves, etc. It's just that they're lined up a little differently now.

I notice the same thing with spiritual alignment. When I'm in the process of forming new habits, or realigning in ways that are healthier for me, I feel uncomfortable for a while. It takes time to adjust to new habits. Even though I have everything it takes to develop in healthy ways already inside me, sometimes I have to realign things so that they function more effectively. When I stand up to give messages, I wonder whether the words I say will be accurate and useful to the person receiving the message. As I develop, I become more and more confident in this process. Sometimes, people come up to me after getting a message to affirm that I'm on the right track. That helps with my realignment, also.

At this time of year, I like to take stock of what might be useful for me to realign. Once again, it appears that I am choosing to learn lessons in patience. It seems that I still get easily frustrated and feel impatient at times. My parents have come to stay in Tucson for the winter and this provides me with many opportunities to practice being patient. The more I stay mindful of love and gratitude, the more I am able to be patient.

Breathing helps. Allowing myself enough time to accomplish what I want to accomplish helps, too. Being realistic in my expectations is also important. I've been doing a dance called West Coast Swing for almost nine years. These days, it's easy and comfortable for me to do this dance. The other night, I went to an Argentine tango class for the first time. This is not a dance that I'm very familiar with. I like the music. I understand about moving on the beat. No problem. But the body position and the way to move and follow what's being lead are totally different and really unfamiliar to me. I felt so uncomfortable. My tendency is to want to give up and just stay with doing what I already know and what already feels comfortable. On another level, though, I understand that if I'm patient with myself and give myself some time, I may grow to enjoy this new dance as much as I enjoy West Coast Swing. I may grow to feel just as comfortable. It helps to remember that when I first started doing West Coast Swing, I felt like Lucille Ball in her husband Desi's chorus line, completely out of place, out of sync, and out of my element. I remember after about six months of taking classes in West Coast Swing, things finally started to click for me, and I "got it" about what I was supposed to be doing. I started to feel more and more comfortable after that.

This is the same process that I go through with spiritual development. When I first started meditating, not much happened that I was aware of. I think I fell asleep more often than not. As time went on, I started receiving more images and "knowings" that made more and more sense to me, and were things I could use on my path of spiritual unfoldment. I've gotten better and better at allowing information to come through to me. I continue to do affirmations on a daily basis. The more "out of alignment" I feel, the more I do my affirmations. That helps with my spiritual realignment. One thing I feel consistently good about is paying attention to my thoughts, words, and actions. I often find myself noticing what other people say, also.

I was talking to a friend of mine the other day, and he said that one of the things he appreciated about me was the way that I made the metaphysical principles applicable to daily life. Keeping them somewhere out in the stratosphere doesn't seem that useful to me. What works for me is to understand them and put them into practice on a daily basis.

Last week, one of the other ministers was talking about how her mother instinctively knew the metaphysical principles. I had a similar experience in my family – I often heard my mother say, "Mama used to say..." and then she would relate adages from my little Italian grandmother for every occasion. One that I distinctly remember was, "Che ti manie, ti ingrida," which loosely translates, "Whatever you put your hands in, you get full of." The first time I remember hearing my mother say this to me, I was making a lemon meringue pie. What I now realize is that this is the distillation of the law of attraction: what you think, what you say and what you do is what you draw more of to you. Apparently, my grandma was able to verbalize that very clearly and instinctively.

Going back to paying attention to words, I have a friend who uses the expression, "I love him to death." That always struck me as strange, and finally, I said something the other day. Why would you possibly want to love someone or something to "death?" Why would you want to create that experience in your life? Doesn't it make much more sense to love someone so much, or just the way they are, or to the ends of the earth, or love them to heaven – or anything other than loving them to death? I have another friend who uses the expression, "It was such a kill," when she has an experience that is really positive and/or exciting for her. That's another one that makes no sense to me. And on one of the dance shows on television, the judge will sometimes say, "You killed that," to indicate that the performance was spectacular. What words are you saying that reflect what you want to be creating in your life and what words could use some adjustment and realignment?

I've been asking myself: What do I want to create in this new year and new decade? The word mindfulness has come to my attention several times recently. One of my best friends gave me a book about mindfulness, and I've been reading a page from it each day, and pondering the concept. How do I form the habit of being more mindful on a day to day basis? Breathing helps. When I take a breath before thinking, saying or doing anything, I am able to be more present and more mindful. I know that my tendency is to multi-task, and I'm certainly good at that, so I do my best to give my attention to one thing at a time and be more present and mindful of what I'm doing in each moment.

From time to time, my sister will call and say, "Can you talk me down?" What she means by this is: can I remind her of what is healthy and positive for her to be thinking, saying, and doing at that moment. Can I remind her of who she really is and who she aspires to be. Can I help her realign herself in ways that are healthy and pleasant, and for her highest and best good. I was describing this to a friend recently, and he asked me who "talks me down" when I'm feeling that way. I told him that I have some very good friends that I rely on to do just that. I also told him that much of the time, I'm able to "talk myself down." The reason for this is because of all that I have learned through studying the metaphysical principles. I know that what I think, say, and do is what I draw more of to myself. If I want to feel happy and positive, I focus on what I am most grateful for and all the love that is in my life. I know that when I'm feeling a little "out of whack," doing affirmations helps me to realign myself.

What kinds of things can you do to remind yourself of who you truly are? I believe that we are spiritual beings having a physical, human experience. The more I connect with that notion, the better I feel. I understand that everything that happens is transitory and that every experience – positive and negative – comes under the heading of, "This too shall pass." I also know that I create all of my experiences and that I always have a choice in how I respond to any situation.

I've also been thinking about the concept of perspective. Just like using a camera, we have a choice of which lens to use when we focus our attention. Do I want to use the wide angle lens or the telephoto lens in any given situation? It's not a right or wrong answer, but more a matter of choice. We are always free to choose our response to any event or situation or encounter. How do we frame it? How do we react or respond to it? What do we choose to think, say or do? Do I want to focus on the details or step back and see the bigger picture? Whichever lens I choose, I do my best to choose love, gratitude, and forgiveness as often as possible. In doing that, I consistently realign myself for my highest and best good.

AND...BACK TO THE LOVING PLACE

2/14/10

Ellen Degeneres has a comedy routine where she talks about getting in touch with spirituality and meditating, then one thing after another pulls her off center, and she keeps having to remind herself "and...back to the loving place." After coming to meditations or services at my spiritual community, I would often find myself getting aggravated in traffic within moments of leaving – I would smile, then say to myself: "And... back to the loving place." How do we get back to our loving place?

Valentine's Day is certainly a time of year and a day when love is prominent in the media and hopefully residing peacefully in our hearts. As we listen to songs, read books, and watch movies, we get to choose how we want to think about love and how we want love to operate in our life. As I was pondering my words for today, some songs about love popped into my head: Put a Little Love in Your Heart, All You Need is Love, Where is Love, Love is All Around, What's Love Got to Do with It, Don't You Want Somebody to Love, The Power of Love, Love Makes the World Go Round, Stop in the Name of Love, The Greatest Love of All. How do we choose to think about love? How do we bring love into our lives? How do we get "back to the loving place?"

When I do Reiki or healing, I believe I channel Divine Unconditional Love. I believe that unconditional love is available to us at all times from the god-self within us. It is our choice whether or not to tune into it and accept it as our own. As humans, the love we feel and express is often conditional in some way. I'm feeling very blessed today to have my parents and my sister here in the chapel – people who I love and cherish very much. The love I feel for my daughters is special and unique also. I am grateful to have very loving friends in my life.

As I've mentioned in some of my previous talks, I've been working on loving myself for the last several years. I've definitely come a long way in this area. I thought I'd made significant progress and that I'd been doing a pretty good job of this. Then some things happened in the last few weeks that shook me and made me look at myself pretty closely.

I've been going through what we call in metaphysics a "breaking down" period. The last few times I've showed up at the spiritual community (and other places), someone will say hello, or hug me, or ask how I am, and I simply burst into tears. At other times, I was snapping at people close to me. It's a little embarrassing. I understand that breaking down is a necessary step in my growth process. I understand that it's a necessary component to change. I understand that I have to release the old to make way for the new. I just don't like the fact that sometimes it's so very uncomfortable.

The way I look at this particular "breaking down" period is that I've been choosing to learn some important lessons about bearing my responsibilities with more ease and releasing burdens that don't belong to me. In several different areas of my life, I've been choosing to learn lessons related to my need to control events and situations. I've been letting go and understanding that "control" is really an illusion. The only things I have control over are my own thoughts, words, and actions and the people, places, and things I choose to surround myself with. A very wise woman said to me recently, there are two things we can do in this life: take responsibility for our own actions and our own reactions. These past few weeks have not been particularly easy. I am truly grateful to the people that have been helping me along the way (especially my sister). I am truly grateful for all the things I've learned here at my spiritual community that help guide my steps in happier and healthier directions.

Someone said, "If you think you are really enlightened, spend a week with your family." My parents are in town for the winter. My interactions with my parents, and especially with my mom, have made me question who I am and who I aspire to be. This has shaken me. Apparently, when I'm with my mom, a different voice comes out of my mouth, and I act differently than I do under any other circumstances. My sister said she hasn't heard this voice from me in about 15 years. She said the good news is that I used to be this way with everyone. These are not words that are particularly easy to hear. Sometimes I think I've come so far on my journey and sometimes I feel like I'm moving through molasses. I know that I've changed and grown, and the fact that I can recognize what I'm doing is an important growth marker. I know that I need to be easy and gentle and especially loving with myself at these times. I need to get "back to the loving place."

In this growth process, I've had to rethink some of the people, places and things that have been in my life for a while. Who do I want to spend time with? Where do I want to go? What do I want to do? In assessing these things for myself, and in letting go of control, in at least some instances, I got some surprises. As I made space in my life, some unexpected gifts showed up in the form of people who really appreciate me and want to spend time with me – just the way I am.

I actually found out how much easier it could be when I didn't feel the need to take charge of everything. There are no vacuums in nature – when you let go of something, it makes room for something new and better to come in.

I was listening to another minister's talk from a couple of weeks ago. She said it had been some time since she'd spoken at the chapel, so she'd asked God what she should speak about and she specified that she wanted it to be new and different and spectacular. She said the answer came back as, "Forgiveness." She said she told God that wasn't new or different and God answered, "It's crucial." I have to agree with her and God. Forgiveness is crucial. I've had to do a lot of that in the last few weeks. Starting with myself. I've had to forgive myself for the way I've acted with my mom. I've had to forgive myself for not always being the person I aspire to be. I've had to forgive myself for being impatient and short-tempered and less kind than I would like. I've had to forgive my mom for not living up to my expectations and to understand that she's doing the best she can. I've had to forgive myself for trying to control events and situations. I've had to forgive my friends for acting in ways that were not particularly pleasant for me. I've had to forgive myself and others and loose myself to my highest and best good.

And, for me, hand in hand with forgiveness is gratitude. As I forgive myself and others, and release things that no longer serve me, I remind myself of the people, places, and things I am most grateful for in my life.

I'm working on balance – the balance between giving and receiving; the balance between taking care of my parents and taking care of myself; the balance between taking care of my parents and letting them be as independent as they choose to be; the balance between work and play; the balance between activity and rest. I am reminding myself to breathe – breathing always helps.

Somewhere along the way, it seems as though I learned, when in doubt, blame someone else for whatever is going on or whatever is too uncomfortable to face for yourself. As I've learned about the metaphysical principles, I've learned to take responsibility for my thoughts, words and actions. Blaming anyone else doesn't work for me at all any more.

So, this cycle of breaking down, changing and growing is all about vibration. We can change our vibration at any moment. We can take a breath. We can smile. We can recognize, release, and replace a thought, a word, or an action. For me, getting "back to the loving place" often involves both forgiveness and gratitude. Paying attention to forgiveness and gratitude are some of the ways that I raise my own vibration. When I get pulled off center, these are some of the ways that I get "back to the loving place."

CHOOSING TO WALK
ON ROSE PETALS

8/29/10

Someone I know recently posted a note on Facebook that she was getting a puppy. Almost immediately, another person commented that that breed of puppy can be very hard to train. Another person has been caring for her nephew. He is now going to live with her mom (his grandmother), and she was expressing worry about whether he would do his home-work properly and whether he would get enough supervision and whether his father would cause any problems. I asked her how it could possibly serve her to think those kinds of nega-tive thoughts. It seems that it would benefit all of them if she imagined him thriving and prospering in the new situation. After all, this woman did raise her! A young mother was pre-paring for her first outing with her new baby and the extended family, and was imagining all sorts of disasters. What if she were to think about the baby sleeping peacefully and being loved and cared for by other family members, and everyone enjoying the experience tremendously. I knew that the worst thing that could happen would be that the baby might cry. Many of the people there were parents and had no problem helping to comfort a baby. Hearing this series of remarks in-spired me to ponder how we create what happens in our lives and what we project in front of us on our paths.

The image that came up for me was a bride walking down the aisle, and the flower girl preparing the way by strewing rose petals for the bride to walk on. Walking on rose petals invites the bride and all those present to imagine a life full of happiness, ease, and grace. That can be our choice in our lives. We can strew our path with rose petals, rather than rocks, thorns, or broken glass. What do you prefer to walk on?

When you wake up in the morning and think about your day, what do you imagine? It is always a choice. Whether you're about to start a new job, move to a new home, have surgery, or place your ailing parent into a hospice facility, you have a choice about how you respond to whatever is presenting itself to you.

A good friend left a note on my refrigerator several years ago that says, "Worry, no matter what its cause, weakens, takes away courage and shortens life." And we know with absolute certainty that worry does not change the outcome of any situation, it only saps our strength and creates negative energy in its wake. It's always better to imagine the best in any situation. It doesn't cost anything. And I'm not suggesting that you just go on your merry way without thinking about what you're doing. I'm saying that you consider any situation, as prudently as possible, take all aspects into consideration, make a wise and informed decision, and then let it be.

I was with someone who was getting discharged from the hospital recently, and the doctor had cautioned her about the risk of wound infection. I heard her say that she had to be very careful about not letting her husband touch her because of the various diseases she might contract, and she began to name them one by one. I encouraged her to stop what she was doing and to focus, instead, on going home to a very loving environment, where she would continue her healing in a powerful and positive way. Rather than worry and stress herself and her family, my friend could choose to take the information that the doctor has given her, and make sure her home and her bedding and her husband's loving hands are clean. She can then go forward with strength, confidence and security, knowing she has the ability to heal herself well and easily. My kids and friends often tease me about never saying the "S" word (that would be "sick.") I almost never admit to being "sick." I may experience a symptom or two along the way, but I always think of myself as healthy and healing myself well – on the road to complete recovery, no matter what. I do my best to think metaphysically, and to affirm the opposite whenever physical symptoms present themselves. I also ask what lessons I am choosing to resolve.

One of my daughter's friends was laid off from work and rattled off facts to me about the unemployment statistics in Arizona and throughout the nation. I told him to just stop for a moment. No matter what seems to be happening statistically, we are always capable of creating our own reality. I choose to think positively and abundantly. In this time of change in the state and the country and the world, it's even more important to maintain a positive attitude, hold the light, and be the change that we want to create. I reminded him of the many skills and talents and successes that he has, and encouraged him to believe that whoever hired him would be lucky to have him. He called to say that he'd been hired for a management position very shortly after that.

Someone close to me actually asked me if I could include the following words in one of my talks. "The greedy are weaving themselves into hell while those who know the charity of minimalism are starting heaven right here!" I really appreciated that he cares so much and wanted to participate, although I don't necessarily agree with what he was saying. I definitely believe that heaven and hell are states that we create for ourselves in each moment, rather than some eternity that we are judged and sentenced to endure or enjoy. However, I do not necessarily agree that minimalism is the path to heaven. I believe that abundance and prosperity are aspects of happiness, health, and wealth. I definitely believe in sharing what I have, but I do not believe there have to be limits placed on what each person has. I believe the universe is abundant and that there is plenty for everyone.

A gentleman I know is contemplating a move to another state, which is contingent upon the sale of his house here in Tucson. He told me he didn't sleep all night because he feels anxious about this. I reminded him that worry doesn't change any-thing about the situation and just causes him to lose sleep. He said that even though he knows that, sometimes he just can't stop himself.

How do we create positive outcomes in our lives? I've often heard my teacher talk about formulating goals and writing them down. That's one constructive thing that works. Pay-ing attention to our thoughts, words, and actions is product-ive and constructive. Affirmations can also be useful. Make affirmations that resonate for you, say them in the present tense as if they're already happening ("I have" instead of "I will have"), and say them with feeling.

I was listening to some Abraham talks the other day. They were saying that if you can hold an undiluted pure positive thought for 17 seconds, that it creates an electrical impulse that connects it to a like positive thought and generates the equivalent of 2,000 action hours of "work." If you can hold that thought for 34 seconds, the effect is tenfold – 20,000 action hours. If you can extend it to 51 seconds, it is com-pounded exponentially – 200,000 action hours. And if you can hold an undiluted pure positive thought for 68 seconds, the amount of energy generated can change your life and your world. Think about that – 68 seconds. It's interesting how challenging that can be. Think about things you have no trouble doing for a minute or more. For instance, when we sing "Let There Be Love" at the end of each service, it takes just over a minute. I notice how many thoughts of various kinds I may have in that time. "Am I singing on key?" "Will I be able to hit both the high and low notes in the song?" "How recently have I polished my toenails?" "What color polish is on other people's toenails?" "Who's singing off key?" "How long is this going to take?" "Can't we sing any faster?" "Should I keep my eyes open or closed?" And this is all in the minute it takes to sing one of the most positive songs I can imagine.

How often do we ask for what we want in one breath, and then tell the universe why we can't have it in the next? What are we creating with our thoughts, words and actions? Take some time during the course of your day to really listen to yourself. Listen to your words and your thoughts and observe your actions. The universe works perfectly in giving us exactly what we ask for. What are you asking for?

When we project negative thoughts about anything that is or may be happening in our lives, it is the equivalent of choosing to walk on broken glass or thorns instead of rose petals. As you imagine anything in your future, whether it's happening five minutes or five years from now, imagine it unfolding in the best way possible. Then, that is the energy that you pave your path with. Positive thoughts create positive outcomes. What we think, what we say and what we do is what we attract more of into our lives. That's "The Secret." Only, it's no secret to metaphysicians. We understand our abilities in choosing how we create each and every moment of our lives. You have the opportunity in each moment to strew your path with rose petals. What do you choose to walk on?

CH-CH-CH-CH-CHANGES

10/10/10

With all that's been going on lately, I keep hearing the song "Ch-Ch-Ch-Ch-Changes" in my head. And I am reminded of the quote: "What the caterpillar perceives is the end, to the butterfly is just the beginning."

For the last several years, there were four people that I attended to on a daily basis, with at least a phone call - my mother-in-law, my dad, my friend Jill, and my mom. They've all made their transitions in the last four months, and people have expressed condolences for all the losses I've had this year. Each of these people held a special place in my heart.

Although I was divorced over 20 years ago, my mother-in-law, Jean, was one of my dearest friends. We had always been close, and after her husband passed eight years ago, I usually talked to her every day and had lunch with her at least once a week. I met her when I was 18 years old and she was a major positive influence in my life. After my divorce, Jean made it clear to me that once I was in the family, I was always in the family.

I loved her very much and she was like a mother to me. She knew she could confide in me about anything. I sat with her in the emergency room and hospital on many occasions and played countless games of Skip-Bo with her. In the last couple of years, we had conversations about how she had enjoyed her life and was ready to go. She had been married to my father-in-law, Bud, for 62 years, and she wanted to rejoin him. In the last few days of her life, her children were all by her side. My relationship with her was very easy and that was the way she lived and the way she passed, quietly, in her sleep, and with ease.

Two days after Jean passed, my father made his transition, at the age of 102. My father was an amazing man. His mind and his memory were as clear and sharp on the day he passed as they had been throughout his life. He only had an eighth grade education, and always felt lacking because of that. He often said he was educated at the "University of the New York Times," putting aside a nickel each day to buy the newspaper even when his salary was only $10 a week. From my perspective, he was one of the most brilliant men I ever met. His depth and range of knowledge was vast, and he never stopped learning. He got his first computer when he was 91 years old because he said he didn't want to live in this age and not understand what that was all about.

He was in very good health up until about 5 weeks before he passed. I think he was just done and ready to leave. His vision was impaired and he couldn't see enough to read or drive. He complained of "existing" rather than living, and feeling useless. He couldn't take care of my mother in the ways that he was accustomed to doing and it weighed heavily on him.

On the day he went into the emergency room in New Mexico, my brother, sister, and I jumped on planes immediately to be by his side. He was so happy to have his children there with him. He recovered enough to move to Tucson briefly, until he went back into the hospital, and then hospice. In the last week of his life, many family members got to come and spend time with him. I was very grateful for all the time I had to spend with him, especially in the last three weeks of his life. My sister, my daughter, and I were with him at the moment of passing. His transition was relatively easy and he was never in any pain.

About four years ago, my dear friend Jill was diagnosed with stage four ovarian cancer that later spread to her brain. The doctor gave her about five years to live. She received chemo treatments every couple of weeks during the last four years. At one point, about 2 ½ years in, the doctor wanted to suspend treatment, but Jill refused. She fought as hard as she could for as long as she could. She had a loving husband and three loving daughters, and wanted as much time with them as possible. She almost never complained. She kept her attitude positive so much of the time. She would downplay the terrible side effects that she experienced from the chemo treatments. She continued to take care of those around her even in her most difficult moments.

The last few months were particularly challenging for Jill. She finally got to the point where she'd had enough because she had lost all semblance of independence and that was intolerable for her. She spent the last three weeks of her life in hospice and that gave her family time to say goodbye to her. She passed gently with her husband, daughters, and her dog, Missy, by her side. I had the honor of conducting her memorial service last week.

And then there was my mom. My relationship with my mom was complicated, to say the least. My mom was diagnosed bipolar when I was 14 years old. In many ways, I felt like I took care of her most of my life. When my dad passed, I knew I would be responsible for my mom for the rest of her life and it scared me a lot. I didn't know whether I was up to the task. Fortunately, I've spent the last 8 ½ years developing at my spiritual community. The last several months have given me the opportunity to learn important lessons in understanding, compassion, forgiveness, and gratitude.

At the end of August, my mom fell and broke her hip, had surgery, then went for rehab. She did well for a couple of weeks, then began to feel progressively worse. Her kidneys, which had been her major health concern for many years, began to fail. A couple of weeks before she passed, my mom made a point to tell me how proud she was of me. She told me I had made the right decision to move her to Tucson because no one else could or would have taken better care of her than I did. She said she saw the kind of heart it took for me to take care of Jill. She said she and my dad had always worried because I didn't have a full time job, but that now she understood what my life's work was and she was very proud of me. I'm so grateful that we were able to get to that point in our relationship. I think it was one of the things that allowed her to go and me to let her go. We were complete in our process.

My mom was unresponsive for the last couple of days of her life. She may have been afraid to let go. There may have been some things in her life that she had not forgiven herself for. When I called my daughter to tell her that my mom had passed, she shared the following information from a meditation she had done earlier that evening.

"I called to my grandmother's spirit to come to the clearing and to come not in her current age but as a young woman around my own age. I then asked the same of my mother. They both came before me standing knee deep in the water and joined hands. I then left them there together in the clearing for a bit. Later I returned to say goodbye. And then my grandmother's spirit evaporated from the clearing and I said goodbye to my mother and returned to my body, and ended the meditation."

This was done at about the time my mom made her transition. I believe my daughter helped my mother to let go, and I am so grateful to her.

People have expressed condolences that I have experienced so many losses this year. I prefer to think that like the caterpillar, my loved ones and I have experienced major changes. When you release something, it creates a vacuum and makes space for something new to come in. That's how I'm choosing to think about things right now. When space is created, amazing things have room to come into our lives. And as I move forward with what I've learned, I remember to infuse my choices with love.

PERSPECTIVE

2/6/11

I've been thinking about perspective, and how it changes my experience. It reminded me of the story about six blind men trying to describe an elephant. Since they have never encountered an elephant, they grope about, seeking to understand and describe this new phenomenon. One grasps the trunk, and concludes it is a snake. The next wraps his hands around the elephant's tusk, and knows that it is a spear. Another finds the elephant's ear, and declares it to be a fan. The fourth explores one of the elephant's legs, and describes it as a tree. The fifth, after discovering the elephant's side, concludes that it is, after all, a wall. The sixth finds the elephant's tail, and announces that it is a rope.

Each one of these men is describing his experience of the elephant, just as each of us describes our experience of our own life, our place in the universe, and our understanding of the concept of "God" from our own perspective.

I have been pondering my perspective on things. Sometimes, I may act as if the universe revolves around me and I am at the center. When I look at things from that perspective, I get easily annoyed when things don't go my way. I don't understand why that driver won't go any faster or just move over and get out of my way. I don't understand why someone won't do what I say without question. I don't understand how I can be on the metaphysical path that I've been on. and say affirmations day in and day out, and still have the kinds of physical problems show up that have shown up in my life.

Recently, I've been changing my perspective and looking at things a little differently. Rather than imagining myself as the center, I am seeing every living thing standing in a circle, with each of us as equal points on the circle. And the center of the circle is where a beam of light from each of our hearts meets to create an orb of healing light. That perspective feels very different. That orb of collective energy is probably the closest I've come to expressing my idea of the concept of "God." I'm feeling a little less like one of the blind men describing the elephant.

This change in my perspective has helped me to move forward on my path. When I imagine all living things as equal points on a circle, I am able to respond to people and situations in a more kind, loving, and accepting way. If I look down on or up to or even through another person, my perspective is very different than if I look into the being that they truly are. My thoughts, words, and actions are guided by this perspective. My understanding of this has been growing stronger every day.

I noticed that I had some unresolved issues and feelings between myself and at least four different people in my life. In the process of learning to know myself, I recognize how easily and strongly I can sometimes react to people and situations. Instead of just going off on people, I have been working on using that reaction as a cue to stop, breathe, and sit with my reaction until a way to deal with the situation positively and constructively shows up in my consciousness.

This is somewhat new behavior for me, and I am enjoying getting familiar with this new habit. Sometimes I can do this within a few minutes, and sometimes it takes months. I am so much more pleased with the results when I take the time and wait for the positive response to make itself known to me. I understand the situation so much better and the other person is usually able to hear what I have to say more easily than if I was just ranting and reacting. I am clearing things up between myself and others in kind, loving, and accepting ways, and I have been really pleased with the results. I am looking into, instead of up to or down at, the people I come into contact with.

I am noticing the ways in which I am changing, which is allowing me to move forward in life with vitality and ease and flexibility. Occasionally, I forget and fall back into my old familiar habits and patterns. And then I notice what I'm doing, take a breath, and stop. I choose how I want to respond, instead of just reacting in the moment. I have been making a conscious effort to change and re-think things sooner and more easily. I notice that if I'm tired or in pain, I'm more apt to fall back into old habits. I forgive myself, and then move forward again as soon as I am able. I remind myself of the perspective of the circle, and that helps me to center myself.

In thinking about coming at things from different angles and perspectives, I was struck by a scene in an improv comedy workshop the other day. The scene was a couple seeing a marriage counselor because the husband was upset when the wife didn't bring him flowers. Their job was to get the person who was playing the marriage counselor to guess this problem correctly, without just coming out and saying those words. They came at it from several angles. The wife explained that she often bought her husband "manly" gifts. The husband said he wanted compliments that were more "colorful." Or perhaps something you could hold in your hand or put on a table. He talked about the vegetable garden and the pretty border he had planted around it to express his feminine side. They went on and on until their scene partner finally got what they were attempting to convey. Our teacher then explained how important it was to come at things from different angles or approaches, if one way wasn't working effectively. It was their job to help the third member to understand what they were trying to convey.

This really reminded me of my dad. When I think about ways to communicate, my dad often comes to mind. My dad taught me that it was always my responsibility to communicate effectively. If the other person didn't understand what I was saying, it was up to me to find a way to communicate it, so that the other person could understand. That was often challenging. I remember being frustrated at times when I was trying to explain something to my dad, and he would make me re-think it and say it, sometimes over and over, until he could finally understand. The end result was always more positive and beneficial for both of us, although the process was sometimes challenging.

The first talk I did at my spiritual community, a little over two years ago, was about Understanding. It is interesting for me to note where I have come on my path since then. I've been experiencing some physical symptoms lately that have challenged my understanding in some ways. How am I moving forward? How am I getting in the way of my moving forward? I really understand that when I manifest something physically, it is the effect, and I look inside to discover the cause, so I can make different choices and create a new effect in the future.

Because the area of my body that is being affected is my hip, I've been thinking a lot about moving forward. I had an interesting thing happen the other night, when I attended a grief support group. At the end of the group, the leader passed around a book called, "Healing After Loss." She asked each person to open the book randomly to any page and read the quote they found. When it was my turn, I read the words, "There is no way out, there is only a way forward." I know and understand that there are no "coincidences." I know and understand that this was exactly the message I needed to hear at that moment.

So, in closing, I invite you to examine your perspective on things in your life, both on the physical plane and on the spiritual plane, and I invite you to join with me in this circle of healing light and love.

COURAGE

5/1/11

Ready, set, go! When the starter pistol goes off, what causes you to take that first step off the line? What moves you from imagination to action? That is your will. And just like starting a race, that's the way it is in life: the only way to get anywhere or do anything is to take that first step. And the only way to take the first step is to have the will and the courage to do so. Whether it is physically taking the first step as you recover from surgery, or emotionally taking the first step of clearing out old habits and patterns to make way for new and healthier choices, it is up to each of us to have the courage and will to take the first step.

My friend Jill was diagnosed with ovarian cancer in August of 2006. She went through chemo treatments every two to three weeks. Two years into the treatments, after having a seizure, she learned that the cancer had metastasized to her brain. She continued with the rigorous chemo regimen for almost two more years, even when her doctor tried to talk her into stopping. She was not ready to give up. She had the courage to face each day as it came along, with all the symptoms and side effects and pain that was associated with her dis-ease and the treatment, day after day. And she continued to think about others – family and friends - and make sure they were taken care of in important ways. She rarely complained and almost always had a positive word for others. She had true courage. She had the will to live despite nearly insurmountable obstacles, for a long time. Then she had the courage to say, "Stop," when it was time, and also the courage to say goodbye to her family and friends.

I spent time with a young girl the other day who was talking to me about her life. She will be 13 on her birthday this month. She is working on learning to speak Spanish, French, and Mandarin Chinese and aspires to learn Italian, German, and Japanese, also. She has thoughts of becoming an international translator and editor. She said she has no plans on leaving the earth plane anytime soon, because she has goals. This caused me to ponder the notion of what gives us the will to live. What gives us a reason to get up in the morning, day after day? To put one foot in front of the other, and move forward along our path?

When I think about courage, I often think about the Lion in the Wizard of Oz. He was called the "cowardly" lion. He was terrified of almost everything, but he put his fears aside and stepped way out of his comfort zone in order to save his friend, Dorothy. Courage is not about doing things that others might consider scary or risky; courage is facing your own fears and using your will to take the first step, when you're not sure you can, and the obstacles may seem insurmountable. It's about being in charge of a high profile university program dealing with mental illness, and revealing your own history with mental health challenges in a newspaper interview. It's about doing another set of exercises when all you want to do is lie down. It's about climbing that 45' telephone pole, when you're really afraid of heights. And you only find courage and will inside yourself. By the end of the movie, the Lion had really transformed himself from cowardly to courageous, through the use of his will.

Another friend has gone through a lot of changes in the last couple of years. She came out publicly with the fact that she'd had an eating disorder for many years. She's been doing emotional clearing work on some things that happened before she was born that have affected her strongly. The challenges in her life might have seemed insurmountable to some people. The courage and will to face these obstacles, and take the steps necessary to make changes in her life, inspire me.

There have been some big challenges in my life in the last couple of years, also. Losing both of my parents last year, as well as my mother-in-law and my friend Jill, was difficult. These were people that I took care of on a daily basis for several years. They've all made their transitions now. I don't have them to take care of any longer, so I ask myself, "What now?" Who am I, if I'm not a caregiver?

Then, I got the news that I needed a total hip replacement earlier this year. I had the surgery a couple of months ago, and have had to dig deep to find the courage to move forward in the face of obstacles that have seemed insurmountable at times. I fell into a deep pit of despair for a while. It takes courage to climb out of that kind of hole. It takes courage to ask for help. It takes courage to reinvent my life while I'm not able to do the familiar things I've been so accustomed to doing. It takes courage to face demons that have been present throughout my life – to shine the light on them and face them as I never have before in order to move forward.

I've had some challenges arise recently in the will to live area. Coping with pain and loss of independence, combined with grief for the losses I experienced last year, caused me to sink very low. I felt like I was in a hole that I wasn't sure I could crawl out of. Some moments, it seemed as if it would be easier to just say goodbye and be done with this. I realized that that was not the answer for me at this time. I choose life and I choose love.

How do we summon the will to live at those dark moments? What I did was to call my sister first. Then I came to my spiritual community and talked to people I could trust. I spoke to another close friend who came right over to be with me. The next day, I called my surgeon to discuss options for relieving the pain. I called my physical therapist to revise the program I was following. I made an appointment to see a counselor. And I proceeded with doing some emotional clearing work which was hard and intense and very worthwhile. I had to be willing to take some action and make some changes, because if I continued doing what I had been doing, I probably wouldn't be standing here at this moment.

In order to face the challenges that arise for each of us every day, it takes courage just to get out of bed in the morning. We have to exercise our will to put one foot in front of the other and move forward. As I pondered the mind power of Will, the willow tree came into my mind. I believe an important component of will is the ability to be flexible and bend with circumstances that arise – like the willow tree bends and flourishes, instead of breaking when the first strong wind comes along.

Just like "ready, set" prepares us for action, we use our will in conjunction with the other mind powers, so that it works most effectively. We use our imagination to create ideas. We temper all our actions with love for the most positive outcome possible. We use our zeal to motivate us and create excitement. We use our knowing to guide us. Then, we use our will to ignite thought into action, and ideally we choose the action that moves us forward for our highest and best good.

ZEAL

6/19/11

Today is Father's Day, and our topic for the month is zeal, so it makes sense for me to start by talking about my dad. As many of you know, my dad made his transition last year at the age of 102. He had a true zest for life and lived well right up until the end.

My dad was born on the Lower East Side of New York City in 1908. His parents had each emigrated from Italy. I didn't know my grandfather, but my grandmother never really spoke English. As the eldest of eight children, a lot of responsibility fell onto my dad's shoulders. His father was apparently not very consistent in his actions. My dad would say that one week there would be a chauffeured limousine, and the next week there would be no food on the table. One of the ways that zeal was manifested for my dad was through work. As we grew up, we always heard stories about him getting his first job when he was eight years old. My dad was constantly on the lookout for ways to bring income into the family. He was creative and resourceful in his efforts. He worked as a messenger on Wall Street in the 1920's, when he was still in "short pants." He was given carfare to deliver the packages, and saved the money he earned by walking everywhere.

My dad had a lot of drive. His goal was to be a millionaire before he was 30. He didn't succeed in that particular goal because the Depression intervened in a big way, but he kept moving forward. He started a number of different businesses with varying degrees of success. He always worked hard and always pushed himself to keep learning. He got his first computer when he was 91 years old because he didn't want to live in this day and age and not know what that was all about.

Just as steel is tempered with heat and other materials to make it stronger, zeal operates best in conjunction with the other mind powers. My dad's life was a great demonstration of zeal tempered with wisdom, power, and will. There was also a large component of love mixed in because much of what motivated my dad was love for his family and wanting to make a better life for his children than what he had experienced.

I miss my dad a lot, and think about him very often. We shared a love of learning. We were both very good at being persistent and following things through to a satisfying conclusion. I learned a lot about leadership from my dad, and know that those abilities count among my strengths. I appreciate so many things that I learned from my dad.

One of the aspects of zeal that my dad demonstrated through his choices was balance. My dad said that the secret to a long life was to do everything in moderation. As I pondered my talk for today, balance kept coming forward for me. It seems like my dad was able to create balance in the use of zeal in his life. Finding that balance has presented some challenges for me. As I contemplate zeal, I think about it in "Goldilocks" terms: how much is too much, how much is too little, how much is just right. How do I find the proper balance?

My teacher wrote about zeal in the newsletter this month: "Zeal has no intelligence or discretion. Guide zeal with Understanding, Faith, and Imagination to get results. Will and Zeal go hand in hand to sustain the results in one's life. Praise Zeal with the power faculty for its great energy. Zeal is tempered with wisdom."

Some of the experiences I've been having lately have made

me think about the importance of balance where zeal is operating, and the importance of tempering zeal with wisdom, understanding, and love. More often than not, I tend towards one end of the zeal continuum. I get very excited about things and have a lot of force in my personality to back it up. As I feel very strong and enthusiastic, I sometimes move ahead too forcefully and at a pace or a style that isn't very comfortable for those around me. Sometimes I speak too quickly or too bluntly. I've noticed that the effect on others is not particularly positive, and it's made me stop and think and reevaluate my choices and behaviors. The image of a bull in a china shop arises sometimes, and I am learning to temper that enthusiasm, so that collateral damage does not occur in the wake of what starts out as excitement.

My intention is generally positive and constructive, and I am working on finding ways to deliver the thoughts I have in more positive and constructive ways. For me, this means taking more time to stop and think before I speak (just like my dad always taught me to do.) To wait for the guidance that allows me to communicate effectively, so that the people around me can absorb and digest the information I may be sharing. I notice that the need to feel like the center of attention affects my actions, and my zeal drives me forward like a steamroller. Lately, I've been quieter in social situations. I'm experimenting with creating different results and observing the effects. I am tempering my zeal with wisdom, understanding and love, to create more positive effects.

I continued reading what my teacher wrote in the newsletter: "Without zeal, there is no zest for living or impulse to go forward, like an electric motor with no current. Energy is zeal in motion."

This has been the other side of things for me lately. I've had some experiences in the last year or so that have practically stopped me in my tracks. Dealing with the loss of so many people that were close to me, then learning that I needed major surgery earlier this year, then the sudden death of a very close friend, and a very bad reaction to some medication recently, have just about overwhelmed me at times. There are days when I don't have enough enthusiasm to get out of bed or open the mail. I've let some things fall by the wayside because I just couldn't face them. At times, grief feels like it's going to overwhelm me. I have to find ways to bring joy into my life and lift my spirit.

There is a song in the movie "Beaches" called "The Wind Beneath My Wings." This is one of the ways that I think about zeal – as the wind beneath my wings. It's useful to take some time to reflect upon what inspires us. What brings us joy and lifts our spirit? What is the wind beneath our wings? For me, dancing is one thing that truly brings me joy. One of the difficulties of going through the physical changes that I've gone through this year has been the curtailment of my dancing. I've found that even though it's not completely comfortable to move in those ways, the joy that it brings to me is worth it. So, I dance a little less often and for a little less time, but I keep dancing and I keep smiling. Dancing is one of the activities that puts the current in the motor of my life. I've also been learning to do improv comedy. Anything that makes me laugh always brings me joy and lifts my spirit.

The applications of being a minister have also been very fulfilling. I've now performed four weddings, and I really love doing those ceremonies and helping to create those special moments in people's lives. The classes and development that I continue to do here at my spiritual community have had a big impact for me, also. The affirmation and validation of what is beyond what we can see, hear, touch, and feel has been very uplifting for me. I keep receiving confirmation that I'm on the right track and moving in the right direction. That's what keeps me going some days.

When it comes to zeal, I encourage you to use it wisely, power-fully, and effectively, and always remember to temper it with love. Then zeal works for you, and with you, and moves you forward on your path. I understand that the zeal that operates in my life is a legacy from my dad. He is the wind beneath my wings.

THE MIND POWER
OF ELIMINATION

12/4/11

Our topic for this month is the mind power of Elimination. The organs of elimination in the body rid waste from the physical body. The function of the mind power of Elimination is to help in ridding mental waste from the system. What constitutes mental waste? Negative thoughts, words and actions. Some of the things I've noticed that constitute mental waste include making people wrong, putting other people down, holding on to grudges and feelings of ill will, making assumptions, gossiping, comparing yourself unfavorably to anyone else, and holding on to things that would serve us far better to let go of.

There is a quote that makes sense to me in thinking about Elimination. "Holding resentment is like taking poison, then waiting for the other person to keel over." What kinds of thoughts might we be holding on to that would serve us so much better if we let go of them? The process is threefold – first, recognize what is not working for you, then release those thoughts, words, and actions or people, places, and things from your life. Finally, replace what you are letting go of with something more positive and constructive.

This topic of Elimination is interesting to me because I spent about a year and a half working for a woman who hired me to help her figure out what to keep and what to get rid of as she prepared to move from the estate where she had lived for 42 years. She knew that what she wanted was someone to help her process her life and bear witness to the important events that the "things" surrounding her represented. There were very few topics that we didn't discuss during the time we spent together. One of the things we came across were all the cards and letters that she had received after her husband had died about three years earlier. She had not been able to cope with reading them at the time, and had just put them away. With time and support, she was able to go through them and then dispose of most of them after she'd appreciated the love that was sent with each one. That's an important part of the journey for each one of us – to take what's important and what matters from each experience, express gratitude for the gifts we've received, and discard what no longer serves us.

I celebrated my birthday this week. For me, this presents an opportunity to reflect on the past year and contemplate the next. What have I accomplished? What am I looking forward to? What do I need to attend to in my spiritual garden? I take time to look at what is flourishing and what needs to be weeded out. Sometimes there are things I think I've eliminated, and it turns out I've just hidden them under some other things, and they pop up unexpectedly. For example, I thought I was valuing myself enough that I was looking for real love in my life. Instead, I settled for something much more superficial. And although it was very stimulating, a large quantity of anxiety lurked just beneath it. I thought I had grown past having those kinds of feelings pop up, but turns out I still have some closet cleaning to do. There are still some issues about self-worth and doubt that I need to attend to recognizing, releasing and replacing. Change is not always comfortable or easy. It seems like it's easier to sit with the pile of trash that is known and familiar rather than actually dispose of it, but it's guaranteed to start to smell sooner or later.

The last couple of years have brought some major changes

into my life. Last year, four people who were very close to me (including my parents) made their transition. Earlier this year, a close friend was killed in a motorcycle accident. I've had three friends in a very short period of time whose brothers have died suddenly and unexpectedly. How we deal with loss is another aspect that comes up for me when I think about elimination. When a person we are close to leaves our lives for whatever reason, we experience loss. This is a type of elimination. How do we cope with loss of this kind? How do we fill the space that is created by that loss? I've been doing my best to appreciate each moment a little more.

What we think, what we say and what we do is what we draw more of to ourselves. This is one of the basic teachings in metaphysics. I do my best to pay attention to my thoughts, words and actions. I was talking to a friend the other night and he mentioned that he'd been having a rough day. When I questioned him about it, he responded by saying he didn't want to dwell on anything negative, that he'd rather focus on positive things in his life. I appreciated and respected his re-sponse. When there is an unpleasant event or circumstance in our lives, we always have the choice about how we respond to it. Do we spend a lot of time talking to others and adopt-ing a victim stance in the matter? Do we choose to wallow in misery and self-pity? Or do we take responsibility for what we create in our lives and move forward from there, doing the best we can and making positive choices in the future? Do we turn our attention to things that bring us joy and lift our spirits to help move us in a different direction?

A close friend of mine was asking about how I was feeling physically. He was checking in very specifically because he's learned that I don't necessarily mention when I'm in pain, even to those closest to me. I do my best to focus on the positive aspects in my life, whenever possible, so I rarely talk about and give much attention to things that are negative.

What we think, what we say and what we do is what we draw more of into our lives... it's important to pay attention to those things as you navigate on your path. Do you want to strew your path with rose petals or walk on broken glass?

Relationships can be some of the more difficult things to let go of. For the longest time, I thought all the relationships in my life were supposed to last forever. I ran myself ragged keeping up with everyone in my life. After a while, I began to realize that some of these relationships were not very reciprocal and, therefore, not that healthy. I was really good at giving, but not so hot at receiving. Consequently, many of my relationships were out of balance, and I was feeling depleted. I began to pay attention to how this was operating in my life and the ways in which I was contributing to the process. I began to say, "Yes, thank you," far more often when someone offered to help or to do something nice for me. I began to spend less and less time with the folks that only called when they wanted or needed something from me. And that brought my life into more balance. Balance can be one of the benefits of using Elimination effectively in your life. As you release things that no longer serve you, you bring your life into greater harmony and balance, and create more happiness, health and wealth in your life.

At my spiritual community, we have the "Hit the Road Jack" box. This contains sheets of paper with the words, "I now let go worn out conditions and worn out relationships. Divine Order is now established and maintained in my world now." Then, there is space on the page to write down what you want to "hit the road." This is a concrete example of using the mind power of elimination. It's an opportunity to do a fearless search of what is working and what is not working in your world. It's time to weed the garden and prune the trees and cut off the dead flowers and branches that are taking away from the new growth. To grow, we have to eliminate things from our lives that hold us back, in order to make room for more beneficial things to come into our lives.

Any negative thoughts that we hold have the potential to create dis-ease in our bodies and our lives. The only way to make room for more positive thoughts is to eliminate negative thoughts. We can clean out our minds the same way we clean out our closets. Examine the thoughts, words, and actions that you do on a daily basis. Look at the people you spend time with, the places you go, and the things that you do. Which ones make you uncomfortable or unhappy or cause unpleasant feelings of any kind to arise? Which ones bring you joy and lift your spirit? Take the time to eliminate the things that are not working for you in your life and make space for the things that allow you to grow as a human being and develop as a spiritual being. You'll be pleased with the results.

THE MIND POWER OF LIFE

1/1/12

Happy New Year! Our topic for this month is the mind power of Life. And in life, EVERYTHING IS POSSIBLE!

This is a time of closure and saying goodbye to what has been, and a time of opening and welcoming what is to come. It's a great time to acknowledge where we've been in the past year because knowing where we've been helps us to know where we're going. Lots of people talk about New Year's resolutions. I think a more beneficial way to think about things are New Year's affirmations.

What we think, what we say, and what we do is what we draw more of into our lives. Affirmations are a useful way to draw more of what we are actually desiring into our lives. Affirmations are created in the present tense, and as if they're already happening in our lives. My personal preference is to say, "With each breath, I enjoy and am grateful for...", and then say what I affirm. The power of affirmations, and especially in saying them out loud on a daily basis, is very strong and constructive. I affirm that I love and accept myself as I am; that I fill this space with love from the inside; that I am wealthful, prosperous and affluent; that I am strong and healthy; and that I am flexible and I am changing. We know that the only thing that is constant in life is change. The more we go along with that notion, with flexibility and understanding, the more we are able to grow and develop in our lives.

In the last couple of days, there have been some posts on Facebook about the New Year that I'd like to share:

One woman states, "Before we pop the champagne and celebrate the New Year, let's stop and reflect on the year that has gone by. To remember both our triumphs and our missteps, our promises made and broken. The times we opened ourselves up to great adventures or closed ourselves down for fear of getting hurt, because that is what New Year's is all about, getting another chance. A chance to forgive, to do better, to do more, to give more, to love more. And stop worrying about what if and start embracing what would be. So let's remember to be nice to each other, kind to each other, and not just on New Year's, but all year long"

Another one says, "Time to look back at the past year and choose what to leave behind and what to pack up and bring into the New Year. Leave behind the pain, disappointments, and hurts. Pack up the joys, lessons learned, and love. Keep the load light. Pack it in a backpack made of hope. Get ready and make room for an awesome 2012 ahead of you!"

It's interesting to see what some people are thinking about. For me, the first day of the New Year is a time to take stock and also a time to focus on gratitude. What are you thankful for in the past year? And what are you looking forward to? What is working well in your life and what would you like to change? Where have you been and where are you going?

Peggy Lee sang a song entitled, "Is That All There Is?" My sister occasionally has what we like to call "Peggy Lee moments" – she questions the meaning of her life and existence. She asks, "Is this all there is?"

I think that if one believes that our existence begins with our physical birth and ends with our physical death, the question of "is this all there is?" comes up more powerfully. I choose to believe that we are much more than just this collection of cells that has a limited existence on the earth plane. I choose to believe that we have always been and always will be, in some form or another. I believe that there is communication between the visible and the invisible world. I believe that we go on and on, and that "this" isn't all there is.

Life force moves through us with each breath. What we choose to make of it and how we choose to direct it, is what makes us individuals. Without Life, there is no momentum and no growth and no forward movement. Without the other mind powers working together, Life is just electrical energy.

What brings us joy and lifts our spirit? What moves us forward most beneficially on our path of unfoldment? What sustains our Life? The mind power of Life resides in the reproductive organs in our bodies. How do the urges that we feel drive us to make choices in our lives? How do we use those feelings to make the most constructive choices possible? How do we sustain our Life force and direct it for our highest and best good?

Towards the end of my father's life, he complained that he was merely existing and not living, and that was not acceptable to him. He couldn't do the things he had been accustomed to doing that made him feel like a man and a productive member of society. He couldn't drive, he couldn't read, and he felt he could no longer take care of my mother. That's when his life force began to seriously deteriorate, and within a couple of months, he had made his transition to the spiritual plane. What sustains Life for us?

I believe that we choose and create all of our experiences. In each moment, we have a choice in how we respond to any given situation. When someone leaves our life for whatever reason, a space is created that was previously filled either with time spent enjoying that person or caring for them or thinking about them or whatever. When that space is created, we have choices about how to fill it. Do we fill it with anguish and grief or do we fill it with something positive and constructive? It's always a choice.

We've just been through a season of intense gift giving. What if we viewed every day that way? What if we viewed every experience as a gift? Whether it's the death of a parent or the end of a relationship or the diagnosis of serious illness in a sibling or the loss of employment, every experience in our lives is a gift. It's an opportunity to grow and learn and change that we have chosen, in order to move forward on our path of unfoldment. Let this year be our golden opportunity to learn from each experience and receive all the gifts that are offered to us in each moment. Pay attention to the gifts you are receiving and learning from this year, take a moment to give thanks, and remember, in life, EVERYTHING IS POSSIBLE!

EMPOWERMENT

2/5/12

Our topic for this month is Empowerment. As I started pondering this, I thought about some of the choices I make as a mom. It was (and continues to be) important to me to do things that encourage my children to be the best that they can be. In contemplating raising children, one of the most important things that their dad and I wanted to instill in them was positive self-esteem. We took time to notice things that they did well and successfully, and focused attention and energy in those areas. We were attentive to asking them what we wanted them to do, as opposed to what we didn't want them to do, to encourage them in positive directions.

In raising my kids, I was aware of the importance of allowing them to make their own choices, and allowing them to make and learn from their own mistakes. Sometimes this is one of the biggest challenges as a parent. But with children or anyone else, the more we tell people what to do rather than encouraging them to think for themselves, the less we empower ourselves or others. When my children were growing up, I often pondered whether a compliant child would grow up to be a competent and successful adult.

When I think about empowerment, I often think of my daughter. When my daughter was about 6 years old, we took a family vacation in the mountains in upstate New York. My brother-in-law was an experienced climber and had all the necessary equipment. My daughter decided she wanted to try the climb, which was up a fairly sheer, steep cliff about 300' tall. She got all fitted out with harness and ropes, and she proceeded to climb up this cliff. At one point, the only way she could advance was to put her back against one side and her feet against the opposite side of this crack in the wall, and inch her way up until she was able to find another handhold. We have all this on videotape. As her mother, I was really nervous watching my little girl do what looked like a very dangerous act. I was assured by the people who had experience that she would be safe, so I gave my permission, love and support to her endeavor. She wanted to quit before she reached the top, but we gave her a lot of encouragement, especially since she was so close, and she ultimately made it to the top. I know that she felt empowered by accomplishing that challenging climb. I know I did my job as a mom that day in putting aside my worries and fears and letting her fly freely.

Yesterday was her birthday. I certainly remember the day she was born. It doesn't seem possible that 31 years have passed already. She's an amazing person. There have been several occasions in her life when she's been offered interesting opportunities for travel and other experiences. She has often turned to me to ask whether she should make the choice to do these things, and I always say, GO FOR IT! – with a lot of enthusiasm. Consequently, she's lived in Africa twice, been to Europe and South America a couple of times, and traveled through Thailand. She's worked at a number of different jobs. She performs acrobatics and contemporary dance, and teaches Brazilian martial arts. I see her as a competent and powerful woman. She inspires me, and I'm grateful for whatever part I played in helping to empower her.

This same powerful woman is now learning to be a chiropractor. She described the process of how she works as removing the interference in the system so that the body's innate wisdom is empowered to heal itself.

This prompted me to think about how we empower ourselves. One of the important ways that we empower ourselves is by acknowledging and igniting the healer within each of us. When we look for the root causes of any physical manifestation or "dis-ease", then affirm the opposite, we ignite the healer within ourselves and acknowledge our authority over our own lives. When I feel pain, and think of having arthritis in any of my joints, my tendency is to feel vulnerable and powerless. When I affirm that I am changing and releasing experiences from the past and creating space in my joints, I feel much better. If I label the sensation in my back and shoulder as pain, I can place myself in the role of victim. If I decide to see it as the place where my wings are sprouting, so that I will be able to fly, it feels much more empowering.

By taking responsibility for all of our thoughts, words and actions, we empower ourselves to be the best that we can be. Every time we take responsibility for our actions and our reactions, we empower ourselves. The process of making choices and forming new habits is an important way to exercise our authority in our own lives. It's useful to think about this as we go about our daily lives. How much more effective is it when we invite someone to participate in a decision rather than telling them what to do and expecting them to just obey.

When we bring our lives into balance with giving and receiving, we empower ourselves. When we bear our responsibilities with ease and release any burdens that don't belong to us, we empower ourselves. When we speak our truth, we feel empowered. Walking our path and developing in the way that is beneficial for each of us is another way to be at ease with being the authority in our own lives.

The way that you know that you are moving in the direction that is most beneficial for you is that it feels easy, it feels natural, it feels right to you. If something feels like a struggle or feels like you're swimming upstream, then it's time to change direction – make a new choice, turn around, follow your intuition and your guidance, and choose the path of ease. If you're in a relationship with someone and they're not comfortable with who you are, then that's not the right person for you. Walk away, and find someone else. If you try to change yourself to fit with someone, neither of you will feel happy or fulfilled. Ease is the key.

The development that we choose to do through classes and other experiences at my spiritual community is another way that we empower ourselves. When we open ourselves to our psychic abilities, we empower ourselves in moving forward on our paths. I was in a class at my spiritual community recently which is called Life Empowerment. After our meditation, we shared our experiences. One of the participants talked about how the music distracted her during the meditation. In believing the music was a distraction, she was giving up her power. The leader of the class very gently encouraged her to think about what happened during the "distractions" as an important part of her experience, and in doing so, handed the power back to her.

In closing, there are many ways that we empower ourselves in our day to day lives. When we take responsibility for healing ourselves, when we take responsibility for our thoughts, words, and actions, when we bring our lives into balance, and when we develop and unfold in the best way we can, we see ourselves as the authority in our lives, and do it with more and more ease.

The only person you can be in this lifetime is yourself, and the more that you are true to yourself, the happier, healthier and wealthier you will be. It's one of the things I admire most about my daughter. Staying in integrity with who you really are is essential to growth. To quote Dr. Suess, "You are you and that is true, there's no one in the world who's you-er than you." I believe that being the best "you" possible is the way to empower yourself and move forward on your path. Here's to "YOU!"

HEALTH

3/25/12

Our topic for this month is Health. Health is our natural state. Health is an attitude and a state of mind. How we think about things and think about ourselves makes a big difference in our health. I am a healthy person and I always think of myself that way. The events of the last couple of years have really pushed my limits, but I keep doing the best I can.

In developing and learning about metaphysics at my spiritual community, I noticed that some of the things I've learned here, I've been doing instinctively for years before. We learn that what you think, what you say, and what you do is what you draw more of into your life. My kids used to tease me because I never used the "S" word. No matter how many physical symptoms I might be manifesting, I would always think and say, "I'm doing better. I'm sure I'll be fine in a minute." This contrasted sharply with their dad who always believed he had a "touch" of whatever anybody else had. He was a little surprised when the doctors thought one of the kids had appendicitis, because he was sure he had a "touch" of whatever she had. Thinking of myself as healthy came pretty naturally to me based on how my dad lived. In 1999, when my dad was 91, he was filling out a medical history form. The only thing he wrote was that he'd had a hernia repaired in 1942. Other than that, he'd always been healthy. And he did live to be 102.

One of the keys to health is knowing yourself, and one of the ways to get to know yourself is to give yourself time and space to be quiet. We need to be quiet in order to tune in to the wisdom that is within each of us. We need to be quiet in order to ignite the healing energy that is within each of us. We need to be quiet in order to think clearly and act accordingly. Many of our lives are busy and full and noisy. Making sure that we make time for ourselves that is quiet promotes balance, and balance promotes health in our lives.

Another very important aspect of life is laughing, having a sense of humor, and having fun. I believe that humor is healing. If we can't laugh at ourselves, we are in "serious" trouble. I think it's never a good idea to take ourselves or anything in our lives too seriously. One of the things I'm most proud of in my life is that I never lose my sense of humor, no matter what challenges present themselves. When my sister was going through treatment for breast cancer, we made each other laugh whenever possible. I believe it's one of the things that helped her negotiate that path successfully. When she was awaiting surgery, and someone came through calling out, "Marco, Marco," we couldn't stop ourselves from responding, "Polo, Polo." I believe that laughter may be the best medicine, and the more we're able to laugh at ourselves and have fun, the healthier we are. One of the things I love about my spiritual community is that in the almost 10 years that I've been coming here on a very regular basis, we always laugh at something. The spirit and atmosphere here is healing and part of the healing comes from humor and being able to laugh out loud. In addition to being a minister, I'm also an improv comedian, and we call what we do "playing." Laughing is one of the healthiest things we can do, and I love being able to contribute to that. I love that one of the things I do most regularly in my life is to "play."

What we choose to put into our bodies is another important factor when considering health. And this means paying attention to what works and doesn't work in your own body. When you eat, what foods give you energy and vitality? What foods don't "agree" with you? What foods make you fall asleep? Or irritate your stomach? Or make you cough or break out in a rash? What foods and in what amounts are best for you? It doesn't matter what books say or what works for someone else. This is an individual process for each person to figure out. You can "eat right for your blood type." You can be "in the zone." You can eat protein or eliminate carbohydrates or follow whatever fad is currently the most popular. Or you can pay attention and listen to your inner guidance and the wisdom of your own body, and make the choices that are most positive and proactive and healthy for you. Knowing what works best in your own body is another important way to know yourself.

Another step on the path of health may be enlightenment or becoming enlightened. A Hawaiian spiritual tradition states that we are each born into this world as a "bowl of light" containing the radiance of heaven. Fear, guilt and unworthiness are like rocks that we place in our bowl that hide our true "light" essence. Becoming "enlightened" is simply a matter of remembering who we truly are, being who we truly are, and removing any obstacles to our brilliance. Anything that works against the full expression of who and what we are may be rocks that we need to remove from our bowl to allow us to be the light that we are truly meant to be.

My daughter is studying to be a chiropractor. She has explained that chiropractic philosophy affirms that the body's natural state is health, and the adjustments that they do remove any interference that exists in the system. When we take the rocks out of our bowls, we are removing the interference in the system that takes away our light. We are transforming dis-ease into ease. What rocks have you placed in your bowl of light? Knowing yourself allows you to remove more rocks and be the "light" that is truly you.

Another way to feel better is to give love to others. "A Course in Miracles" teaches that the two primary emotions are love and fear, and they cannot exist in the same space at the same time. When we choose to give love or nurturing or reach out to another, this is one of the things that is most healing to ourselves. When you are hurting in some part of your body, mind, or spirit, one of the best ways to heal yourself is to reach out and give love to someone else. Make a phone call, pet your cat, go visit someone in a hospital or nursing home, do healing energy work on someone else, and you will definitely focus on love instead of fear. Know yourself well enough to know when it's time to reach out in order to ignite healing within.

Recently, I went to see Shirley MacLaine. It was a very entertaining evening. It almost felt like she'd invited us into her living room to show us photos and film clips, and tell stories from her life. She's had some wonderful experiences in metaphysics and spirituality. Her parting message was: "Allow the intelligence of what you've chosen to be your teacher." She counseled the audience that one of the most important things we can do is to know ourselves. There are many ways to do this, as we've talked about today. Meditate, go inside, search out your inner wisdom, laugh, and give love to others. I believe this is the way to "know yourself to health."

(I found a lot of inspiration for this talk in the book, "A Deep Breath of Life" by Alan Cohen. This book has a page for every day of the year and I've been reading it on a daily basis for almost 10 years.)

AT ONE MENT

4/15/12

I had an interesting reaction to this month's topic. When I got the schedule for topics and I saw the word "Atonement", I immediately thought, "AT ONE MENT." Then, when I got the attachment with the themes and ideas, sure enough, it said, "AT ONE MENT," which was very affirming. As I was stopped at a red light last week, I noticed a sign on the church across the street which read, "Experience God's love Sundays at 10:30 a.m." This struck me particularly strongly because of the things I've learned at my spiritual community and the things I've found to be true for myself. Why would anyone want to be associated with a place that thinks you can only experience God's love on Sundays at 10:30 a.m.?

In pondering AT ONE MENT, I started thinking about what brings us together and what moves us apart. About 20 years ago, I remember noticing some aspects of myself that I was not especially pleased with or proud of. I labeled these attributes impatient, intolerant and entitled. I noticed how these things were affecting my interactions and relationships with people, and the choices I was making in my day to day life. As I became more familiar with my thoughts, words and actions, I started to make different choices. As I reflect back now, it becomes clear that in order to justify feeling any of those things, one must feel separate and different from everyone else. If I see myself in a different or better position than anyone else, separation is implied. If I truly understand and acknowledge the connection with all that is, I cannot see myself as separate, different, and, most importantly, better than anybody else. My needs cannot take precedence over anyone else's. I have no more right to drive at any particular speed or to acquire any material thing or get to the front of the line faster than anyone else. We are all one, and the more we acknowledge that and live in cooperation and harmony with each other, the better off we all are. And it may not feel that way in one particular moment, but in the long run, it's definitely a better and more loving choice.

When I think about myself and reflect on the way I operate in the world, I see myself as an "inclusive" person. When I invite people to events, I generally have a "more the merrier" outlook. I like to make people feel welcome. I've had some lovely feedback from the dance club I belong to from people who've shared experiences of feeling welcomed and encouraged. I hate the feeling of being left out. It's one of my earliest memories of unhappiness. I never liked being the one who was picked last for a team, or wasn't picked at all. When I read about someone's gathering on Easter, I felt bad that I hadn't known about it, because I ended up being home alone, and I had celebrated with them last year. When I feel left out, it touches the little girl inside me and I feel small, sad and scared. I much prefer to feel connected and loving, rather than left out and alone.

When I reflect on connections, I sometimes think about the kids from elementary school. Through the magic of Facebook, I have reconnected with some of the people I went to elementary school with. I went to a small Catholic school, and was in the same class with the same kids from kindergarten through eighth grade. There are so many memories of those times. Recently, we've all been discussing the experiences that we had with some of the nuns, who were definitely abusive at times. We've talked about the May processions, and the traditions we had for celebrating birthdays. We remember our gym teacher so fondly. For me, those are un-breakable bonds and connections. I feel very loving whenever I see their faces and their comments. Even though I haven't seen many of them in about 45 years, I still feel very con-nected to them, and I love and appreciate those connections.

Another internet connection is online dating. On one of the sites that I've visited, one of the questions asked is what is the first thing people notice about you? Responses are things like eyes, hair, tattoos, smile (I admit I'm kind of partial to arms myself) and other physical attributes. People rarely write about their loving spirit, kind heart, or inner beauty as being the first thing people notice. It takes more than just looking at a photo and reading a few lines to make a meaningful con-nection with someone and truly get to know them. When we look beyond physical attributes and the perceptions of age or race or ethnicity or intelligence or economics to the innate humanness of each of us, it is much more difficult to feel sep-arate and different. When we get in touch with the ways in which we are alike, rather than different, we feel much more connected, much more AT ONE.

I was watching a TV show the other night, and someone re-ferred to our outward appearance as a dust cover, like we put on our books when we were in school. And this dust cover can take on any appearance. It can be a brown paper gro-cery bag. It can be decorated with personal art or stickers and cartoons. But no matter what the outward appearance of the "dust cover," what is inside is our true essence, the being that we truly are. And the being that we truly are is part of a whole, and completely connected to all that is - not just other human, physical beings, but all that is and all that ever was or will be. Sometimes people can cover up who they are very effectively with loud voices, obnoxious behavior, piercings or jewelry, and many other physical trappings. It is our job to see past the "dust cover" to the essence, and then respond from our higher self to their higher self, and connect in a loving way.

In addition to feeling connected to others, it is also important to be connected to ourselves, which leads to being "AT ONE" with ourselves. For me, this means living in integrity with who I am and what I believe. It is important for me to treat people the way I want to be treated, with love and compassion. When we choose things that are healthy for our bodies, we are at one with ourselves. When we choose people, places and things that bring us peace and help us grow and develop, we are at one with ourselves.

Our connections with each other and our connection with ourselves leads naturally to thinking about our connection with God. As I went through the seminary a few years ago, what was challenging for me was the notion of God and what I did or did not believe. I keep coming to terms with what that means in my life. Here at the my spiritual community, we are taught that God is everything and everyone, and there is no separation between us and God. That's the principle I've been adjusting to, after having been raised Catholic and being taught to experience God's love on Sundays at 10:30 a.m. Now, I know that there is more to this life than just this physical body and this physical existence. Now, I know, because of the experiences that I've had, that there is communication and connection between the visible and invisible. I have definitely felt the presence of my dad and others that have made their transition, especially here at my spiritual community during meditations. I know that the messages I receive are "transmissions" for the other person, as I tune into their frequency. And these "transmissions" are coming from something beyond myself. In some cases, when I give messages to someone I've never met before and technically "know" nothing about, and they give me the feedback that the messages are right on, I know beyond a shadow of a doubt that there is a connection beyond whatever I can rationally understand or explain. I know that we are AT ONE.

I recently read a quote that moved me (and not just because it was from Johnny Depp) that I'd like to share - "There are four questions of value in life: What is sacred? Of what is the spirit made? What is worth living for, and what is worth dying for? The answer to each is the same. Only love." When we choose to be open to the love and connection that exists between each of us, and to be in touch with the essence that we truly are, we are AT ONE.

INTEGRITY

6/24/12

Our topic for this month is Integrity. When I think about integrity, people like Martin Luther King and Gandhi come to mind. People who stood up for what they believed in, despite huge personal consequences. For me personally, integrity is about being consistent with the person who I am and aspire to be, no matter what anybody else does. I treat people the way I want to be treated and in harmony with the person I want to be, even when they are acting in ways that on the surface might not seem to merit being treated that way. When I make an appointment to meet somebody, I do my best to arrive on time. When I make an agreement to do something for or with somebody, I do my best to make that happen. When I say I'll call, I call. I notice that sometimes, there is a temptation to be petty or spiteful when there is some perceived slight or wrong. I understand that that does not serve me or anyone else, and I pay attention when those kinds of feelings arise. One of my favorite sayings is, "Holding onto resentment is liking taking poison, then waiting for the other person to keel over." Sometimes I do better with this than others. Instead of reacting negatively when someone does something that bothers or irritates me, I do my best to sit with it until a constructive solution presents itself. Then I do my best to forgive myself and the other person. That is part of staying in integrity for me.

When I think about integrity, I often think about my daughter. She had an experience recently of being held up, and having her iPhone stolen. Fortunately, she was not physically harmed in any way. In talking to her about this, to process the experience, she said it lead her to examine the small acts of "stealing" that happen in her life. She noticed the tendency to sometimes take little things from stores if she thought she could get away with it, or to keep things that she found that belonged to someone else. She said she's looking at these behaviors and changing them in her life. I was really proud of her for her willingness to look at that experience from that perspective. She was home for a visit recently and I observed the way she goes about her day to day life. She chooses to eat in a very healthy manner on a consistent basis. She and a couple of friends have challenged each other to be more physically fit, and she's been consistent in her physical efforts. She's in school, and has made time to study and practice, even though she's on vacation, and would like to be out having fun. She speaks her mind and her truth, even though it's sometimes very uncomfortable. She's preparing to go on a chiropractic mission trip to El Salvador because she believes in what she's doing, and believes in the importance of service in one's personal and professional life. These kinds of behaviors are what constitute integrity in my mind.

Another person who I think about when it comes to integrity is a young man who is a member of the dance community. He became pretty famous a few years ago when he won the title of "America's Favorite Dancer" on So You Think You Can Dance. Recently, he came out as being a gay man. He did a 2 hour interview on Mormonstories.org about being a Mormon and coming to terms with his own sexuality. He talked about having had a female fiancee for a while, in his attempts to fit in to the model that he'd been taught. He talked about wanting to die at some points because he felt as though he was going against the teachings he'd believed all his life. As a devout Mormon, he had gone on a mission for a year, and that was a very impactful experience in his life. In his exploration of his sexuality, he had chosen to remain chaste in order to be consistent with his religious beliefs. He followed all the prescribed rules, and was forthright and open in his conversations with his bishop. He went through a process of what might be called "penance" in coming to terms with who he is. He did his best to effect change from within, in order to stay within the structure of the church that he loves so much, and believes in so deeply. Ultimately, he chose to leave the church and live in integrity with who he knows himself to be. Family is extremely important to him, and he fully expects to have a family, but it will be one with two dads. In listening to his sharing of the process that he went through, I was so moved, and knew that I wanted to incorporate his story as part of my talk on integrity. He is a truly shining example of what integrity means to me – living in consonance with who you are, no matter what.

For me, integrity is about telling the truth and honoring yourself for the being that you truly are. One of the most important people to tell the truth to is yourself. Next, is to be truthful with those close to you. In understanding and living the metaphysical principles, I truly believe that what we think, what we say, and what we do is what we draw more of to us. From that perspective, I really pay attention to what I think, say, and do. I have learned to affirm the opposite, and practice that on a regular basis. When my knee hurts, I say, "I am moving forward with flexibility and ease." And when people ask how I'm doing, I usually say, "Fine," or "I'm doing great," or something of that nature. Consequently, most people see me as strong and capable and competent and together and able to handle things easily. Which is true, on the one hand. On the other hand, I'm also someone who is sensitive, and feels things really strongly, and feels sad and scared and upset and challenged by things that happen in my life. It sometimes feels like a challenge to me to reconcile using the metaphysical principles in my life, and at the same time letting people know who I truly am and what I'm really feeling.

There are a number of things that I don't talk about much. Almost every movement I make, from sitting to standing to getting in and out of a car to dancing causes me pain. I am alone far more often than not, and I feel really lonely sometimes. I function best when I have a best friend and/or romantic partner who I talk to every day and share everything with, and I haven't had either for quite some time. I'm really sensitive, and get my feelings hurt very easily. My mother-in-law, my parents, and one of my best friends all died in four months a couple of years ago, and I am still so very sad about that sometimes. I don't dwell on these things, but wanted to share them in this moment as a way of being in integrity with myself. I know that I am strong and confident and smart and capable, and also someone who depends on the loving support of family and friends.

In order to be in integrity with yourself, you have to know yourself. That's one of the things we focus on here at my spiritual community – knowing oneself. There are many ways to know yourself – spending quiet time with yourself, and allowing thoughts and feelings to arise is one. Being aware of your thoughts, words and actions is another. Noticing the people you spend time with, the places you go, and the things you spend your time doing informs you about your choices. As you get to know yourself, you can begin to make choices that make sense for you. If something is not working for you, notice the people you're spending time with, the places you're frequenting, and the things that you're doing, then figure out which ones are bringing you joy and lifting your spirit. Figure out which ones keep you in integrity with who you are and who you want to be. There was a quote on Facebook the other day that made sense to me. "Respect yourself enough to walk away from anything that no longer serves you, grows you or makes you happy."

And there was also a quote from Mother Teresa that echoed

my thoughts:

"People are often unreasonable and self-centered.
Forgive them anyway.
If you are kind, people may accuse you of ulterior motives.
Be kind anyway.
If you are honest, people may cheat you.
Be honest anyway.
If you find happiness, people may be jealous.
Be happy anyway.
The good you do today may be forgotten tomorrow.
Do good anyway.
Give the world the best you have and it may never be enough.
Give your best anyway.
For you see, in the end, it is between you and God. It was never
between you and them anyway."

In closing, take the time to get to know yourself. Be true to
yourself and truthful with others. Live in a way that is consistent with how you see yourself and how you want to be. Be in
integrity. You're worth it.

PROSPERITY

7/22/12

Our topic for this month is Prosperity, and Prosperity is, first and foremost, a state of mind, just as thoughts of lack are a state of mind. Prosperity is not about your bank balance, it's the consciousness you have about your life. Prosperity is happiness, health, and wealth. I feel really lucky, and know that I have abundance and prosperity in my life. Every day, I affirm that I am wealthful, prosperous and affluent. A number of years ago, I read those words in a book called Spiritual Economics by Eric Butterworth, and they really resonate for me. I like thinking of myself in that way. I like having Prosperity consciousness.

I do affirmations on a daily basis. I firmly believe that what we think, what we say and what we do is what we draw more of to us. I noticed that I was saying and thinking, "I'm so disappointed," on a surprising number of occasions. I know that this is a thought of lack, and I choose to have prosperity consciousness. To transform that thought, I added a new affirmation. I say, "I am peaceful. I am content. I am loved. I am enough." I find that when I get "wound up" about something that is happening in my life or notice myself thinking about being disappointed, if I stop and say those words, "I am peaceful. I am content. I am loved. I am enough," it changes my consciousness and calms me down and I feel better. Sometimes, I have to do it several times a day and even several times in a row, and it does really work.

In thinking about Prosperity, I asked myself the question,

"What is enough?" How do we know how much is enough? And how do we fill ourselves? I have noticed that sometimes I try to fill myself with food. Recently, I was experiencing a significant amount of "daughter drama" in my life. I noticed that I was eating way more than I needed to, and sometimes compulsively traveling back and forth to the kitchen, long after my actual physical hunger had been satisfied. I needed to stop, and breathe, and think about what was going on, and make a different choice, because I have learned that, ultimately, food is not going to fill whatever is happening inside me. I needed to affirm, "I am peaceful. I am content. I am loved. I am enough." I affirm that I fill this space with love from the inside. I change how I think and that changes what I do.

About nine years ago, when I was taking classes at my spiritual community, one of the teachers talked about tithing and what it meant to her. Why do we give 10% of what we earn to the place that promotes our spiritual development? Her talk impacted me so much that I started doing just that. Whatever money I earned, I immediately adjusted the check I wrote each Sunday to reflect a 10% donation. I wondered occasionally what effect this would have on my finances. Would I still have "enough" money to take care of my needs? I found that I had even more abundance. At times when I wondered if I would have enough money to pay certain bills, something would happen, and suddenly there would be plenty of money in my checking account.

Affluence is defined as an abundant flow. In the same way that we can put a rheostat on a light switch, and regulate the flow of energy and the amount of light that is shed, our prosperity is all about our consciousness. The electricity and our affluence are always there. Our consciousness is what regulates the flow. Giving freely is one way to open the flow of abundance. I find that when I give fully and freely, abundance flows to me more easily. When we give thanks before the Love Offering, we put into effect the law of tenfold return to those who give freely and from the heart. That means that whatever you give is returned to you TENFOLD or more! We bless what we give. One of the definitions of the word bless is "to confer prosperity." Blessing everything and giving thanks is one way to turn the rheostat of abundance all the way open.

For me, another aspect of prosperity is allowing your good to come to you. It is about allowing your life to be full of happiness, health, and wealth. It is about knowing and affirming that you are worthy to receive. When I had my hip replaced last year, I chose some very important lessons in both asking for and accepting help. It was a real challenge for me, especially at first. I know all about giving to others. The challenge was allowing others to give to me. I got a lot of practice with the words, "Thank you." Magical words really. I also got to learn about and understand the gift we give to others in allowing them to give to us. The first step is asking for help, the second step is allowing the good to be given to you, and the third step is being grateful and expressing gratitude.

Gratitude is a really important component in abundance and flow. I began my fifth year of keeping a gratitude journal last week. Every night, I write down at least five things that I am grateful for. When I pay attention to what I am grateful for, the flow of abundance is strong and there is no room for thoughts of lack. Prosperity is not about how much money you have, it's about how you think about things. It's about allowing and accepting an abundance of happiness, health, and wealth in your life, and then giving thanks for that abundance.

I got a call from a close friend the other day telling me that her grandma was going into hospice. I've known this family for over 20 years, and love them all very much. The next morning, I went to visit Grandma at the hospice. When I walked into the room, she was surrounded by family members, all of whom really love her. She has requested that I do her memorial service, so I was talking to people about their thoughts about her. In every case, her family members talked about how Grandma would do anything for you, and often had. Her generosity of spirit impacted each one of their lives. To me, that is the essence of Prosperity – feeling the abundance of happiness, health and wealth in your life and being able to share that fully and freely with those you love.

As many of you know, my dad lived to be 102 years old. People often asked him what his "secret" was. I believe that part of his "secret" was prosperity – happiness, health, and wealth. My dad was really loved by family and friends. He was very healthy for all of his life. He was wealthy in many aspects of his life – he had a large, loud, loving family, and many lifelong friends. He was truly generous. He gave freely to people in need. When he loaned money to others (which was a frequent occurrence), it was always with no strings attached. This is important in developing prosperity consciousness. Giving freely is part of the essence of prosperity. When I trust that the universe is abundant, I can give freely of myself because I understand that there is never any lack nor need for any thoughts of lack. Prosperity exists in our consciousness, not our checkbook. Believing in abundance is the first step in creating prosperity.

I have a book called, "A Deep Breath of Life," that has a page for each day of the year. Recently, I read a page that was all about letting your life be easy. The author asked the question, "What would you be doing differently if your life was about ease?" This doesn't mean sitting back and expecting others to do things for you, it means honoring yourself and doing what you love. It means choosing to do the things that bring you joy and lift your spirit. It means choosing to do the things that make you feel most alive and refusing to participate in anything that does not serve you. It means allowing the flow of abundance and affirming that you are a whole being in a whole universe. Prosperity is not about your bank account or your job, it's about your consciousness. With each breath you take, remember to choose happiness, health and wealth, and allow the flow of abundance in your life to be opened up to the max.

AUTHORITY

8/12/12

Our topic for this month is Authority. Words like authority and command are often "charged" with energy and can easily push buttons for some people. I know that I personally have a fairly strong history of resisting authority. For a long time, the best way to get me to do something was to tell me I couldn't. I saw that as a challenge, and I often accepted that challenge. One of the things that used to be so important to me was that I really needed to be RIGHT! I would argue every little detail with someone, especially when I knew or thought I knew that I was "right." I thought that being confrontational and winning every point that I could was the way to exercise my authority.

Fortunately, I have grown. I have learned to be much gentler. If there's a point of minor disagreement, I choose to say things like I may or may not have heard you correctly or I may or may not have said or done that. Some of the affirmations that I have learned here at my spiritual community include, "I am the authority in my life, and I am at ease with that authority. I am in command of my life and I am at ease with that command." Ease being the operative word.

During an experiential weekend in high school, I remember getting a book mark (which I still have) that says, "What you resist runs you." (And for us Star Trek fans, the Borg told us, "Resistance is futile.") I do my best to pay attention to what I give my energy to. From time to time, I sit back and look at what, if anything, I'm resisting, and how I'm letting it run me. The choices we make, and the experiences we create, and the people we draw to us, are a reflection of ourselves. When we resist authority figures, what is it reflecting about us? The more secure I am with myself, the less I feel the need to resist others. I can just be. I am secure in the authority within myself. I am at ease with my authority.

When we are at ease with our authority, we don't feel like we have anything to prove to anyone else. We know who we are. We know what we want. We know how to proceed in going about our lives. We don't have to waste energy resisting other people's authority, and we don't have to set ourselves up as "authority figures" that invite resistance from others. We can just be ourselves – in the profound words of Dr. Suess, "You are you and that is true, there's no one in the world that's you-er than you."

Part of my training in becoming a Reiki Master Teacher was learning how to lead meditations. I had already been doing meditations at my spiritual community for a little while, so I was pretty sure of myself in this area. After my practice meditation, my teacher commented that my style was kind of like grabbing someone by the throat and dragging them forward whether they liked it or not. He suggested that I think about Bugs Bunny in the Looney Tunes cartoons, when an enticing scent wafts out of the window, and Bugs is irresistibly drawn towards it. It's an invitation rather than a demand. When you invite someone to participate in an experience, it's very different than demanding that they do something or ordering them to comply.

Where does authority originate within ourselves? When we have confidence, we act with authority. When we believe in ourselves, we are much more able to act with authority. When we use our own wisdom, discernment and guidance, we are at ease in knowing what is right for ourselves. I read a quote from Gautama Buddha that says, "Believe nothing, no matter where you read it, or who said it, no matter if I have said it, unless it agrees with your own reason and your own common sense."

When we trust in our own knowing and infuse our actions with love, our authority comes forth with ease. When our authority comes forth with ease, we can invite people to participate instead of demanding that they comply. As I pondered this talk, I kept hearing the verse from 1st Corinthians, "If I speak in the tongues of men and of angels, but have not love, I am only a resounding gong or a clanging cymbal." Being Sicilian, Sagittarius, and from New York, I know how to be a "clanging symbol" in order to get people's attention. I've been working on learning to be softer and more gentle and quiet in my leadership, and working on leading by example, instead of volume. When I smile as I lead my meditations, I feel more gentle. When I infuse my words with love, they are much easier for others to hear.

There are times when it is useful to be very confident with your authority, and express it strongly and clearly. I was going to perform a wedding last year, and at the rehearsal, the wedding coordinator was telling everyone what to do, and where to stand. I observed what she was doing and accepted it with good humor, especially when she told the groomsmen to "stagnate" themselves on the steps. But when she commanded me to ask, "Who gives this woman away?", I decided to take a stand. I asked the bride if that was what she wanted. After all, she was 40 years old, had been living with her husband-to-be for a few years, and they already had a 2 year old son. So I didn't think anyone needed to GIVE HER AWAY! I asked her if that was what she wanted, because I was completely willing to respect her wishes. When she said that wasn't what she wanted, I spoke with a lot of authority, and told the wedding coordinator that we wouldn't be doing that.

When you speak with authority, and it is infused with love, people listen and respond. My daughter was teaching a partner flips class to the Bay Area Derby Girls. It was in a big warehouse space, and it was really noisy. There were lots of women in the class, so when they started practicing what my daughter had explained, I went down to the opposite end of the practice area from where she was, and gave tips and encouragement to the women there. Now, I don't know anything about partner flips, but I had listened to my daughter's explanation, so I was able to say things like, "Move in closer, point your toes, bend lower, etc." And because I speak with authority, they listened. My intentions were for the highest and best good. I wanted them to have the most successful experience they could in the safest way possible. I exercised my authority and infused it with love.

When I affirm, "I am the authority in my life and I am at ease with that authority," it feels good. There are many things in this world that I notice, but I have absolutely no control over. What I always have control over are my own thoughts, words, and actions. I cannot change or affect anything anyone else does, but I have absolute control and ability to choose my reaction and my response. Just as we build our physical muscles through training and exercise, we build our mental, emotional and spiritual muscles through practice also.

I've been taking the Life Empowerment class at my spiritual community. One of the purposes of this class is to remind and encourage us to know that we are the authority in our lives. When we take full responsibility for our thoughts, words and actions, we are active in how we're creating our lives. As we develop awareness of what we think, say and do, we know and understand ourselves better. I read a beautiful quote from the Dalai Lama recently, "When you think everything is someone else's fault, you will suffer a lot. When you realize that everything springs only from yourself, you will learn both peace and joy."

We empower ourselves when we take responsibility for ALL

of our thoughts, words and actions. We are the creators of everything that happens in our lives. We empower ourselves when we acknowledge that our choices belong to us and are the seeds that create our lives. We also empower others when we take responsibility for ourselves, leaving them free to be responsible for themselves.

"I am the authority in my life and I am at ease with that authority." As we affirm those words, we understand and affirm that we are the creator of all of our experiences. We are in command and at ease with that command. We exercise our authority in the most constructive way possible, and always infuse our choices with love.

HONOR

9/2/12

Our topic for this month is Honor. Echoes from my childhood showed up immediately - Honor thy father and thy mother. I was thinking about my dad. Recently, I was visiting family in California. I was telling my 10 year old great-niece a story about my dad (who was her great-grandfather and who she loved.) During World War II, my dad was stationed in Sicily, and early one morning, a very large bomb dropped into the house where he was staying. Miraculously, it did not go off. My dad always celebrated that day as a second birthday, and this year, I honored him by sharing that story with the next generation of our family.

I honor his memory frequently. He was so special to me and I think of him often. For years, I called my parents every day and now, two years after their transition, I wake up many mornings just wishing I could call them. So, I honor their memory in that way, too.

I showed my great-niece how to play a fun piano piece that my mother taught me when I was little. It involves running your knuckles over the keys, and I thought she would enjoy it. She picked it up very quickly, and I told her it was one of Grandma's favorites. It felt good to share something special about my mom.

In addition to honoring our parents, I believe it is also important to honor our children. I have two daughters, who I love and appreciate very much. I'm proud of the close relationships I have with them. I believe one of the reasons for that is the amount of honor and respect we have for each other. I believe we have two ears and one mouth so that we can listen twice as much as we talk. When my children talk to me about things that are happening in their lives, I always ask permission before giving them input. If they don't want it, I keep my opinions to myself. (Although occasionally I am accused of thinking really loudly.) When I offer my opinion, it is with the understanding that ultimately, their choices are their own, and I support them in their choices, even when they differ from what I might have chosen. We have keys to each other's houses because we know that we treat each other's space with respect, and don't enter without permission. We honor each other in that way.

It is important to honor our friends. We honor our friendships by staying in touch, being available when friends need us, and making time for each other. We also honor our friends by telling them the truth, even when it's hard to hear. We honor our friends by creating a safe space for them to vent their feelings when they need to, and by listening supportively in those moments. We have compassion for the feelings of others. We honor people when we put our trust in them.

Sometimes the best way to honor somebody is by saying no. We often think we have to "be nice" to someone, and do what they ask, even if it's something we really don't want to do. We think they won't like us if we don't do what they ask. We actually serve ourselves and others best when we are honest about things. It is much better to say something like - I care about you and support you, but I can't help with this particular thing at this particular time, than to do something we really don't want to do, and then feel resentful after the fact. Being true to ourselves serves ourselves and others best in the long run. And someone who doesn't like you because you won't do something for them that isn't right for you, isn't a true friend anyway. We honor others when we respect their opinions, and their right to express them. We don't have to agree, just show respect.

It's important to respect our own and other people's ways of doing things. Everyone processes things differently. It's important to honor ourselves in the way that we choose to process events that occur in our lives. Grief is an important example. Everyone processes grief and loss in their own way and in their own time. It does not serve us or anyone around us to be critical or judgmental about the way someone else deals with grief. One person may need to wail and express themselves loudly and often. Another person may need to withdraw and seclude themselves. One person may take years and another may take days. Sometimes it can feel hurtful when someone else processes an experience very differently than we do. It's useful to honor ourselves and them in allowing them to walk the path that is most beneficial for them. And sometimes that means removing a photograph that is too painful to look at for a while, or choosing to limit or eliminate contact with that person for whatever period of time makes sense.

It is also important to honor ourselves. We have a physical body, a mental body, an emotional body and a spiritual body. How do we honor each aspect of ourselves? We take care of ourselves by paying attention to what we eat and drink, how we move our bodies, using sunscreen, getting enough rest and enough activity. We pay attention to what we think, what we say and what we do. We choose what we read, what we watch, and what we listen to. We choose the people we spend time with, the places we go and the things that we do. We choose friends and partners who support us in being the best we can be. We meditate and have quiet time to reflect, and allow our guides and teachers to communicate with us. We create balance in our lives. We honor ourselves when we affirm "Peace I am Still." The more we create harmony in our lives, give ourselves time and space to breathe and think, and the more we surround ourselves with light, love and beauty, the more we honor ourselves.

We honor ourselves when we make positive healthy choices about the people, places and things in our lives. We honor ourselves when we choose what we know is right, even when it is not what's easiest.

The way we allow ourselves to be treated is a reflection of how we feel about ourselves. When we feel good about ourselves, we draw people to us who treat us with respect, and honor us for who we are. If we don't feel so good about ourselves, we may choose people who treat us poorly. We accept that kind of treatment because we don't value ourselves highly enough. If you're not happy with the way someone else is treating you, it is useful to stop and look at how you're treating yourself.

Recently, I read a Facebook post which said, "The law of attraction is this – you don't attract what you want, you attract what you are." When we treat ourselves with respect, we draw people to us who treat us respectfully.

We honor ourselves when we allow ourselves to become most fully who we are, whatever that might be. We don't have to make excuses or apologize to anyone for being who we are. We honor ourselves when we follow our own personal path, no matter where it leads us. Ask yourself – what is your passion and how are you following it? How are you allowing yourself to grow in the ways that are most important for you? What is the price you pay if you don't choose to follow your gifts?

No one was more surprised than I was that I became a minister. Although I'm very comfortable with the path I've chosen, and continue to grow and develop, the echoes from my childhood still crop up. Because of my upbringing and the baggage

I still carry about "religion," I think twice when I meet people before telling them I'm an ordained minister. I qualify my statement by explaining that I'm very spiritual and not at all religious. I'm not trying to convince anyone of anything, and not trying to convert anyone to my way of thinking. I'm not sure why I still feel the need to do that, but possibly it's because of my own reaction when confronted with anything of a "religious" nature. I tend to back up as quickly as I can, and distance myself from it. I'm not entirely sure why I still have that reaction, but I'm sitting with it, noticing what happens and moving forward in my process. I'm honoring myself by allowing myself to grow.

In closing, honoring and respecting others and honoring and respecting ourselves is a constructive way to go through life. Giving ourselves the time and space to breathe, and process whatever is going on in our lives, and checking in with our own wisdom before making a decision or commitment, is such an important way to live our lives in an honorable fashion.

MANIFESTATION

10/14/12

How often do we hear people say, "Well, nobody's perfect." My response to that is, "Everybody's perfect." Because that's the truth – we are all perfect, in that we are all manifesting exactly what we are creating for ourselves. Our life is a garden, and we harvest what we plant. If we are manifesting abundance, it is because our thoughts, words and actions are abundant.

In our Life Empowerment class, the teacher has created a chart that shows a bean from the time it's planted to the time it's harvested, in each of its stages. After it's planted in the ground, it germinates and there's a lot of action under the ground, but not much is visible on the surface. Then it begins to sprout, but doesn't look like much, and it isn't ready to eat. Given the proper amounts of sunshine, water and weeding, eventually it grows tall and strong, and produces an abundant crop that can be picked and enjoyed. This is the cycle that we constantly create... cause and effect. Because we are always creating, these cycles can overlap. So, once upon a time, we may have had a thought of lack or "dis-ease" that is mani-festing in the present. At some point, we changed the way we were thinking, and created thoughts of abundance and ease. We wonder why we're experiencing lack when we are living with abundance thinking now. It's just the cycle playing itself out. The more we can stay in the cycle of abundance and posi-tive thinking, the more we will manifest abundance and other positive things in our lives.

Recently, one of my friends commented, "I can't get anywhere on time." Because of the kinds of conversations she and I consistently have about metaphysics, and particularly abundance, and because I know she is very aware of her thoughts, words and actions, I told her that saying that she can't get anywhere on time is a thought of lack, and encouraged her to change that statement to something that makes sense for her, like, "Time works perfectly for me" or "I arrive at each place in just the right time." That way, she manifests abundance instead of lack.

Everything that is created starts with a thought. We imagine something. Then we think about it. We might draw or paint or build or shape it in some way to make it manifest into physical form, but it always starts in our imagination.

And we have to be patient in order to see things come to fruition sometimes. We have to stick around in order to see the harvest of what we have planted. Sometimes, it happens in an instant, but it can also take the fullness of time to manifest.

Manifesting is creating, and we are constantly creating. One of the strongest experiences I've ever had in my life was the creating of my second child. After my first child was born in February of 1981, I knew there was a second child, and I knew that child was going to be born in March of 1984. It was one of the strongest things I've ever experienced. Even though things were not going particularly well between her dad and I in the spring of 1983, I knew this soul needed to come through us. Sure enough, my second child was born in March of 1984 and after that, I knew beyond a shadow of a doubt, that I was done having children. I had manifested exactly what I was supposed to, and was complete with the experience.

Choosing our thoughts, words, and actions is what we use to create the effect we desire. The other night, I really wanted to be in two different places at the same time. I made a choice to spend most of my time at one place, then go to the other for the tail end of the second event. The first event took longer than I was anticipating, and I found myself getting a little impatient and frustrated, and was really ready to go by the time it was over. I was feeling kind of tense when I got into my car. As I drove across town, the drivers in front of me were going "too slow." So I started swearing at them. Then every light I came to turned red just before I arrived at the intersection, so I started swearing even more, and banging my hands on the steering wheel, and generally getting myself all worked up. Part of me was encouraging myself to change my behavior, to affirm that I am peaceful, content, loved and enough, but I was ignoring that part and telling it that I didn't want to hear that stuff at that moment. I just wanted to be mired in my frustration and childishness.

I finally arrived at my second destination. There was a guest instructor there, and I went up to her to introduce myself and thank her for being there. She shared that she'd recently had a concussion. Immediately, my energy shifted, and I offered to do energy work on her. We went outside and I did some Reiki on her, and then shared the information that came up for me to tell her. It was a totally positive connection for both of us. Then, I went back in and danced for a while. My mood had shifted completely, and when I left there and drove to my next destination, the trip was smooth and relaxed and, amazingly, all the lights were green.

We are responsible for absolutely everything in our lives. We create everything. Blaming someone else serves nothing and no one. We manifest exactly as we are, and the more we accept responsibility for our lives, the more we empower ourselves.

And sometimes, it's helpful to "act as if" something that we desire has already been manifested. I was talking to a friend who applied for a new job. She said she'd learned that even though it's a behavioral health position, the employees wear scrubs. She decided to go out and buy some scrubs, and "act as if" she already has the job and is preparing to go to work there. "Acting as if" is a very powerful tool. When we act as if something is already happening in our lives, we use our creating energy to manifest our desires.

Affirmations are a wonderful example of "act as if." We affirm what we desire in the present tense, and as though it is already happening. To increase the power of my affirmations, I learned from my teacher to begin each statement with the words, "With each breath, I enjoy and am grateful for..." Gratitude is another important component of the creating energy. I am so thankful for so many things in my life and I express that on a daily basis, literally with each breath I take.

Something else that is particularly important to pay attention to is using the words: "I AM." "I AM" is one of the most powerful creating energy statements we can make. When we say, "I AM" - it is essential to pay attention to what follows, because that is what we are creating. That is what we are manifesting.

One of the most important beliefs that we have as metaphysicians is that what we think, what we say, and what we do is what we draw more of into our lives. This is the basis of manifestation or creating energy. Pay attention to the words you say, the places you go and the people you spend time with. If you want to manifest something different, you actually have to change something in your life.

Affirm and know that we are always perfect, and always creating perfectly. What we manifest is our choice, and we have the power to change that with each breath. You are the authority in your life. You are in command. The choices we make are the seeds that we plant, and the harvest that we reap. If you're not content with what's happening in your life, the one thing you truly have the power to do is to change something in yourself that will then change what you manifest. It's always within our power to choose what we create.

PROSPERITY LAWS – CREATION AND ATTRACTION

11/4/12

Our topic for this month is the Prosperity Laws. There are several Prosperity Laws and I'm going to talk about the Laws of Creation and Attraction this week.

Abundance is about flow. It's important to open up a faucet in order to allow the water to flow freely. You can look at it for as long as you want. You can tell it what an amazing faucet it is, and how you know the water stream will be powerful. You can affirm that the water flows freely and abundantly. But until you actually turn on the tap, the water doesn't flow. One of my friends told me her husband just got a job working at IHOP. He's been unemployed for a while, and although he's a highly knowledgeable computer person with very specialized skills, he hasn't been able to find work in his field at this moment. Taking the job at IHOP is one way to open up the flow. I firmly believe that he will be surprised at how fast he attracts a job in his field, now that he's allowed himself to get into the flow of abundance by taking a job that brings in income. He will also feel better about himself as he interacts with others and is in a service position. Sometimes the best way to feel better about yourself is to serve others.

I went to visit someone at TMC last week. It still affects me to walk past the hospital room where my father was when we got the news that he was going into hospice and only had days to live. I was re-experiencing that loss, so I called my sister for support, which always helps. I told her I was going to make meatballs, and she thought that was a good plan. (What she actually said was, "That's good because with us, it's either food or vendettas.") I proceeded to make 5 lbs. of meatballs (which is a lot of meatballs), and then bring them to friends and family. The more I shared them, the better I felt. Four days later, I repeated the whole process again. And, again, the more I shared, the better I felt. Sometimes, the best thing I can do for myself when I'm feeling down is to do something nice for someone else. Giving can be the best way to receive.

When I'm feeling the worst, stepping outside myself and giving to another person can make all the difference in the world. When I was little, we used to sing a song that went like this: "Love is nothing till you give it away, give it away, give it away. Love is nothing till you give it away, you'll end up having more. Love is like a copper penny, hold it tight and you won't have any. Lend it, spend it, you'll have so many, they'll roll all over the floor." That's the great thing about abundance. The more you give, the more you get.

And that's the principle behind tithing. I remember when I first came to the chapel and I would put a dollar or a five dollar bill as a donation. Then, one of the ministers came to the Self-Realization class I was taking and talked about tithing. This had a really big impact on me. It totally changed how I thought about giving, and totally changed my behavior. I started giving more every week. Whenever I earned any money, the first thing I did was to calculate 10%, so I could factor it into my check on Sunday. Although it took me a minute to develop the habit, and to quiet the voice inside my head that asked, "Will I still have enough?", what I found was that I had more abundance than ever. When we say the blessing before we give, we usually invoke the law of tenfold return to those who give freely and from the heart. That means that whatever you give to the place or places where you receive spiritual support is returned to you TENFOLD and more! I'll tell you a secret. I feel so good about abundance that when I say that prayer, I always say ten thousandfold return. I'm willing to open up and receive all that and more.

One of the things I've been working on is treating myself well. I've always been good at giving to others and taking care of them. It's taken me a while to expand my generosity to include myself. Now, whenever an opportunity to treat myself well presents itself, I always say YES! I go ahead and order that menu item that I really want instead of the cheapest one. I buy the Groupon for the massage for myself. I stay the extra day on the trip that means so much to me. I've been working on accepting the good that comes to me. As a minister, when I perform services and people ask me what I charge, I used to say, "Oh, that's not necessary." Now, I usually say, "It's by donation, and you decide what fits for you." I'm amazed at how generous people are. I am learning to accept this good, and just say thank you. I saw a quote by Robert Kiyosaki that said, "It's not what you say out of your mouth that determines your life, it's what you whisper to yourself that has the most power." I've been doing my best to whisper powerful and positive things to myself more consistently.

This also reminds me of one of my friends. Recently, she commented, "I can't get anywhere on time." Because of the kinds of conversations she and I consistently have about metaphysics, and particularly prosperity, and because I know that she is very aware of her thoughts, words and actions, I told her that saying that she can't get anywhere on time is a thought of lack, and encouraged her to change that statement to something that makes sense for her, like, "Time works perfectly for me" or "I arrive at each place in just the right time." That way, she creates and attracts prosperity instead of lack.

Another friend has been talking to me about being very frustrated in her current position at work. She's applied for a new job, but in the meantime she's feeling buried under the mountain of paperwork associated with her current position. And every time she thinks she's got it down, they throw something new at her or change the way it's supposed to be done. She said she recently got back a form that she thought she'd filled out correctly. It had little comments scrawled all over it by the clinician in charge of scrawling little comments on forms. We cannot control what anybody else does. We always have a choice in how we react. Instead of feeling overwhelmed, she has the choice to imagine the clinician with a big red clown nose and big clown shoes. And every time something new gets thrown at her, she can imagine going, "Honk, honk!" and just laugh out loud. There will always be hoops placed in front of us. Our choice is in how we jump through them. Do we slog and plod and trudge and complain, or do we fly through them doing a double somersault in the process and stand proudly with our hands in the air like Olympic gymnasts when we're done? It's a choice. My friend decided to give herself an attitude adjustment, and I got a message from her a couple of days later saying the new job was now ready for her. Her change in attitude changed what she attracted into her life.

And gratitude is always the most important piece that completes the puzzle. We are always creating, and we are always creating exactly as we are. Giving thanks with each breath makes sense. The more we pay attention to what we are grateful for, the more we draw positive energy into our lives. It's always our choice, so why not choose to take responsibility and to be grateful.

What we think, what we say and what we do is what we draw more of to ourselves. That is one of the most basic beliefs that we hold as metaphysicians. There is a book and movie called, "The Secret," but it's no secret to anyone who has studied metaphysics. We are constantly creating – the question is, "What are we creating?" The answer is very simple – just look at your life and you will see and know exactly what you are creating. Prosperity is happiness, health and wealth. If you want more of that in your life, that is how you have to live...as if your life is full of happiness, health and wealth.

PROSPERITY LAWS –

IMAGINATION, GRATITUDE, AND FORGIVENESS
11/18/12

This month, we're talking about Prosperity Laws. Today, we'll give our attention to Imagination which is the spark of ignition for all ideas, Gratitude which increases the flow of heart energy, and Forgiveness which clears the way for Prosperity to flow freely in our lives.

As some of you know, I am a member of a local improv comedy troupe called Not Burnt Out Just Unscrewed. Recently, the founder wrote a note about how the troupe started. He'd auditioned for another troupe and wasn't accepted, so he had the idea to start his own. From some people gathering in their homes or in public parks to rehearse, and performances in small venues where sometimes the players outnumbered the audience members, we have grown to a non-profit corporation that had a 10th Anniversary Reunion Fundraiser Show with 300 people in attendance. We are now about one-quarter of the way towards our goal of opening our own performance and training space. All this came from an idea, just as anything and everything we envision in our lives starts with our imagination.

The subject of the first talk I did at my spiritual community, about four years ago, was Imagination. At the time, my dad was 100 years old, and in preparing for my talk, I asked him about some of the things he couldn't have imagined that had become reality within his lifetime. He talked about things that many of us take for granted like jet airplanes, television and computers. He also mentioned Social Security, unemployment insurance, interstate highways, the United Nations, and advances in medicine. He was talking about changes that had taken place over the course of a century. As we progress, ideas come to fruition in weeks instead of years. And they still all start with imagination.

One of the steps to Prosperity is goal setting. And goals also begin in our imagination. We think about what we want to have happen in our lives, then articulate that in the form of goals. Writing down our ideas (on paper, whiteboard or mirror) gives them shape, form, physicality, and energy. When we take something from the abstract to the concrete, we move forward on our path of actually achieving what we set out to accomplish. Because just like the faucet I talked about a couple of weeks ago that doesn't work until we turn it on, ideas and imagination only become reality when we take action. We use our imagination to envision the life we want, then set the goals to achieve it, and ignite Prosperity.

As our ideas and imagination become reality, the second step is gratitude. It's great to think about gratitude with Thanksgiving coming up. An attitude of gratitude transforms our lives, and is essential for opening our hearts, and creating the flow that is Prosperity.

One of my favorite things about Facebook is when people share very positive things that are occurring in their lives. I've noticed people posting 30 days of gratitude. I love reading what people are grateful for. I've been keeping my gratitude journal since a close friend of mine bought one for me in 2008. I sat with it for a while, then got it out one night and started writing. There are five lines for each day of the year. Some days, I write in the margins and on the extra pages because there are so many things I'm grateful for. Some days, it's hard to get started. I find that as soon as I start the flow of gratitude, it pours out of me easily. The more thankful I am, the better I feel. The more I focus on gratitude, the more I attract positive energy and abundance into my life. I have given a number of gratitude journals to people as gifts because I so strongly believe in the power of gratitude to open our hearts and transform our lives.

In the aftermath of the comedy show I mentioned, the first words that kept coming out of my mouth were, "Thank you." I was grateful for everyone and everything associated with the show. It felt really good to thank everyone, and my gratitude was truly heartfelt.

Imagination and gratitude seem very logical in thinking about Prosperity. At first glance, the next step may not seem as logical. This is the power of forgiveness. I know that I've come pretty far on the road of forgiveness. It's something I've been working on for more than ten years in a pretty concerted way. One of my favorite sayings is, "Holding resentment is like taking poison and then waiting for the other person to suffer." I know how powerful it is to really let go of hurt and anger, and truly forgive myself and others. Even two years after her death, I still get triggered by my mother at times and am still working on forgiveness with her.

In preparing to speak today, I read Edwene Gaines book, "The Four Spiritual Laws of Prosperity," and got a whole new perspective on forgiveness. Some of what Edwene said was consistent with what I know and have been using in my own daily spiritual practice. I understand that forgiveness is not something we do for anyone else. It is something we do for ourselves. She talks about forgiveness as emotional housecleaning that allows us to make room for the good we desire. We have to clear out negative thoughts that hinder us from moving forward, in order to make room for new and positive things to come into our lives, including Prosperity.

Edwene goes on to explain how judging and blaming others

gets in the way of our spiritual development. She says that some people believe that what we condemn in others in this lifetime, we condemn ourselves to experience in the next. Whenever we see a high profile murder or celebrity trial, we tend to form our opinion about it, even though it has nothing whatsoever to do with us, and is completely none of our business. She says that as humans, it's our nature to want to fix things. Forgiveness frees us from the need to blame and allows us to focus on how to be happy, healthy and wealthy. Instead of asking, "Who can I blame?", our question becomes, "How can I serve?"

And how much should we forgive? The answer is absolutely everything, fully and freely and without reservation. Not for anyone else's benefit, but for your own. If you blame someone else for anything that happens in your life, you cast yourself in the role of victim. And how does being a victim ever serve anyone? It's so much more powerful to take responsibility for everything that happens in your life, and make the story serve you.

Edwene says that she suffered abuse as a very small child. She says that one of her teachers suggested that in order to heal this childhood trauma that she create a new story about it. Perhaps, she came into this lifetime to be a woman of power, and the misuse of power she experienced very early in life allowed her to become a woman of power in the world, knowing that she would never misuse or abuse power. And in the process she gained a most valuable spiritual gift – the understanding heart. Edwene says that little by little, she was able to embrace this new story, and reorder her personal history. It made her feel powerful rather than helpless, and allowed her to give up the victim role permanently.

This book was so inspiring. Incorporating the daily forgiveness techniques that Edwene suggests makes a lot of sense to me. If we expend our energy judging and blaming, all it does is hold us back and prevent us from having prosperity in our lives. Even though I feel pretty good about prosperity in my life, it's so helpful to have reminders about ways to continue to grow and prosper. It's so valuable to remember to use imagination, gratitude and forgiveness on a daily basis to help us on our path to Prosperity.

PEACE

12/2/12

My daughter is in chiropractic school, so I've been learning a lot about chiropractic care. The basic philosophy is that the body's natural state is health, and chiropractic adjustments remove any obstacles to the natural state of health. As metaphysicians, we know that our spirit's natural state is peace. There are many adjustments we can do to return ourselves to our natural state of peace. I believe that most of the time, it's simply a case of reminding ourselves about our natural state, and remembering to be at peace.

When someone walks into our spiritual community, one of the first things they see are the words, "Peace I am still." This is a fantastic reminder of our natural state. Just saying those words, "Peace I am still," reminds us to breathe and to be at ease. I do pretty well with this when I'm here at the spiritual community. I'm working on remembering this more often when I'm behind the wheel of a car. Several years ago, some friends and I drove to Phoenix a couple of times a month to dance. I told my friends that one day, I would be able to be completely at peace while driving, and then I would have achieved whatever I needed to accomplish in this lifetime, and I would probably be assumed straight into heaven. One of my friends commented that he wasn't worried about that happening any time soon!

I know this about myself. I give myself little pep talks all the time. I know that if I allow myself enough time, I stay much more peaceful. It's when I feel pressed for time that my impatience skyrockets, and my swearing capacity goes off the scales. I notice that I feel more peaceful when I feel like there is enough, particularly enough time. When I allow enough time to complete whatever task I've set out for myself, I feel more peaceful. When I allow enough time to get wherever I'm going, no matter what the traffic conditions, I feel more peaceful. When I allow enough time to think about whatever is on my mind, I feel more peaceful. When I allow myself enough time to write my talks before Sunday, I feel more peaceful. I also feel more peaceful when I remember to breathe. Breathing is so important. And not just shallow breaths, but mindful breaths. I have been affirming, "I am peaceful. I am content. I am loved. I am enough."

When we feel like we have enough, and we are enough, we feel peaceful. We know that we are on our right path. A friend called the other day to tell me that his father had made his transition to the spiritual plane. He moved back to Alaska several months ago, with the express purpose of being there to take care of his father. He took him to his appointments, and was intimately involved in his day to day care. He did his best to be fully present. At the moment of his father's final breath, my friend said he experienced a deep feeling of peace. I know that this is partly because he followed his guidance in the last year, and took the steps necessary to go home, and be there in the complete way that he was for his family. He knew that he had done enough. When we are on our right path, we are at peace. It's one of the markers we can use to tell whether we're doing what's best for us.

We feel peaceful when we allow ourselves time and space. I was talking to one of my cousins recently. He said he had decided to go to church one day. He does not describe himself as religious in any way, but what he appreciated about being in church was the peacefulness. He loved being quiet, and being by himself. He said he felt the presence of my father and his father as he sat there. When we allow ourselves time and space for peacefulness, so many wonderful things have the opportunity to show up for us.

Being at peace is always beneficial, and even more so when there is turmoil around us. I read about a member of a Native American tribe whose role was that of "Faithkeeper." The job of the "Faithkeeper" is to hold the higher vision, remembering the light, and holding peace. I love this concept. I make the choice in my life to not read newspapers or watch the news, for the most part. When people discuss challenges in their personal lives, or major events that happen in the world, I do my best to be the "Faithkeeper," to remember the light, and to hold peace in my heart. I think it is most important to do that at times when people are struggling to remember that for themselves. I observe my teacher doing this very consistently, and keep his peaceful energy in mind at those times.

It was my birthday this week. Good a time as any for self-reflection. In thinking about Peace, I was paying attention to the things that make me feel peaceful. Saying "Yes" is a good place to start. In doing improv comedy, one of the first things we learn is to always agree and add, to always say "Yes, and..." It's a reasonable way to be in life, also. When we say yes, our energy changes. It's very different than saying no, or even maybe. We open up possibilities when we say yes to positive things in our lives.

Recently, I read a quote on Facebook that said, "Every sixty seconds you spend angry, upset or mad, is a full minute of happiness you'll never get back."

A few weeks ago, a close friend asked when he and our other friend could take me out for our annual birthday dinner celebration. He made a big deal out of not telling me where we were going this year, insisting that it be a surprise. In the past, I have resisted suggestions from him, and I decided to just be as peaceful as I could, go along with whatever he had planned, no matter how goofy I thought it was, and say yes. He told me that he would call at a specific time, and let me know where to go. I was still doing my best to stay peaceful. The appointed time came, and the phone rang within a few minutes. After some confusion about where we were actually going, we found my friend at McDonald's sitting with someone I didn't know. My friend tried to convince me this was someone I knew, and didn't remember, but he's played this trick on others before, and I just wasn't buying it. I was pretty irritated by this point, despite my resolution to remain peaceful. He made comments about eating at McDonald's because it was cheap, then gently guided me out the door, and said, "Let's go to Paradise Bakery instead."

I didn't really want to go to Paradise Bakery. I wasn't sure there would be anything on the menu that fit with what I could eat. I was feeling very resistant, and not very peaceful at all. I was thinking I just wanted to go somewhere else, and get a burger. I was grumbling and not particularly pleasant. Then, he insisted we go in through the Exit door that clearly said, "Use front entrance." That just about put me over the edge. We walked through the door, and I was so caught up in my own negative thoughts that it took me a minute before I realized that a whole group of my friends was sitting there, and that, in fact, I was walking into a surprise party that my friend had organized just for me.

Within a moment, my whole energy shifted. I took a deep breath and smiled. I couldn't believe that my friend had pulled off this surprise, and that I had absolutely no idea. And that none of my friends had leaked a word of it. I was so happy. I felt so loved and cared for and so grateful. Suddenly, I felt all the tension I had been holding dissolve, and felt completely peaceful and happy. I couldn't believe I'd wasted all that time being negative. When we get wrapped up in expectations and irritations, we remove ourselves from the moment. When we allow ourselves be fully present in any given moment, we find peace. "Every sixty seconds you spend angry, upset or mad, is a full minute of happiness you'll never get back."

At this time of year, it's especially important to remember to look beyond the petty frustrations and irritations that arise because they are obstacles to our spirit's natural state of peace. The more we can be present in each moment, the more we can fully appreciate it, be happy, and live in our natural state of peace.

PEACE – PART 2

12/30/12

We end each service here at our spiritual community by singing, "Let there be love on earth, and let it begin with me." The topic for this month is Peace, so today I'm singing, "Let there be peace on earth, and let it begin with me." The only way to let peace begin with us is to make that our choice. It's always our choice.

Every thought, every word and every action is a choice. Earlier this year, I had pain in my neck and shoulder that went on for several weeks and was pretty intense. I tried everything I knew from chiropractic adjustments to stretching to heat and liniment to pain relievers and nothing seemed to help. I was increasingly more and more stressed about it. I was having trouble sleeping because of it. I wondered if it would ever go away. Then, one night, I was in the Life Empowerment Circle, and during the meditation, the pain went away. Just like that. Months later when I felt the pain again, my reaction was completely different. I knew that it would go away before long, and I just stayed peaceful. It didn't last long at all. When we are familiar with something, we are often able to be more peaceful with it, even when it might be an unpleasant experience. The more peaceful we are able to remain, the better we feel in the long run.

Interestingly, my own talk from earlier this month has had a big impact on me. I keep reflecting on the statement, "Every sixty seconds you spend angry, upset or mad, is a full minute of happiness you'll never get back." It's actually made a big difference, especially when I'm driving. I start to get all worked up, then remember to breathe and shift my focus and calm down...sometimes. What obstacles to peace do we create for ourselves and how do we replace them with ease?

I seem to be attracting some lessons in the opposite of peace as a learning tool. I've been especially challenged while driving. I've allowed myself to be thrown off balance by things my kids have done, which are, in fact, none of my business, but I get worked up nonetheless. I do my best to allow these situations to be reminders to pay attention to my own behavior, to breathe and to relax.

The holiday season has raised lots of issues for me. About being alone and feeling lonely. About the things I am longing for in my life. About allowing myself to get my feelings hurt. Then at other times, I'm able to look at my life and be deeply grateful for all the people who do love me and all the people I feel very connected with. It's been kind of a seesaw time for me. And even though I have all these tools in my tool box, sometimes it's really hard to remember to use them at the moments when I need them the most.

I have been reflecting on the things that allow me to feel more peaceful. When I understand something, I am more able to be at peace with it. In friendships and relationships, I often find myself asking people to just tell me what's going on. I can deal with anything when I know what's happening. It's when I have to guess, that I make things up that are usually far worse than the reality of whatever's actually going on. When I feel like I understand a situation, I'm able to be more peaceful with it.

As I mentioned in my last talk, I feel more peaceful when I give myself enough time to do something with ease. And sometimes, even when I have enough time, I struggle with being peaceful when I'm behind the wheel of the car. I can't tell you how many conversations I've had with myself, especially in the last month. I get all worked up and frustrated at whatever's happening with traffic. Then I remind myself that it's such a waste of time. Then, sometimes I'm able to sit back and relax and enjoy the scenery or listen to music or just have some positive thought in my mind. And at other times, I just act like a crazy person who's completely out of control. I don't get it myself.

I was driving to get a massage last week, and although I was only traveling about two miles, I hit every red light, and it seemed as though every "stupid" person on the road chose that moment to drive in front of me. I did a lot of swearing and got myself all worked up...and for what. I still got where I was going eventually. I got my massage and felt better. The next day, I drove back to the same place by the same route. I allowed extra time, just in case. This time, every light was green, the long left turn line moved freely, and I got there in just a few minutes, feeling peaceful and relaxed, instead of stressed out and angry. Both reactions were my choice.

A friend was telling me about a situation where one of his daughters pushed his buttons so far that he completely lost his temper, and threw her out of the house using very colorful language. This is very uncharacteristic behavior for him, and he was feeling pretty bad about it. He was complimenting me on how I'm always the calm voice of reason and always have just the right thing to say to soothe the participants and bring peace to the situation. I laughed and said that while I appreciated his perception, I had to confess to the moments in the past week where I lost my temper, and there was plenty of screaming and crying involved with my own family members. We all do the best we can at any given moment. It's wonderful when we can remind ourselves to choose peace. I do use my affirmations on a very regular basis: I am peaceful. I am content. I am loved. I am enough. And I apologize and take responsibility for my actions when I know I've behaved in ways that are less than ideal.

In preparing to talk about Peace this month, thoughts of my mother kept coming up for me. My parents both died in 2010, so the holiday season still brings up grief issues for me. I've found myself crying on quite a few occasions for a wide variety of reasons, including moments on so-called "sitcoms." I miss my dad a lot. I think of my mom at odd moments, and still struggle to be at peace with her, even though she's been gone from physical form for over two years.

My relationship with my mother was very challenging, for many, many reasons. Although she died more than two years ago, there are still things about her, and memories of interactions, that trigger strong feelings for me. I am in the process of truly allowing her to rest in peace, and allowing myself to be at peace, also.

My mother chose a lot of interesting lessons to learn in her life, and I chose some interesting lessons by coming in as her daughter. She was the youngest of 10 children, and from all reports, many members of the family catered to and "spoiled" her for much of her early life.

My father was married to my mother's older sister, who died in 1950, and then my father married my mother. I think it took many years for her to believe that my father actually loved her. I think he really did, especially later in their lives.

Another challenge that my mother chose was the label "manic-depressive." My mother was diagnosed with this illness when she was 46 years old. I was 14 at the time, and I worried for a very long time about whether or not I would turn out like her. It weighed on my mind. I observed any behaviors that I thought were indicators. As I got closer and closer to the age of 46, the worry escalated. I am built very much the same as my mother was physically, and I worried that I might have the same kinds of mental issues. Finally, after lots of reflection, I realized that I had much more in common with my dad in terms of temperament, outlook on life, and behavior, and that I was not much like my mom at all. Over time, I made peace with that aspect of my life, and have felt much better in recent years. I have let go of that worry. Worry is a genuine obstacle to peace.

Forgiveness is so important in choosing peace. We have to fully and freely forgive ourselves, and fully and freely forgive others, and allow them to fully and freely forgive us, in order to move forward on our path, and return to our natural state of peace. I am still working on this with my mother, and with myself. I do my best to choose peace on a more consistent basis.

As we step into the New Year, let us support and encourage each other to make this choice: "Let there be peace on earth and let it begin with me."

IMAGINATION

2/3/13

Throughout the course of this year, we're going to be talking about the 12 Mind Powers. Our topic for the first month is the mind power of Imagination, and this seems very appropriate to me. Imagination is the creating energy. It is the spark which ignites, and is the genesis of every thought, every word and every action that we produce. When someone tells you that it's "just your imagination," that's the highest compliment they can pay you. And as we use our imagination, we then infuse our ideas with the other mind powers: love and wisdom, zeal and power, strength and life, faith and will, divine order and understanding, and elimination of anything that does not serve us.

When I think about imagination, I often think of my dad. My first talk at my spiritual community was about imagination. At the time, my dad was 100 years old, and I had a conversation with him about the things he couldn't have imagined in his lifetime, that had come to pass. Some of the things he talked about were things that most people would probably come up with, like jet airplanes, television and computers. Some of the things were a little more surprising, like Social Security, unemployment insurance, interstate highways, and the formation of the United Nations. He mentioned advances in medicine, and how so many soldiers simply died from diseases, rather than injuries, in WWI. He talked about the ability to get an education, and the cost of getting that education. He was amazed at how things had changed. There were so many things that had transpired that he couldn't have imagined even 50 years ago. And they all started with a spark from someone's imagination.

Along the same line, there was a post on Facebook recently that asked the question: If someone from the 1950's suddenly appeared today, what would be the most difficult thing to explain to them about life today? The answer was, "I possess a device, in my pocket, that is capable of accessing the entirety of information known to man." Who could've imagined this even 5 or 10 years ago?

And, it may seem simplistic, but when I think about imagination, I often think about food. There are so many foods that we eat on a regular basis, and so many ways to prepare food, that it's staggering to think about who had the idea in the first place. One food that I'm fascinated by is the egg. So, a chicken produces an egg about once a day. Think about the imagination that went into someone seeing an egg that probably cracked open accidentally, looking at that slimy mess, and thinking, "That might taste delicious." Someone figured out that you could add heat, and cook eggs over easy, scrambled, or hard boiled in the shell, to name a few ways. Or you could beat the egg, then dip some bread into it, cook that, and call it French toast. Or you could combine it with milk and sugar, and bake it, and produce custard. Or you could mix it with flour and sugar and chocolate, bake it, and have cake. It's quite a leap from a chicken's natural by-product to a souffle!

All these things from eggs benedict to the internet were the product of someone's imagination. Someone had a thought, then acted upon it to bring it into physical form. We have thoughts, we have words and we have actions. Thoughts are the creating energy. Words are the expression, and actions bring things into reality. If we can see it, we can be it.

Goals are such an important part of our growth process. And

goals begin with imagination. We have to see ourselves as we want ourselves to become, in order to set goals, and then accomplish them. We use our imagination, in conjunction with our other mind powers, to bring our thoughts and words into action. When we write down our goals and ideas, we bring them into physical form. We can imagine water coming out of a faucet all day long, but until we turn it on, nothing actually gets wet. That is true of our mind powers, also. We can imagine something all day long, but until we use our other mind powers, and bring an idea from conception to action, nothing actually happens.

As I have said on more than one occasion, no one was more surprised than me that I became a minister. There was definitely a time when I could not have imagined this. Now, it is such an important expression of who I am. I love all the aspects of the ministry – speaking at services like this, doing readings and messages, doing energy healing, and performing weddings and celebration of life services. Doing each of these things has allowed me to become more fully who I am. And a few short years ago, I couldn't have imagined this.

Part of the reason this was such a stretch in thinking for me was because of my history with religion and with God. I was raised Catholic, and my mother's mental illness manifested in religious fanaticism, at times. In 2002, I had a reading done, and the medium told me that the biggest loss I was suffering from in this lifetime was the loss of my relationship with God. I know that if I had heard that at any earlier time, I wouldn't have been able to accept it at all. I spent so many years resisting Catholicism and my mother's craziness, and God was all wrapped up in that. But at that particular moment, I was open to receiving those words. A few weeks after that reading, a series of events lead me to my spiritual community.

From the moment I walked in, it felt like home to me. In the more than 10 years that I've been coming on a very regular basis, I have learned more here than I've ever learned any-where else in my life. When I went through the seminary, I really came face to face with my beliefs about God. I was not at all sure I believed in God. The word "God" is still one that I'm not entirely comfortable with. I feel easier when I refer to Spirit, Source, Universal Life Force, the All-Knowing or things of that nature. Maybe it's because of my own personal history. I know that I am clear now that there is more to life than just ourselves, more than just our physical being, more than just this lifetime of experience. When I give messages, I know that they are coming from somewhere greater than me. When I do healings, I know the energy comes from something beyond myself. If that's "just my imagination," I'm fine with that because it makes perfect sense to me.

These days, I have a much greater understanding of "God" as everything, everyone and all that is. I truly believe that there is no separation between ourselves and God. I am much more comfortable than I ever have been in the past. The notion of "God" is still something I spend time pondering, and I value the use of my imagination in the process, as I continue to make sense of it for myself.

Without our imagination as the spark of creating energy, nothing can change. So, the next time someone tells you that it's "just your imagination", simply say thank you, because that's the best compliment they could possibly give you.

WILL

3/13/13

In the Star Wars movies, the very wise Yoda tells his Jedi student, "There is no try. There is only do." That is the essence of the Mind Power of Will... "There is no try. There is only do."

This year, we're focusing on the 12 Mind Powers, which are all inter-related. The topic for this month is the mind power of Will. Will is action. I've used the faucet metaphor in some of my talks. We can look at a faucet all day long, and believe or have faith that water will come out of it. We can love how clean the water makes our bodies and our dishes. We can get excited, and demonstrate our zeal, and cheer it on. We can understand the complexities of plumbing, and know how the water comes from the main line into our kitchen sinks. We can imagine the cool, clear water flowing into a glass, then quenching our thirst. But until we actually open the tap, water doesn't flow. We can think and affirm and believe all day long, but until we take action, nothing ever happens.

Action is necessary in order to move forward on our path. If you want a new job, you have to take the steps necessary to get one. You have to look in the want ads. You have to get whatever education and/or certification is required for the position you desire. You have to apply for each job that interests you. You have to dress appropriately for an interview, and be prepared for whatever questions might be asked of you.

If you want to learn to do something, you have to take action. You have to research or take classes or find a mentor or whatever it takes to learn what you want to learn. Thinking about it, dreaming about it, imagining it, talking about it, and hoping it will happen, won't make it happen. You have to actually get up and move, and do something active. You have to exercise your will.

We have a choice in each moment how to react and respond, no matter what anyone else says or does. We know that what we think, what we say, and what we do is what we draw more of to ourselves, so we always have the ability to choose our thoughts, words and actions. Each thought, word and action is a seed that we plant. If we want to harvest happiness, health, and wealth, those are the seeds we need to plant, and then weed, water, and nurture them for the fullest harvest possible.

One of the most important things we do in our lives is to know ourselves. We do this by paying attention to our thoughts, words, and actions, and the people, places, and things that we spend time with in our lives. If we want something to be different in our lives, we have to actively change what we're doing.

At our spiritual community, we learn the concept of recognize, release and replace. We all experience feelings. We all have our thoughts, words and actions. These are the only things that we can actually control. If we find ourselves spending time with people, places, and things that are not particularly beneficial, we have the choice to walk away. We recognize a behavior, thought, feeling, or action. We release that which no longer serves us. Then, we replace it with something that is more positive and conducive to growth. The replacing piece is where our will comes into play. It is where we take action to change what is happening. Until we take action, nothing changes.

There's a wonderful story in the book, "A Deep Breath of Life," that tells of Ralph who prayed to God every day to help him win the lottery. Each week when he didn't win, Ralph became more and more frustrated, and he grew angry at God. Finally, Ralph went to church, stood before the altar, shook his fist and shouted, "If you are a true God, how can you say that prayer works? I have been praying for a long time to win the lottery, and now I have less money than when I started! Why have you not helped me?"

Suddenly, a deep voice from above the altar boomed, "The least you could do, Ralph, is to buy a lottery ticket!" We can pray and affirm, wish and hope all day long, but unless we buy a ticket, there's no way for us to win the lottery. We must exercise our will to move forward on our path.

Wishin' and hopin' and prayin' and dreamin' are great song lyrics, but they won't get you where you want to go. In order to get somewhere, you have to take action, and move forward to achieve your goals.

Continuing with our faucet metaphor, if we are power washing a house, full blast works. If we are trying to water a delicate plant, it doesn't serve us to turn the water on full blast and as hot as it can be. If we turn the water pressure on too hard, water just splashes all over everything, and can be destructive, instead of being directed to where it can do the most good. We use the mind powers of Power, Wisdom and Zeal in conjunction with Will to create the most beneficial effect possible. For many people, exercising the mind power of Will is about taking stronger and bolder action than they may have been accustomed to doing. For me, sometimes the opposite holds true.

Being Sicilian, Sagittarius and from New York, I have no problem with turning the water pressure on full blast. What has been important for me to learn about, and practice, is activating the mind power of Will to just sit still, and be quiet and reflective, especially when things happen in my life that cause me to have a strong dramatic or negative reaction. In the past, I would just go off on the person who was involved in the interaction with me. Now, I do my best to sit with my feelings and reaction until a constructive solution presents itself. Sometimes it takes a few minutes, and sometimes it takes a few months. When the time is right, I use my Will and take appropriate action for the highest and best good of all concerned.

Everything in our life is a choice. We create our reality with each breath we take. We empower ourselves when we take responsibility for what we have created. People often raise the question – when are we going to have peace in our world? The answer is when peace is what we focus on. When each of us is peaceful inside ourselves. When we make peace with those close to us. When we let go of anything that is unlike peace. We each play a part in how our world is created in each moment.

There are often themes or patterns that recur in our lives. When we notice ourselves moving through them a little more easily or quickly, those are indicators that we are growing spiritually. We are always going to have situations that affect us in one way or another. How we choose to deal with them, and how quickly and easily we move through them shows us how far we've come on our path of unfoldment. Peace is the ability to walk through turmoil and see the solution.

So, as we walk on our path of unfoldment, we use all of our mind powers to create our lives. We are wise, loving and powerful in our actions. Just like Captain Picard in Star Trek, we use our Will to "make it so."

ZEAL

5/12/13

Happy Mother's Day.

Our topic for this month is the mind power of Zeal. Bruce Springsteen tells us, "Can't start a fire without a spark." Zeal is the spark. Zeal is enthusiasm. On the other hand, Smokey the Bear reminds us, "Only YOU can prevent forest fires." We always use the mind powers in conjunction with each other, and this is especially important with zeal. Can't start a fire without a spark, but we don't want to start a forest fire when we just want to roast marshmallows or warm our hands. Zeal can be constructive or destructive. Fire can warm us and inspire us or burn everything in its path to the ground. Zeal has some of the same components. I read a book last week called, "Collateral Damage." This reminded me of using the mind power of Zeal – when we use it with wisdom, understanding and love, it is a positive, motivating force. When it gets out of control, there can be significant amounts of collateral damage.

Without zeal, our thoughts and imagination might never take shape into action. We have to find ways to motivate ourselves to get up in the morning, to exercise, to complete tasks that we set out for ourselves, or that others set out for us. Few people love to clean their houses, but it's necessary and important, and we need to activate zeal in order to accomplish most things.

On the other hand, being over-zealous can cause problems. I notice that my mind often works very quickly. When a situation arises, or a problem presents itself, I can often see a solution quickly and easily. My tendency is to just blurt things out sometimes, when the wiser course of action is to allow the other person to figure things out for themselves, or for me to just give an indication, then let the other person take it from there. Sometimes, I have ideas for things in situations where my opinion is neither solicited nor invited. Again, I have to use my wisdom to contain my zeal for the most positive effect overall. I remember the wise words of Nelson Rockefeller who said, "Never pass up the opportunity to keep your mouth shut."

Balance is the key in so many areas of our lives. If we sit around all day watching television and being a "couch potato", that is not healthy for our minds, bodies, or spirits. On the other hand, if we spend all day in the gym, and overdo our exercise program, we become sore, and may even injure ourselves. Balance is the key with zeal.

My mother was an interesting example of two of the extremes of zeal. There were times when her mind raced so fast that she couldn't sleep for days and days at a time, and her thoughts were not particularly coherent. Then, there were other times when she couldn't even get out of bed because the depression, or lack of zeal, that she experienced was so debilitating. Zeal was out of balance in her life at times. In contrast, my dad represented much more of a balance when it came to zeal. His philosophy in life was to do everything in moderation, and he accomplished that very successfully. I notice aspects of both my parents in my own life, and my use of zeal in my life.

Interestingly enough, today is the third anniversary of the day my dad made his transition from the earth plane. When I looked back at the last talk I did about Zeal, it was two years ago on Father's Day, and I talked a lot about my dad. My dad had many amazing qualities, and like all of us was human, and had his foibles. He had a tendency to be critical and judgmental. I notice this tendency in myself, and I'm working on changing that.

Sometimes role models appear for us at just the right moment. Last week, I met a man who told me a story about picking up a hitchhiker on a drive from Yuma to Tucson. He said when the man first got into his car, he was shaking his head randomly and practically drooling – that he appeared to be seriously mentally ill. The driver said he felt like God spoke to him in that moment, saying – don't judge, just love him. So, he concentrated on being loving, and before long the two men started to have a conversation. The conversation deepened and lasted for the entire four hours of the drive. The passenger was completely coherent, and seemingly "normal." When they arrived back in Tucson, the driver let his passenger out of the car, and observed the people around him making judgments and derogatory remarks. Almost immediately, the man began shaking his head randomly and drooling again. His ability to function normally evaporated in the absence of the loving environment.

One of the most valuable things that we are encouraged to do at our spiritual community is to know ourselves. Knowing myself has been especially important for me in thinking about Zeal. While attending a memorial service the other day, I found myself criticizing and judging many of the people who walked into the church. "Nice outfit to wear in a church." "That haircut looked fantastic...in the '80's." "Great idea to let your children play on the steps where people are trying to walk." And so on. I realized what I was doing and stopped. I decided to be more like the driver in the previous story, and just be loving. So, I turned my enthusiasm to being loving, and it really transformed my mood. I found myself being happier and more relaxed, and sitting and smiling, instead of fuming. This has come up a few more times this week, and as I find myself being critical, I just stop. I choose to be more loving in that moment, and especially to be forgiving, loving, and accepting of myself, as I move through my own growth process.

My intentions are usually positive, but the results are not always positive. It is so important to temper Zeal with Wisdom, Understanding, and Love in order to create the most beneficial effect possible. For me, breathing is often a helpful step. Taking a breath before plunging into a discussion or situation is very useful, and sometimes provides time for the guidance and wisdom that is within each of us to emerge.

I had a situation in my life where someone that I had a fair amount of regular contact with was treating me in a manner that I experienced as hurtful and unpleasant. I was pretty upset about it, and my first reaction was to just berate him in return. I had a lot of imaginary conversations with him that involved name-calling and cursing and putting him in his place. Fortunately, I made the choice to keep those conversations in my head. Instead of lashing out at him, like I thought I wanted to do, I kept putting his name in the healing box at my spiritual community, and sending positive energy to him and to our interactions. A few weeks after a particularly negative interaction, he apologized to me in a very sincere and heartfelt manner. I accepted his apology completely, and have forgiven him. I feel comfortable being around him again. There are still moments when he acts in ways that I consider less than ideal. Instead of taking it personally, I choose to smile and send love to him. This choice feels so much better.

I've mentioned the notion of "going in quietly" in a couple of talks that I've done. For me, that exemplifies the balance that I seek in using the mind power of Zeal. I know how to go in big. I'm learning how to go in quietly. As I contemplate zeal, I think about it in "Goldilocks" terms: how much is too much, how much is too little, how much is just right? If a diva is belting out an aria and wants the people in the second balcony to hear clearly, a different level of enthusiasm is required than someone trying to soothe a fussy baby to sleep. Both skills are important and valuable. It's knowing the time and the place to utilize them for the most beneficial effect. This is where the other mind powers come into play to temper and balance zeal, and have it be used as effectively as possible.

In thinking about Zeal, fire is a powerful metaphor. It takes a balance of kindling, sticks and logs to make a fire that burns strong and long and steadily. If you just throw a lot of paper on and light a match, there's a large blaze that burns out quickly. If you try to light a large log, there's not enough spark to get it going. If you build a stable structure with logs and sticks and kindling, the spark ignites, then the flame burns steadily and for a long time. That's the key with zeal – it works best when balanced with wisdom, power, strength and love.

POWER

6/30/13

At the beginning of each service, we say the Invocation which includes the words, "...our choices belong to us and are the seeds that create our lives." What a powerful expression. Our choices belong to us and are the seeds that create our lives. Our every thought, word, and action is a choice. We have the power to create our lives with each breath we take. When we take responsibility for our choices, we affirm that the power is within us. Recently, I read a post on Facebook that made a lot of sense to me: "A bird sitting on a tree is never afraid of the branch breaking, because her trust is not on the branch, but on her own wings. Always believe in yourself." This is the essence of affirming our own power. Believing in ourselves, and knowing that our choices belong to us and are the seeds that create our lives.

I've been paying close attention to the choices I've been making lately. I've been observing my thoughts, words, and actions. I've been noticing a pattern that is less than ideal, and am working on changing that by making different and more constructive choices. I've been noticing how I choose to react when I'm driving. I get myself all worked up. My pulse races, my heart pounds, my face gets red. There is often very creative swearing involved. It is not a pleasant experience for anyone. I have developed a new affirmation for myself: "I create ease and flow with each breath I take." I do this affirmation on a daily basis, usually in the morning after I wake up. I am usually feeling peaceful at those times. Sometimes, I'm even able to remember to do it when I'm behind the wheel of my car, before the heart pounding, red face, and angry gestures begin.

I feel really foolish when I let myself react in those negative ways. I know better. I know how to make different choices. I feel so much better when I can sit back and relax, and affirm that I create ease and flow with each breath I take.

As I think about the statement "our choices belong to us and are the seeds that create our lives," it is important for me to remember that this applies to each of us. I have complete control over my own choices, and zero control over other people's choices. There is someone who is very close to me, who sometimes make choices that I perceive as less than ideal. I do a pretty good job of keeping my mouth shut much of the time, although keeping a poker face is not my strong suit. When I feel particularly concerned, I make some kind of comment, that in my mind is gentle and loving and constructive. That happened last week. My comment was not received well, to say the least. The other person got very defensive and critical in response, berating me for making assumptions. That response triggered anger and frustration in me. Then, I got in the car and within two minutes had two nasty altercations with other drivers and pedestrians. I had to just stop and look at my behavior and my choices. "Our choices belong to us and are the seeds that create our lives." What am I choosing and what am I creating?

When I got home, my neighbor was outside, and I went over to talk to him and shared what had happened. His wise response was to remind me that each person is on their own path, and has to come to their own decisions in their own space and time. This helped me to breathe and calm myself. I was then able to make a different choice. I texted an apology for having made assumptions. The other person then apologized for becoming so defensive. I was able to move forward with much more ease and peacefulness.

When we affirm our power, an affirmation we may say is, "I am the authority in my life and I am at ease with that authority. I am in command and I am at ease with that command." In affirming our power, sometimes it is useful to notice when and where we give it away. In general, I consider myself a fairly powerful individual. However, there are times when I am instantly drawn back into being called into the principal's office because I'm "in trouble."

I've been attending the Life Empowerment Circle since it began. I've gotten so much out of this class, and really respect the teacher. Although we started coming to the spiritual community around the same time, I have often looked to her for guidance, and consider her one of my teachers. A few months ago, she asked me to meet her for lunch. I had no idea why, and was filled with anxiety and trepidation. I wondered what I had done wrong, and what she was planning to speak to me about. We sat down and ordered and chatted and shared, and I kept waiting for the "other shoe to drop," and for her to tell me the real reason she had asked me to go to lunch. Finally, I shared with her what I was thinking and feeling, and she started laughing. She confessed that her agenda had simply been to have lunch. Everything else was what I had created in my own mind.

In another recent instance, another teacher asked if I had time to talk after the service. I agreed. Then, I spent the next hour wondering what I had done wrong, and how it was going to be addressed. I had a complete exit strategy planned for how I could leave the meeting and even how I could leave all my responsibilities at the spiritual community, if necessary. We sat down to talk, and he shared some things he'd been thinking about for himself, and we had a very pleasant conversation. My adrenaline returned to normal levels, and I was able to go on about my day.

Both of these situations were great reminders that I am the authority in my life. I continue to work on being at ease with that authority. And both were examples of the importance of affirming our own power and believing in ourselves.

Another aspect of power that I've been noticing and working on for myself is the power in letting go of the need to be right all the time. This is an issue I've worked on in one form or another for much of my life. In my twenties, I had an overwhelming need to be right. I've let go of that to some extent, gradually over time. Recently, I noticed a new shift. I was at dinner with people I know pretty well, and the hostess was recounting some events that were part of my life. She was not accurate in her descriptions, and I noticed myself kind of tensing and getting ready to pounce and correct the story. Then, I took a breath and just let it go. It felt right to just let her have the moment. There was nothing life-altering in the story. It felt very empowering to let go of the need to be right.

A few days later, I was having a conversation with someone, and he was telling me that one of the kids in his class had said the reason he was taking the class was because, "Rosanne said he had to." I didn't recall having that conversation with the kid. I felt the tensing and preparing to argue feeling come on, then just stopped. First of all, I only had this person's perception and recollection of what happened, which might or might not be what actually transpired. I know that this person sometimes enjoys being able to "get a rise" out of me. It was empowering to just breathe, let go, and let him have that moment. It was much more peaceful and powerful to just smile and say that I was so glad that the kid was enjoying the class.

As I move through challenges and growth experiences, I am so grateful for the tools I have learned as I have developed as a metaphysician. I take full responsibility for all my thoughts, words, and actions. I do not point any fingers or blame anyone else for anything that happens in my life. I know that I am the authority in my life, that I am in command, and that every thought, word, and action in my life is of my own choosing.

I continue to create affirmations that allow me to make more positive and constructive choices. And I continue to work on remembering to use them at the moments that are most powerful. I continue to use my gratitude journal on a daily basis. Gratitude is a most powerful and transformative tool. And I forgive myself, fully and freely, and loose myself to my highest and best good. Gratitude and forgiveness are two of the most powerful tools in any spiritual tool belt.

And just like Dorothy in the Wizard of Oz, who realized that she had the power within her all along, we always have the power within us. Our choices belong to us and are the seeds that create our lives.

THE MIND POWER OF LOVE

7/28/13

As I started to think about my talk on the Mind Power of Love for today, I looked back at some of the other talks I've done. The one from February 2010, called "And... Back to the Loving Place" stood out. In that one, I shared about Ellen Degeneres having a comedy routine where she talks about getting in touch with spirituality and meditation, then one thing after another pulls her off center, and she keeps having to remind herself, "and...back to the loving place." I mentioned that after coming to meditations or services at the chapel, I would often find myself getting aggravated in traffic within moments of leaving – I would smile, then say to myself: "And... back to the loving place." I asked, "How do we get back to our loving place?"

I said that sometimes I think I've come so far on my journey and sometimes I feel like I'm moving through molasses. I acknowledged that I know that I've changed and grown, and the fact that I can recognize what I'm doing is an important growth marker. I reminded myself that I need to be easy and gentle and especially loving and forgiving with myself at these times. Along with Ellen, I recognized the importance of getting "back to the loving place."

So here I am, three plus years later, still working on some of the same issues. Sometimes I think I've come so far, and sometimes, as a dear friend used to say, "I keep re-learning things with stunning regularity." It's a little discouraging some-times, but then I remember the importance of being loving and accepting and forgiving with myself.

This has been a year full of feedback from friends. Recently, I got feedback from a very dear friend about the ways in which the negative comments that I would make under my breath were really starting to bother her. She did not want that en-ergy coming towards her. She wanted to be able to come into the setting and just have fun. She didn't want to know about what was going on behind the scenes, and she certainly didn't want to hear any disparaging remarks about anyone there. It has really made me stop and think. I realized that she's right, and it's not particularly useful for me to be operating in these ways. I need to get "back to the loving place."

I know exactly how and where I learned to be critical and judgmental: from my father and my mother. They were masters of the craft. This week, I decided to do something different. Whenever I noticed a negative or critical thought arising, I would come up with the most loving thing I could possibly say at that moment about the person or situation that I was reacting to. It totally changes the experience to choose a loving thought over a negative thought.

There have been many songs written about the power of love. (I'll save the "Lookin' for Love in All the Wrong Places" for an-other talk.) Huey Lewis's lyrics speak to this notion:
"The power of love is a curious thing
Make a one man weep, make another man sing
Change a hawk to a little white dove
More than a feeling that's the power of love."

When we are able to open ourselves up to being loving, it transforms us. When a person or situation that we find irritat-ing in some way presents itself to us, we always have a choice in how to respond. If we can step outside ourselves for a moment, and get in touch with our higher self, and connect with their higher self in a loving way, the outcome can be very surprising. The more we can get "back to the loving place," the more we are able to heal ourselves.

The cycle of breaking down, changing, and growing is all about vibration. We can change our vibration at any moment. We can take a breath. We can smile. We can recognize, release, and replace a thought, a word, or an action. For me, getting "back to the loving place" often involves both forgiveness and gratitude. Paying attention to forgiveness and gratitude are some of the ways that I raise my own vibration. When I get pulled off center, these are some of the ways that I get "back to the loving place."

The power of love is one of the most healing and transformative forces in the universe. In order to be open to receiving love, we must first learn to love ourselves. The opening words of the song that we sing at the end of each service are, "Let there be love on earth and let it begin with me." Learning to love ourselves is the first step in letting love begin with us.

I started learning Reiki about 11 years ago. Reiki is a Japanese word that loosely translates "universal life force energy." I learned (and believe) that as a Reiki practitioner, I open myself up as a channel for divine unconditional love. In my Level One Reiki training, the teacher gave us a handout called "Learning to Love Yourself." I know that one of the reasons that I chose her as my teacher was because learning to love myself was something that was so important for me to work on. I would like to share the words of this affirmation that has been so helpful in my process of learning to love myself.

I love and accept myself as I am.
I love my physical body as it is in this moment.
I honor my emotional body and allow my feelings freedom to flow.

I open to my creative body and allow my life to flow in bliss and abundance of happiness, health, wealth, wholeness and love.
I am full of happiness, health, wealth, wholeness and love.
I allow my Divine Core Essence to surround
and support my being with every breath.
I deserve the best in life.
I have the best in life.
I deserve love.
I have love.
And I love myself.
I completely love and accept myself.

Letting love begin with ourselves means loving and accepting all aspects of our body, mind and spirit. It means forgiving ourselves, fully and freely, with each breath we take.

The challenge is to continue to be loving and forgiving to ourselves, rather than being critical and judgmental, and wondering why we keep choosing the same lessons over and over. It's useful to notice that as we raise our vibration, we attract different people, places and things into our lives. The spiritual tools that we gain along the way help us to move forward on our path of unfoldment. One of those tools is meditation.

Recently, a meditation by a local integrative wellness doctor, called the Heart Center Meditation, came to my attention. The premise is that there are four attributes to the Heart Center. She says the first is Compassion – oceanic, limitless, boundless compassion. The second is Innate Harmony, the calm in the midst of chaos or the still point or the eye of the hurricane. The third is Healing Presence, the desire and longing toward healing. It's the first movement in the universe, love in action, drawn toward healing. The fourth is Unconditioned, Unconditional Love. It's reverence. It's the ability to perceive each thing for what it is. It's not personal love. It's the ability to appreciate each thing for exactly what it is, without trying to change it. She suggests placing the right hand over the heart chakra area, and the left hand over the right with the thumbs touching, and then calling in each of the four attributes. When we open ourselves to these attributes of the heart center, we take steps towards healing ourselves. All healing begins from a place of love.

So, my message today is to pay attention to getting "back to the loving place" - for that is the place where our own wholeness, growth and healing begin.

ORDER

9/15/13

"To everything, turn, turn, turn...there is a season, turn, turn, turn...and a time to every purpose under heaven." Although I eventually realized that this was a Bible verse, my strongest association was with the song that The Byrds recorded in the 1960's. "To everything there is a season" is an excellent way to introduce the Mind Power of Order. The verse continues, "A time to be born and a time to die." This is, of course, true for all of us. Metaphysically, we refer to it as a transition – either into or out of the earth plane of existence. It's interesting to notice how the way we make the transition out of the earth plane often mirrors the way we began. As newborn humans, we are completely dependent on others to feed us, attend to bodily functions, and make sure we are safe and well cared for. As we exit, we are often dependent on others for the same kind of care. As humans, we often celebrate the transition into the earth plane and have a harder time with the exit, when in fact, both represent Order operating just right, as it always does.

I have noticed that I am changing. Of course, we're all changing, but the changes are becoming a little more noticeable to me, of late. I used to be able to dance all night long and not give it a second thought, then turn around and do it all again the next night. Not so much anymore. Now, I plan my time in a way that fits more with my current reality. I still have a lot of fun. I just take the condition of my physical body into consideration in a different way these days.

A few months ago, my daughter shared her news with me that

she is pregnant. I'm going to be a Gramma. In some ways, I feel like I've been waiting for this for my whole life. It feels so right. It's another way that I'm changing. I'm accepting that I'm in a very different stage in my life. Because my father lived to be 102 years old, my perspective on life and aging is sometimes a little skewed. I'm going to celebrate my 60th birthday this year, and I'm very aware of actually feeling like I've gone past the halfway mark in my life. It's not always easy to deal with what this feels like for me.

One of the things that helps is the development I've done by studying and understanding metaphysics at my spiritual community. In learning about the Twelve Mind Powers, I've come to understand what "Order" means for me. That everything happens in the proper sequence and in the proper time. In the invocation we say at the beginning of each service, we affirm, "Our choices belong to us and are the seeds that create our lives." This clarifies what Order means for me.

I firmly believe that we choose and create every thought, word, and action in our lives. Everything that's happening today is the effect of all the thoughts, words, and actions that we've done up until this moment in life. We are responsible for what we think, what we say, and what we do. We are creating our experience with each breath we take. We affirm that Order operates perfectly in our life. Everything happens in the proper sequence and in the proper time, just as we have created it.

I've been listening to and noticing some things that people around me have been saying related to Order. One friend shared that on a camping trip, they were headed to another place, but it got too late. They ended up unexpectedly finding a beautiful spot where they spent the weekend. One friend was celebrating his 32nd birthday, and said he thought he was kind of old to be starting medical school. One friend shared that he was feeling stressed because he's been working on building a client base, and may choose to leave the area temporarily for a different and potentially lucrative business opportunity. Another friend shared that she was feeling pressure because of life choices that she is contemplating that may significantly change her living situation and relationship.

When we are able to affirm that Order is operating perfectly, each situation makes sense. Sometimes when you're looking for one place, you come upon another that is even better. You can spend the next several years doing anything...why not become a doctor if that's your calling, no matter what your chronological age. You might not know where a particular business venture may eventually lead you. When you get a job offer that feels right, everything else will fall into place. Order always operates perfectly in our lives.

I've been taking a Numerology class. We learned about tendencies that were connected with each number. Then we learned about what happens when those tendencies are out of balance or destructive. We learned about a calculation for a birth date that indicates how we see ourselves, then the next which indicates how others see us and what our destiny is, what we are working towards. When I read about my destiny number, the first words were: "Must cultivate patience." I notice how often I've been choosing to learn lessons in patience, as I move through this lifetime. It's been kind of a key word for me for a long time.

I know that this is really important for me to be working on. I know that I've made some strides in this area. When thinking about the Mind Power of Order, patience comes up very strongly for me. Things happening in the proper sequence and in the proper time. Sometimes, I'm not great at waiting. Sometimes, I'm able to be very patient. Doing a talk on Order is a great reminder to myself to be patient. To understand that things are unfolding just right.

I've been working on affirming that I am receptive and I am ready, instead of pushing or chasing after whatever it is that I think I want and need. This helps me with patience. I'm allowing people and things to come to me in Divine Order. I'm doing more observing and less pushing. I'm being quieter and softer and gentler in my interactions with people. I recently came across a box that had letters that I had written and received in the early '70's. In one of the letters to my sister, I described how I was working on "gentle-ing" myself. P.S. I'm still working on that, and I'm proud to report progress.

One of the areas where Order is very apparent in our lives is in our physical bodies. We have physical, mental, emotional, and spiritual bodies. When something manifests physically, it means it has moved through all the other areas. It means we have worked through the issue, and can now say thank you and goodbye. For any physical manifestation, there is a root metaphysical cause. One of my favorite source books is Louise Hay's book, "Heal Your Body." It lists many physical symptoms, the root cause, and then suggested affirmations. In dealing with physical "dis-ease," it is always useful to affirm the opposite. If my knee is bothering me, it is useful to affirm, "I move forward in life with flexibility and ease." What we think, what we say, and what we do is what we attract more of into our lives.

Order is part of natural law. It is always operating perfectly, whether we are aware of it or not. When we are able to allow our lives to unfold and not rush to arrive at a destination before the fullness of time, we are affirming Order. If events appear to unfold in ways that seem unexpected, Order often allows that the new opportunities that present themselves are even more beneficial than what we thought we anticipated or had planned. Affirming Order can mean not jumping to where you think you want to go, but rather allowing yourself to get to the place where you need to be.

"Our choices belong to us and are the seeds that create our lives." Our thoughts, words and actions are the seeds that we plant. We reap what we sow, always and perfectly. If something isn't working well in your life, you can trace it back to the seeds that you planted. If you want to change something in your life, you have to plant different seeds, and then be patient as they grow, and allow Order to unfold. "To everything there is a season. And a time to every purpose under heaven."

THE MIND POWER OF LIFE

12/22/13

Sometimes when I ask for guidance, I hear songs. In preparing for this talk, I heard Liza Minelli singing, "Life is a cabaret," Frank Sinatra singing, "That's life," and the cast of Fiddler on the Roof, singing: "L'Chaim, To Life!" Our life force is always active within us. In thinking about our topic for this month: the Mind Power of Life, it seemed useful to contemplate the things that make our life force flow freely and the things that create obstacles to our life force.

Each time I prepare to give a talk at my spiritual community, the process looks kind of like this: what's the topic and what do I have to say about it...it's getting closer and I don't know what I'm going to say...what do I have to say that someone else will find worthwhile...will I have enough time to write a good talk...and so on. Then, I remember to trust the process, and know that I will be inspired, and have just the right words when the time comes. When I remove the obstacles to the creative energy, it flows perfectly.

Sometimes our life force feels powerful. We feel motivated, active, energized and outgoing. Sometimes our life force can feel diminished. We feel tired, anxious, fearful, or sad. For me, when I remember that I have enough and that I am enough, the life force flows much more freely.

The holiday season can be a challenging time for people, and that is sometimes true for me. I've had some days lately where I've felt like throwing myself a little pity party. I've been missing my parents. I won't be with one of my daughters for Christmas this year. I don't have a romantic partner in my life at the moment. My brother and sister are in Paris for Christmas. And so on. If I focus on what I imagine is missing in my life, I feel sad and depressed, and my life force feels very constricted and limited. When I remember who I am, and what I actually have in my life and am grateful, my energy changes completely. When I am able take it a step further, and move beyond my own individual perspective, and find ways to reach out and give to others, that helps even more.

One of the things that I find useful is to ask yourself what brings you joy and lifts your spirit. Take time to pay attention to the things that enhance and expand your life force. One way to do this is to really get to know yourself better. One aspect of getting to know yourself is to notice the people, places, and things around you, and your thoughts, words, and actions. If you feel lethargic, unhappy, or are experiencing any form of dis-ease, notice what you're doing, where you're doing it, and who you're doing it with. If you want to change the way you're feeling, you can choose to change the people, places, and things you surround yourself with, and you can change your thoughts, words, and actions.

This can be a small gesture or a major life change. We might decide to say an affirmation, to smile more frequently, to pay a compliment to a friend. Or we might decide to move across the country, change careers, end a marriage, or have a child. Knowing yourself, and trusting your own guidance, allows you to make the choices that are most beneficial and for your highest and best good.

Life is always what we make of it. We are responsible in every way for our lives because we are constantly creating with our thoughts, words and actions. I make references to Facebook at times, because social media has become a powerful force in our culture. I'm very aware of people who constantly post negative things about being sick or angry or upset or blaming others for whatever is happening in their lives or who did what to whom. I limit my contact with those kinds of people. I'm really conscious of what I put out, because I know whatever energy I put out is what returns to me multiplied.

One of my favorite people to enjoy on Facebook is a young man who is so full of positive energy. He frequently posts uplifting and encouraging messages. He got married earlier this year, and he and his wife have a powerful, loving and supportive connection that is a pleasure to observe. He takes this energy that he has, and uses it to inspire himself and others to be the best they can be. He's been in the process of starting a business, but still took the time to organize a trip to bring health care to people in a very underserved area. He lives his truth fully and freely, and is an inspiration to those around him. The life force is very strong within him.

Life is about choices. We are constantly choosing everything. We are choosing our thoughts, words, and actions, and therefore, creating our experiences. When we value ourselves, we feel better. When we remember to feel and express gratitude for what we have, rather than complain about what we do not have, we feel better. Our life force flows much more fully and freely when we focus on prosperity instead of lack.

As we observe and implement ways to keep our life force flowing freely, an interesting phenomenon may occur. We want our life force to be powerful and healthy, so we make choices to do things in our lives that are positive, uplifting, and expansive for our life force. We choose to form more positive habits. We might decide to eat more healthy foods, exercise, communicate more clearly with a partner or friend, practice yoga or meditation. We notice that we start to feel better. Sometimes, once we start to feel better, we stop doing the things that allowed us to get to there in the first place. It's important to know yourself, in order to know what works and what doesn't, in maintaining a more positive flow of life force energy. It's important to follow through with positive habits, in order to sustain positive changes in our lives.

Some of the things that have been working for me in this area are beginning each day by doing Reiki on myself, saying positive affirmations, and taking quiet time to meditate. A friend shared a Heart Center meditation that focuses on compassion, innate harmony, healing presence and unconditioned, unconditional love, that has been very powerful and transformative for me. The way I end each day is by writing at least five things I'm grateful for in a gratitude journal. No matter what has gone on during a day, focusing on what I'm thankful for always changes my vibration in a positive manner. I dance as often as possible. I spend time with friends. And I do improv comedy. There's only one rule in improv – always make your scene partner look good. The rest are guidelines: Say, "Yes, and..." Listen. Make eye contact. Be present. Tell the truth. These are great guidelines for life, and when I practice these things regularly, I feel better, and the life force flows more freely.

As we come to the end of the year, it's a useful time to reflect on the things that work and don't work in our lives. Notice the things that bring you joy and lift your spirit, and enhance your life force. Do more of those, and reduce or eliminate the things that do the opposite. Here's to us, and here's to Life!

SELF-ESTEEM

2/16/14

Our topic for today is Self-Esteem and the stumbling blocks that can impede us. The way we feel about ourselves, as everything in life, is a choice. No matter what we have been told or what we have been taught, in this moment, we can choose to feel good about ourselves, just as we are. Do we choose to put up a "mime wall" imposing limitations or do we choose to see ourselves as the beings that we truly are, perfectly creating in each moment?

Self-esteem begins really early in life. When my kids' dad and I were preparing to be parents, we talked a lot about self-esteem and how important it was to promote healthy, positive self-esteem in children. We did our best to help our daughters feel good about themselves. Which was not exactly the way I was raised. Criticism was the norm in my family. If there was something negative to be said about anyone or anything, my mother could be counted on to be the first to bring it up. It seemed to me at times, especially as a teenager, that in order to feel good about himself, my father needed to put other people down.

Weight was such a big issue in my family. My mother was on a diet for as long as I can remember. I can still see, smell, and taste the Metrecal wafers that she ate on a regular basis. And I remember, when I would reach for a roll in the bread basket, my father saying, "We're going to have to roll you home." Not particularly helpful in developing positive self-esteem.

The theme of "I'm not good enough" seemed to run through my life for a long time. Although I was voted the smartest kid in my class, when I brought home my report card with a grade of 99%, my father always said, "Why didn't you get 100?" When I was married, my husband repeatedly talked about how much "potential" I had. Although he may have meant that in a positive way, in my head that translated to "I'm not good enough now." I was not in the habit of choosing to feel good about myself.

When our perception of ourselves is skewed, this is a stumbling block. A close friend of mine was talking about some of his issues with meeting women. He said he didn't feel like he brought much to the table. I asked him what he thought others "brought to the table." He said they were intelligent, interesting, active, fun, and attractive. I was truly shocked because he is ALL of those things. It's just that his perception of himself is inaccurate. He's not choosing to see the best in himself. His self-esteem is lacking, and he needs to be reminded of who he really is. Sometimes we have to rely on our friends for help.

About 10 years ago, someone whose opinion I really valued told me that I looked exactly the way he liked a woman to look. That really surprised me. I didn't think that was possible because when I look at magazine and television ads, the women who are portrayed as beautiful, most definitely do not look the way I do. And the media is a powerful force at this time in our society. After he said that, I spent time looking at myself through his eyes, and it gradually changed the way I thought about myself.

At one point when I was feeling pretty down on myself, I thought about some of the people in my life who I really love and respect, and whose judgment I really trust. I reminded myself that they all treasure me as their friend, and if I really love, respect, and trust their judgment about most things, why not choose to believe the best about myself?

When we compare ourselves to others, the result is rarely productive. When I look at someone else and think – why does she have so much money or why do men fall all over themselves around her or why are her psychic messages so much better than mine, how does that serve me? When we compare ourselves to others, the result often leaves us wanting. None of us knows the path that another has walked or what price has been paid to attain some kind of position or status or even skill level. We are much better off choosing to appreciate who we are and what we have, and giving great thanks in each moment, rather than envying or resenting anyone else's good.

Forgiveness is another really important tool. Over time, I have gradually learned to accept and embrace the fact that I make mistakes. The key is in forgiving myself, and giving myself permission to change, and grow, and move forward. Forgiveness is such a powerful tool, and it is most important to begin with forgiving ourselves. In my daily affirmations, I say, "With each breath, I fully and freely forgive myself, and loose myself to my highest and best good. I fully and freely forgive everyone and everything, and loose them to their highest and best good. Everyone and everything fully and freely forgives me, and looses me to my highest and best good." Forgiveness means truly letting go and moving on. Not holding on to any remnants because, "Holding resentment is like taking poison, then waiting for the other person to keel over."

It is useful for us to pay attention to the things that trigger us. Our primitive brain is essential for keeping us breathing, and preventing us from running into telephone poles. The primitive brain is not always so useful for processing emotional information. We can sometimes be triggered by other people's behavior. If a person that you are romantically involved with suddenly changes the game plan, your primitive brain may be triggered, and a downward spiral may begin. What's necessary in that moment is to identify the trigger, recognize the habitual reaction, then redirect your energy in a more positive and constructive direction. The only things we ever have control over are our own thoughts, words, actions, and reactions, and we always have the choice to recognize, release, and replace.

When I took my first Reiki Class about 12 years ago, I knew I had chosen the right teacher when she brought out a handout called "Learning to Love Yourself." Learning to love yourself is both the key and the first step on the path of developing positive self-esteem. I would like to share this affirmation with you:

I love and accept myself as I am.

I love my physical body as it is in this moment.

I honor my emotional body and allow my feelings freedom to flow.

I open to my creative body and allow my life to flow in bliss and abundance of happiness, health, wealth, wholeness and love.

I am full of happiness, health, wealth, wholeness and love.

I allow my Divine Core Essence to surround
and support my being with every breath.

I deserve the best in life. I have the best in life.

I deserve love. I have love.

And I love myself. I completely love and accept myself.

I have been saying this affirmation every day since I first learned it, and it has really made a difference in how I think about myself, how I look at myself, and how I treat myself. It has reminded me on a daily basis to choose to love myself.

Going back to our "mime wall," the reality is that nothing is holding us back except ourselves. We imagine that we are or are not a certain way, do or do not have a certain look, do or do not possess certain traits or talents, and then create a box for ourselves that does not serve us. When we use the tools at our disposal to dismantle the "mime wall," we realize that we are free to embrace and enjoy the being that we truly are. That we are free to fully acknowledge the concept of "I AM," and can choose to raise our self-esteem for our highest and best good. We can choose to love ourselves with each breath we take.

CLEANSING

Our Daily Bread
3/23/14

Our topic for this month is Cleansing, and this week specific-ally: Our Daily Bread. For a minute, I wasn't sure what that was supposed to mean. Then, I decided to choose to know. In the same way that we physically clean our body, our hair, our clothing, and our home, it is also important and necessary to attend to cleansing our mind and our spirit. How do we do that? By paying attention to the thoughts, words, and actions that we choose to fill ourselves with.

In thinking about Our Daily Bread, I was reminded of the Cherokee legend regarding a man teaching his grandson about life. "A fight is going on inside me," he said to the boy.
"It is a terrible fight and it is between two wolves. One is anger, envy, sorrow, regret, greed, arrogance, self-pity, guilt, resentment, inferiority, lies, false pride, superiority, and ego."
He continued, "The other is joy, peace, love, hope, serenity, humility, kindness, benevolence, empathy, generosity, truth, compassion, and faith. The same fight is going on inside you - and inside every other person, too."
The grandson thought about it for a minute and then asked his grandfather, "Which wolf will win?"
The old Cherokee simply replied, "The one you feed."
So, which wolf do you feed? We have a choice in each moment about this. I have been a member of a local improv comedy troupe for about three years. I attend rehearsals consistently, attend classes regularly, and perform in live shows each week.

I get good feedback about my skill and my progress, and often hear laughter when I perform. The other night during a singing/rhyming game, for the first time on stage, my mind went completely blank, and I absolutely could not think of a word that rhymed with "slow." I felt embarrassed. I heard negative self-talk going on in my head for a long time after the show ended. I know that it wasn't a problem for anyone else. I told my sister that I was "stupidly beating myself up," and she asked if there was ever a time to beat yourself up that was not stupid. After a while, I finally decided to let go of it. I decided to give myself credit for doing well so much of the time, and to be gentler and kinder to myself.

That same night, after I left the show and was driving to get to a dance, I got pulled over because I was speeding. I was really angry at the officer who pulled me over. I was really angry at myself for getting caught. I shared this with a good friend the other night, and he said to just write the check and be done with it. He said not to give them any piece of me. As I thought about his words, I decided not to give away any of my peace, p-e-a-c-e. Is there anything that is worth giving away our peace?

When I affirm that I am the creator in my life, I affirm that I create for my highest and best good and the highest and best good of all others. I want everyone to prosper, and be the best they can be. When I maintain abundance consciousness, I know that there is plenty for everyone. I want everyone to succeed in the best ways possible. If we envy what someone else has or does, we put ourselves in lack consciousness. The more someone else achieves, the more I know what is possible.

How do we go about cleansing our consciousness? There are many different ways that people choose to detox themselves. There are cleanses, there are treatment programs. In doing a spiritual detox, it is useful to look at our thoughts, words, and actions, and the people, places, and things that we spend time with in our lives. At a workshop I went to a number of years ago, the facilitator suggested that for any experience or decision in our lives, we ask ourselves, "Does this bring me joy and lift my spirit?" These are really valuable and useful questions to ask yourself on a consistent basis. If you are feeling tired, unhappy, or resentful, take a look at how you're spending your time and energy, and do your best to make choices that bring you joy and lift your spirit.

I visited a friend recently who's gone through a challenging time after her husband made his transition last fall. She has been learning some new coping skills. As I listened to her, I realized that she's being much more selective in the people, places, and things that she fills her life with. She has also been clearing out space in her home, and eliminating things which no longer serve her. This is making room for her to have a meditation and yoga room, as well as an exercise and art studio. These are really healthy choices for her to be making in sustaining the changes she is incorporating into her life.

What do we choose to feed ourselves? When we look in the mirror, what do we say to ourselves about our physical bodies? A friend very bravely shared what has been going on in her life in a blog called, "The Dependopotamus." She is a military spouse, and has relied on being supported in every way for some time. She also shared that she has gained a significant amount of weight, and is not feeling very good about herself. She has begun to initiate changes, including going to the gym. In a comment, I suggested that it was already time to change the name of her blog to reflect the person she is becoming, rather than the person she is leaving behind.

In choosing to operate in positive ways, one way that I choose to feed my spiritual health, is to do daily positive affirmations. This promotes positive growth and development, and sets the tone for each day. I've been doing Reiki for many years. A little over a year ago, I started doing Reiki on myself every day. It's made a difference to start my day with a dose of very positive energy.

Energetic protection is another topic worth mentioning. When I teach Reiki classes, one of the first things we talk about is protection. There are many ways to do this for yourself. Imagine a light, a color, a fabric or netting, a shield – whatever makes the most sense for you – running in and around and through you, so that only the highest and best can come through for your highest and best good. This way you do not give away your peace to anyone or anything. You bubble your energy so that it goes where you want and when you want it to go, rather than being scattered or stolen or absorbed in ways that are not of your choosing.

When I find myself in conversations that are negative or gossipy, I do my best to either change the subject or extricate myself from the situation.

I am the creator of my life. What an empowering statement that is. When we take responsibility for absolutely everything in our lives, we are accepting and acknowledging that we are powerful, and that we are the creators of our lives. You may notice people around you that spend time blaming others for what happens to them. I do my best to take responsibility for everything that happens in my life, from a hang nail to a speeding ticket to an argument or a lottery ticket win. What we think, what we say, and what we do, is what we draw more of into our lives.

Every thought, every word, and every action in our lives is our choice. We can choose to be positive or negative with each breath we take. We are the creators of our lives, and what we experience is a reflection of what we choose and create. Which wolf do you feed? The one you feed is the one who will win.

UNDERSTANDING

4/27/14

Our topic for this week is Understanding, with the theme for the month being K-I-S-S, the acronym for "Keep It Simple, Sweetie." In the most simple terms, we are the creators of our lives. We are responsible for everything that happens in our lives. With each thought, word, and action, we create our experiences.

Coming to my spiritual community felt like the most natural step for me to take. I felt like I belonged here from the first moment. The steps I have taken on my path have felt like becoming more and more of who I am. The things that I have learned here make sense to me. What we think, what we say, and what we do is what we draw more of to ourselves. If we are really wanting watermelon, and we plant corn, we cannot be surprised when the harvest is an abundance of corn. No matter how much we said we wanted watermelon. In order to harvest watermelon, you have to plant watermelon. Our thoughts, words, and actions are the seeds that we plant in each moment. Are we planting seeds of doubt, fear, anger, and lack? Or are we planting seeds of confidence, love, peace, and abundance? It is our choice.

We read things like, "All I really need to know I learned in kindergarten." For me, much of what I need to know I learned in studying metaphysics. What we think, what we say, and what we do is what we draw more of to us. We choose every experience that we have. We are the creators of our lives. This week, I've spent some time releasing. First, my body and head felt achy, and all I wanted to do was sleep. Then, my appetite disappeared for a while. Then, some elimination was going on. I've been traveling a lot in the last four months, primarily spending time with my daughter and new baby grandson. This period of release was much gentler than I've experienced at other times in the past. My body told me to slow down, stay home, keep things very simple, rest, and re-group. Not in an extreme way, but in a gentle way, which I was very grateful for.

Knowing where we've been can be helpful in knowing where we are, and where we're going. As I re-read my talk on Understanding from last year, I was relieved to note that I've made progress on my path. I haven't been experiencing the kind of upheaval that I was going through last year. Some of the things that I am still working on have to do with my need for attention, my need to look good in front of others, to look or feel important, to feel like I'm "in the know," to stand out from the crowd. As I assess my behavior and experiences, I notice that when I operate from a place of being loving, centered, grounded, and grateful, my life works much better. I have been affirming that I think before I speak, and I think before I act. I acknowledge the missteps that I may take, and I forgive myself. I move forward doing the best I can, with each breath I take.

If I am finding someone else's behavior so irritating that it makes me want to scream, it's time for me to look in the mirror, and to look inside myself, to see what's really going on. And I ask myself, what is my goal? If my goal is to simply vent, rant, and potentially look foolish in the process, then I should definitely go with my first instinct, and just react. If my goal is, instead, to be effective, to grow, to create change, and to learn, it is worth my while to take the time to understand the situation as fully as I can, and to make my response in the most thoughtful way possible. Understanding allows me to take responsibility for my part in creating the situation.

One of the most challenging parts of my relationship with my father was that he was SO critical. And yet, I often find myself operating just like that. Fortunately for the people around me, much of that critical dialogue goes on internally. By the time it makes its way out, I have filtered it through lots of screens, taken responsibility for what's actually going on, and am able to communicate in a much more reasonable manner. I'm still working on modifying the internal process.

When we understand things, we can be at peace with them. As I move through this journey of growth, sometimes things are not immediately apparent to me. If I take the time to sit with an experience for a while, and see what's really going on, it's often easier to understand the situation. Watching my daughter be a mother has been a really interesting experience for me. It's provided some excellent lessons in letting go – letting go of my own preconceived notions of how things should be. My daughter and I have always been close. When she was planning her home birth, and choosing her birth team, she was including me. Several weeks before the baby was due, she told me she'd changed her mind, and didn't want me in the house during the birth – which was, of course, her right, and I supported her decision completely. However, I was devastated by the news. I felt rejected and left out. Then, when she went into labor, I stopped by the house very briefly a few hours in. I watched her go through two contractions. Then, I went outside, and cried for half an hour. It was so difficult to watch my baby be in pain. I was SO grateful that she had made the decision for me not to be there. Later, she shared that part of her decision was based on not wanting the energy of my "birth story" (which was not easy in any way) in the house during her birth process. It all made perfect sense, and her experience turned out to be very peaceful and beautiful. She was surrounded by loving women friends who took such good care of her and supported her completely. I was welcomed shortly after the birth, and then I was at peace with the experience.

The Mind Power of Understanding is located in the feet. Think about taking a step back so that you can see something more clearly, see the bigger picture. When you only look at one piece of a puzzle, you can only see that piece. When you step back, you can see the whole picture, and then the single piece makes sense in a whole different way. Understanding, as all aspects of development, evolves continually.

We are the creators of our lives. Every thought, word and action is a choice. If we look at the people, places and things around us, they are a reflection of ourselves. The more irritating we may find a person or situation to be, the more we have to learn from them. What aspects of ourselves are they reflecting? We are the creators of our lives, and in developing our understanding, we acknowledge that the only way to change anything in our lives is to make a change in ourselves.

CHANGE

GIVING UP WHAT BELONGS TO OTHERS
6/22/14

As I thought about the topic for the month - Change, and for the week – Giving Up What Belongs to Others, a couple of affirmations came to mind. "I bear my responsibilities with ease, and release burdens that do not belong to me." And, "I see clearly and act accordingly." As metaphysicians, we are encouraged to recognize, release, and replace, as we work to know ourselves and make changes in our lives. Many of us do a credible job at recognizing what's going on in our lives and the things that we might want to change. The next step is releasing, and sometimes that presents more of a challenge. The third step is essential – that is replacing. If we don't replace what we've been doing with something different, we just get better at doing what we've already been doing. If we don't form new habits, we just strengthen our old habits.

As humans, when we become aware of a problem, often our response is to want to fix it. I've noticed that when a challenging situation comes to my attention, my brain works analytically, and generates solutions. Whether it's appropriate to share those solutions, and whether those solutions are invited and/or welcomed by others is another story.

Last year, a close friend of mine pointed out to me that I was choosing to operate in ways that were not particularly healthy in relation to one of my daughters. I was taking responsibility for her life. I was getting her mail, making sure her bills were paid, following up with anything that had any kind of a deadline, making decisions for her, and being ready with financial support at a moment's notice. I was doing myself and her a big disservice by not allowing her to take responsibility for her own life. After some contemplation, we met and came up with a new plan for how we would operate with money and responsibility together.

At first, it was really challenging for me to make these changes. I had been in the habit of acting in a certain way, and thinking about her in a certain way, for a long time. I gave myself credit for small, incremental steps as I was able to take them. I called my friend at times for guidance, to check and see if I was making the healthiest choice in the moment. Over time, my daughter and I adjusted to our new arrangement. Amazingly enough, she is perfectly capable of managing her own life. She might not always do it in the way that I would, but she does it in her own way, and in her own time. Letting go of these burdens that did not belong to me has freed me. Our relationship has evolved in ways that are much healthier and more positive.

Another way to bear responsibilities with ease is to just listen. As a people who are hunters and gatherers, we go through life gathering things into our "baskets." Sometimes, people's "baskets" are full, and they simply need to empty them. Sometimes, the way to best serve someone is to just listen in a loving, supportive, and reflective way. To allow them to "empty their basket," without offering solutions, can be a true gift. The respect that is offered in listening warmly and supportively can be the most valuable and useful thing to do in any given moment.

Recently, a friend called to discuss a challenging work situation. There were several options that occurred to me, and I put forth a couple of gentle suggestions. Mostly, I just listened to her, and told her that I loved and cared about her, and was willing to listen and be supportive at any time. She responded very positively, and I did not take on those burdens that did not belong to me.

When we hear about the challenges that someone else is experiencing, sometimes the solution seems fairly obvious. The internal response we may have is: how come they can't see that this is what they need to do? And why won't they just do what they need to do? The answer is that everyone has their own path, and makes their own choices. No matter what I think someone else should do, they have to come to it in their own way and in their own time. The lessons they are choosing are theirs to learn at this moment, and each person has to figure out how to do that in their own way.

At the beginning of each service we affirm: "Our choices belong to us and are the seeds that create our lives." One of the most important things to give up to others is the freedom to make their own choices, the freedom to create their own lives, and even the freedom to make their own mistakes. As we look around at our lives, sometimes we see doubt, worry, anxiety, insecurity, fear, and anger growing in our garden. That's the signal that it's time for some spiritual gardening. It's time to weed, prune, turn over the soil, and plant new seeds. Each person does that in their own way and in their own time.

There is a Hawaiian spiritual tradition that states that we are each born into this world as a "bowl of light" containing the radiance of heaven. Fear, worry, and insecurity are like rocks that we place in our bowl, that hide our true "light" essence. Becoming "enlightened" is simply a matter of remembering who we truly are, being who we truly are, and removing any obstacles to our brilliance. Anything that works against the full expression of who and what we are, may be rocks that we need to remove from our bowl to allow us to be the light that we are truly meant to be.

My other daughter is a chiropractor. She has explained that

chiropractic philosophy affirms that the body's natural state is health, and what chiropractors do is make adjustments to remove any interference that exists in the system. When we take the rocks out of our bowls, we are removing the interference in the system that takes away our light. We are transforming dis-ease into ease. Releasing burdens that belong to others, and choosing ease, allows you to remove more rocks, and be the "light" that is truly you.

The only way to change anything in our lives is to change something in ourselves. A very close friend has been going through a challenging time. She called herself a "hot mess" (in even more colorful terms than that.) I told her that it did not serve her in any way to speak or think that way about herself. She got it right away. In thinking about what's going on in her life, she realized that she needed to make some changes in order to feel better. She needed to go to sleep at some regular time, wake up at some regular time, eat in a more consistent manner, do some form of exercise, and speak positively to herself, in order to change how she was feeling. She has a plan for implementing these changes for herself, which includes writing everything down as a tangible reminder. She is affirming that she sees clearly and acts accordingly.

Thinking about change reminds me of the Michael Jackson song, "Man in the Mirror." To paraphrase his lyrics, we can say:

Start with the person in the mirror
Ask yourself to change your ways
And no message could have been any clearer
If you want to make your life a better place
Take a look at yourself, and then make a change.

As we recognize, release, and replace things that we wish to change in our lives, giving up what does not belong to us, we are free to move forward, grow, and become our highest and best selves in each moment.

HONOR AND HUMILITY

7/27/14

Our topic for this month is Honor, and this week Humility. I was so honored to have had a friend who was a shining example of these qualities. I met Bob in the 1990's, when he was already about 75 years old. There was never anything ostentatious about Bob. He wore black t-shirts and jeans in warm weather, and added flannel shirts when it got chilly. He preferred to share a sandwich for lunch. His smile was always warm and welcoming. At the time that I met him, I was working for a woman in Tucson. She and Bob had known each other many years before when both had been married, and both their children had been in pre-school. Bob and his wife and four sons had moved to Florida for about 20 years. His wife had passed, and Bob moved back to Tucson, to be closer to one of his sons. As soon as Bob learned that this woman he had known so long ago was now single, he began courting her immediately. That's how I got to meet Bob.

I got to know Bob very gradually, and mostly learned details of his life through things other people would share. Bob had a Ph.D., and had had a fairly illustrious career in both academics and local government in Arizona and Florida. Bob had served in World War II, landing on the beach in Normandy within days after D-Day. Bob and his best friend had been very involved in our spiritual community in the 1970's, and Bob had a deep and rich spiritual life. Bob continued to love learning throughout his life. He educated himself extensively about the stock market. He continued to read books about metaphysics. I never saw him without a book close by. His sons and others relied on him for the sage advice that he was willing to offer, if asked.

He and the woman got married in the late 1990's. Although there was some divergence in their financial situations, that didn't affect Bob in the slightest. He preferred to eat beans and rice at home most nights, understanding and supporting his wife's choice to eat in fancy restaurants when she wanted to. Their vacations together consisted mainly of road trips to visit their respective children and grandchildren. He loved her for who she was, and was completely devoted to her. Her wealth didn't matter to him in the slightest.

In the last few years of his life, he began to be more and more forgetful, to the point where sometimes he would wander away and not remember how to get home. His wife did everything possible to protect him, and keep him in familiar surroundings, while making sure he was safe. Eventually, he lived in a beautiful room in an assisted living home that was designed to keep people in Bob's condition safe and comfortable. He gradually lost the ability to find the words that he wanted to use to express himself. But he remained kind and loving throughout the process.

Last fall, his health began to deteriorate rapidly. In the last several days of his life, the only way he was able to be calm and comfortable was if he was holding tightly to someone's hand or arm. I was honored to be one of the people to spend a little time with him during those days. I talked to him about the people who loved him, reassured him that it was OK to go, and sang him songs from the eras that had meaning for him. His wife and sons were with him as he made his transition.

Bob served his country with honor, and without hesitation.

He was a loving husband and father. He accomplished a great many things, that one only learned about through talking to others. For me, Bob was the ultimate model of honor and humility, in the simple and straightforward way that he lived his life. He used the gifts that were given to him in very effective ways. For me, this is another important aspect of Honor – how we choose to use the gifts that are given to us.

Developing our gifts can be a very valuable and important process. We may have spiritual, mental, emotional, or physical gifts. It's important to recognize the gifts that we are given, and then develop them in the highest and best ways that we can, to honor ourselves and Spirit.

Last year, a friend shared a meditation about the Heart Center that has had a major impact on my life. The premise is that the Heart Center has four attributes, and we can ignite each one of them for our highest and best good. The first attribute is Compassion - oceanic, limitless, boundless compassion. When we operate from a place of compassion, we open our hearts to feel and understand what others may be experiencing. Instead of judging, we are loving and accepting. We imagine what it is like to be in any situation, and act accordingly in dealing with others. We honor our connection with all that is.

The second attribute is Innate Harmony – calm in the midst of chaos, the still point, the eye of the storm. When we operate from a place of innate harmony, we choose to bring our lives into balance. We choose the solution that is the highest and best for ourselves and others at any given moment. To paraphrase Rudyard Kipling, we choose to keep our heads when all about us may be losing theirs. We choose to be the voice of reason.

The third attribute is Healing Presence – love in action, drawn toward healing. When we choose to operate from a place of healing presence, we can be the balm to any wound, we bring peace where there may be disharmony, and ease where there is dis-ease. We can choose to bring out the best in ourselves and others.

The fourth attribute is Unconditioned, Unconditional Love – loving everyone and everything exactly as they are, without needing to change anything. This is so very powerful. When we choose to operate from a place of unconditioned, unconditional love, we honor everyone and everything for the paths they have chosen, for the gifts they are expressing, and for the lessons they are offering. We honor ourselves and others for the beings that we and they truly are.

As I have mentioned on a number of occasions, one of the most important things in my life is gratitude. I just began my seventh year of using a daily gratitude journal. At the end of each day, I write down at least five things that I am grateful for. Focusing on gratitude has been a huge gift in my life. It has been a transformative process for me. In paying attention to the things we are grateful for, we have the power to change any situation or experience into something positive.

I am so grateful for having been given this topic to ponder and speak about this week. I recognize that I can get caught up in feeling like the center of the universe at times, and can feel impatient, intolerant, and entitled. When I honor the connection with all that is, and know that I am simply part of a greater whole, it serves me and those around me much better. I am so grateful for having known Bob, and for being able to honor him by sharing a little bit about his life today. Thinking about Honor and Humility has been a very valuable reminder for me to have perspective on what's important in a little different way, to remember to honor myself and others, and to remain humble and be grateful for the gifts that I have received.

CHOICES AND CHANGES

9/27/14

The only constant is change, and this has been particularly true for me this year. Since my daughter gave birth to my beautiful grandson in January, I've been traveling to see them every month, and adjusting to my new role as "Gramma." I've been taking a significant break from the improv comedy troupe that I've been involved with for many years, in order to refresh my perspective. And the spiritual community that has been my home and my center has gone through major changes in the last month or so. In some ways, all these changes have felt disruptive to me. I have felt a sense of turmoil and upheaval, and have been feeling somewhat out of sorts. When I was talking to my sister the other day about how I was feeling, she exclaimed, "We don't do change well!" Which made me laugh, and is also somewhat true. As I thought about it, I realized that what is true for me is that I don't necessarily do change quickly. I need time to adjust to change.

Everyone has had experiences of sudden and/or unexpected changes that we may or may not feel prepared for. Everyone adjusts to changes in their own way and in their own time. No matter what works for someone else, it is important for us to pay attention to what works for us. Someone else may adjust immediately, while I have to take time to work through my thoughts and feelings. There is no right and wrong, just what is for the highest and best for each person.

I believe that the body is a reflection of what has gone on in the spiritual, emotional, and mental realms. Each part of the body represents a metaphysical aspect. When we manifest physical symptoms, that is the final step in working through and letting go of issues. Saying positive affirmations helps us to move through the things we are working on. Given the way that I adjust to change, it is no surprise that I have had significant issues with my hips. I keep affirming that I move forward in life with vitality and ease. I have also been keenly aware of my knees, and know that flexibility is being ignited for me in a big way. I keep moving forward. I keep affirming that I am flexible. I understand that things change. I'm working on it.

How do we adjust to change? One of the things that I've been doing is really utilizing my quiet time. In one of the meditations that I do on a daily basis, Innate Harmony is ignited. Imagine calm in the midst of chaos, the still point, the eye of the storm. This has been helpful during this time. To really focus on the still point, and allow whatever comes up to just arise without conscious thought or control. In allowing ourselves to enjoy quiet time, we give ourselves the opportunity to process changes that are happening in our lives in the ways that serve us best. Recognizing, releasing, and replacing are very useful tools in this process.

There are many things in our lives that we have no control over. What we always have complete control over are our thoughts, words, and actions. In each moment, we get to choose what we think, say, and do. The choices that we make are the seeds that create our lives. In looking at our lives, it's useful to examine which choices are positive and constructive, so that we can grow and nourish those areas, and to look at which choices no longer serve us, so that we can release and/or eliminate them. In moving forward with the changes in our spiritual community, I noticed that, at first, I was feeling angry and resentful. In classic Italian fashion, I really wanted to blame someone else for what had occurred.

Then, I remembered to breathe (always a good plan.) And I remembered all the things I've learned along the way in studying metaphysics. We are responsible for everything in our lives. We choose and create every experience that we have. Then, we choose how we respond to each situation. It took me a minute, because of the way I handle change, to recognize the ways in which I contributed to creating this situation. I take responsibility for my thoughts, words, and actions. I know that it does not ever serve me to blame anyone else for anything that happens in my life. I truly believe that things happen for the highest and best good of all concerned. I do my best to recognize the gifts that exist within any challenge that occurs.

What we think, what we say, and what we do, is what we draw more of into our lives. When we recognize and acknowledge that we are the creators of our lives, we empower ourselves. When we take responsibility for absolutely everything in our lives, we are accepting and acknowledging that we are powerful, and that we are the creators of our lives. If we blame someone else for anything that happens in our lives, we are choosing to give up our power. When we accept responsibility, we affirm our power.

Another step for me in adjusting to change is forgiveness. It is so important at these times for me to be very forgiving. Each day, I affirm that I fully and freely forgive myself, and loose myself to my highest and best good. I also affirm that I fully and freely forgive everyone and everything, and that everyone and everything fully and freely forgives me. It is essential in moving forward to let go of anything that may hold us back. Forgiveness is one of the most important tools in letting go and moving forward.

Sometimes, there are triggers from the past that cause us to react in less than ideal ways. It's useful to pay attention to these triggers, so that we can make different choices in the present. Growing up, we are taught many things by our parents, teachers, friends, and society. Sometimes, these ideas become deeply ingrained, and we operate from assumptions that may or may not be valid for who we are in the present. It's useful to do a mental inventory, and really check in with our beliefs to see which ones serve us, and which ones need to be changed or eliminated. The process of recognizing, releasing, and replacing is so valuable to implement.

In thinking about the changes that we have gone through in our spiritual community, it has been helpful for me to see it as an awakening, and an opportunity for change and growth. I have been noticing what worked, and what didn't, as we move forward. What gifts do we want to carry with us, and what burdens do we want to release and leave behind?

And, for me, gratitude is always an essential step in adjusting to change. I am so grateful for all the things I have learned from the many teachers who have come into my life. I am grateful for my friends who support and love me, no matter what is happening in my life. I am grateful for having found a space where we can gather together. I am grateful for the tools I have learned, and for remembering to use them as I move forward.

We all have a variety of tools in our physical, mental, emotional, and spiritual tool boxes. It is important to remember to use them in ways that are most beneficial. As we move forward on our path, taking responsibility for our thoughts, words, and actions, we remind ourselves to recognize, release, and replace things that no longer serve us. We remind ourselves to nurture and cherish the things that are for our highest and best good and the highest and best good of all others. We do our best to be loving and forgiving as we move forward on our path. And we give thanks in each moment for our ability to continually make choices and change.

ILLUMINATION

10/19/14

With Halloween coming up, and thinking about spooky things that go bump in the night, it seemed like a good time to explore fear, and how to illuminate our way past it. One of the acronyms for the letters: F.E.A.R. is that it stands for "False Evidence Appearing Real." If fears were real, then all of us would be afraid of the same things. In fact, one person may shudder and hide when they hear thunder, while another stands outside with arms outstretched, embracing the energy of the storm. One person may shriek in terror at the sight of a spider, and another may enjoy tarantulas crawling up their arms. One person may be terrified to speak in public, and another seeks every chance to get on stage and be in the spotlight. What causes us to be fearful, and how do we change that?

Sometimes things are learned very early on, from our families of origin. My mother's Italian family pinned Faith, Hope, and Charity charms on babies to ward off the "Mal'occhio" or evil eye. And there was a whole procedure involving mixing oil and water that was passed down to counteract the Mal'occhio. What strategies do we employ to deal with our fears?

We may create rituals in order to convince ourselves that we are safe. There are people who feel compelled to knock and say the name of the person on the other side of the door three times before entering a room. Or they may feel compelled to wash their hands over and over, or check to make sure every light and appliance are turned off before leaving the house. In a more positive and proactive way, metaphysicians invoke spiritual protection by imagining light or color flowing in and around and through us, and knowing that only the highest and best can come through for our highest and best good. We also develop and say positive affirmations, in order to attract what is best into our lives.

"A Course in Miracles" teaches that the two primary emotions are love and fear, and they cannot exist in the same space at the same time. In each moment, we have the opportunity to choose love or fear, to choose illumination or darkness. What causes us to lean in one direction or another?

In Star Wars, Yoda tells us that "fear is the path of the dark side." What represents the "dark side" in our lives, and how do we counteract darkness with our light? When someone is overcome by the "dark side," they may choose to end their own lives. Robin Williams' transition is an example of this. Even though he was so incredibly beloved by so many people around the world, and even though he brought so much light to others, his own "dark side" overwhelmed him. A good friend shared that her 19 year old nephew had nearly succumbed to his dark side. It affected her a lot because she had been in the same place a number of years ago. There have been times when the "dark side" exerted a powerful pull in my own life. When we feel like darkness is closing in, how do we bring ourselves back into the light? How do we illuminate ourselves?

Think about what happens when we lift up a rock or fallen tree limb on the forest floor. Anything that existed and flourished in the darkness scatters and runs away when exposed to light. It's the same way in our own lives, when we expose our fears, doubts, and insecurities to light, they can no longer grow and flourish.

And sometimes, we may think that as one individual, we cannot possibly make a difference in contributing light to the world. Imagine being in a completely dark space. Striking one small match illuminates the space enough to take a step forward. And taking one step can make all the difference in the world. Lighting one candle can allow you to walk for hours with your path illuminated. One pebble can change the course of a river. One voice can change history – just look at Dr. Martin Luther King. And one thought can change the way you operate in your life. If someone like Robin Williams had been able to say, "I'm OK," for the space of one breath, the outcome might have been very different. Sometimes it's essential to give voice to the thoughts that we have. Even if it feels like we're the only one thinking or saying something, when we speak our truth, it may resonate to another person, and then another, and then another. Sometimes our voice can be the catalyst for someone who has not yet been able to find their voice.

How do we illuminate ourselves? For me, at the times when I feel the pull of the "dark side" most strongly, there are a number of tools that I use. Twelve Step programs encourage people to get through one day at a time. I find it even more effective to know that I only have to get through one breath at a time. Talking to others and bringing our fears out into the light can also be helpful. Creating and saying positive affirmations aloud is an effective tool. Saying daily affirmations has really contributed to learning to love myself, and to illuminating my days. Gratitude is a powerful tool. Every night, I write at least five things I am grateful for in my gratitude journal. Paying attention to the things I am grateful for changes my attitude, and makes me feel lighter. And forgiveness is always a key factor in moving forward. The first person it is most important to forgive is ourselves, and then everyone and everything else. When we truly forgive and let go, we lighten our load.

There is a Hawaiian spiritual tradition that states that we are each born into this world as a "bowl of light" containing the radiance of heaven. Fear, worry, and insecurity are like rocks that we place in our bowl, that hide our true "light" essence. Enlightenment is simply a matter of remembering who we truly are, being who we truly are, and removing any obstacles to our brilliance. Anything that works against the full expression of who and what we are, may be rocks that we need to remove from our bowl, in order to allow us to be the light that we are truly meant to be.

One of my favorite quotes, from Marianne Williamson, casts an interesting take on fears, light, and darkness: "Our deepest fear is not that we are inadequate. Our deepest fear is that we are powerful beyond measure. It is our light, not our darkness that most frightens us. We ask ourselves, Who am I to be brilliant, gorgeous, talented, fabulous? Actually, who are you not to be? You are a child of God. Your playing small does not serve the world. There is nothing enlightened about shrinking so that other people won't feel insecure around you. We are all meant to shine, as children do. We were born to make manifest the glory of God that is within us. It's not just in some of us; it's in everyone. And as we let our own light shine, we unconsciously give other people permission to do the same. As we are liberated from our own fear, our presence automatically liberates others."

What false evidence are you allowing to appear real in your life? When we shine the light that we truly are on our fears, we allow them to dissipate and be transformed. When we acknowledge the mighty spiritual beings of light that we truly are, we empower ourselves to be the best that we can be. When we bring our light together, our illumination becomes so much greater. The name "Community of Light" reflects our intention. Thank you for sharing your light as we walk forward together on the path of illumination.

LOVE

2/8/15

Our topic for this month is Love. Have you noticed that sometimes people who need love the most will ask for it in the most unloving of ways? Think about the inner city kids who walk around blaring their boom boxes. Think about a little one throwing a tantrum. Think about the young woman who dresses so scantily that she's barely covered. Often, these kinds of behaviors, and others, are a call for love and attention. And sometimes, when we are most in need of love, or comfort, or attention, is the most difficult time for us to reach out and ask for it in a positive and straightforward way. As we move through our lives, it is useful to pay attention to ourselves and those around us. Who are you noticing (including yourself) that might be in need of some love?

I know for myself, that sometimes when I'm feeling down, or challenged, or lonely, or any of those difficult types of feelings, I wish someone would just magically know what's happening, and either call or show up at my door with a hug. Recently, when I was having one of "those" days, I really thought about reaching out to a couple of friends. I wasn't able to do that in the moment, but the next day when I saw one of my friends, I shared what had been happening, to at least alert her to the possibility. She was warm and open, and encouraged me to call next time I was feeling that way. What stops us from asking for what we want and need? Sometimes, it is fear. We fear rejection, among other things. When we are most vulnerable, it is most difficult for us to open up and risk being rejected.

"A Course in Miracles" states that love and fear are the two primary emotions, and that they cannot exist in the same place at the same time. In every situation, we have the opportunity to choose love or to choose fear. When we choose fear, we feel small, inadequate, powerless, helpless, and unable to function. When we choose love, we are capable of anything. And the more love we choose, the more love we have.

There was a song my kids used to sing in pre-school that said, "Love's not love until you give it away, give it away, give it away. Love's not love until you give it away, then you end up having more. Love is like a copper penny. Hold it tight and you won't have any. Lend it, spend it, you'll have so many, they'll roll all over the floor." Metaphysically, love and fear represent abundance and lack. Fear says we are not enough. Love says we are everything. If we think of love as a limited commodity, we are living in fear and lack. If we know that love is unlimited, abundant and self-replenishing, we embrace prosperity – that is happiness, health, and wealth.

In the words of the song from the musical, Oliver, "Where is love?" I would like you to point to yourself. Look around and notice how many of us pointed to our hearts. In ancient Egypt, when mummifying bodies, the heart was left intact because the Egyptians believed the heart was where the essence of a person resided. Since the Egyptians considered the brain unimportant, it was thrown away. Our heart represents the love center of our beings. When we choose to proceed from a loving place as we walk through our lives, we are full of love, and full of life.

Love is all around us in a wide variety of ways. There are probably more songs written about love than any other topic. Whenever I prepare to speak about Love, songs run through my head. Are we "Lookin' for Love in All the Wrong Places?" Do we feel that "All You Need Is Love?" Do we believe in the

"Power of Love?" Are we prepared to "Stop in the Name of Love?" Are we recognizing "What I Did for Love?" How do we choose to express and receive love?

There is a book called, "The Five Love Languages," by Gary Chapman. The premise is that people express and receive love in different ways. It is useful to recognize the ways in which you express love, and the ways in which the significant people in your life express love, in order to communicate more effectively. As you recognize these love languages, you are more able to express love, and to receive the love that is being shown to you. The author believes that there are five primary ways that people express love:

Words of Affirmation, Quality Time, Receiving Gifts, Acts of Service, and Physical Touch.

Words of Affirmation are simple, straightforward compliments and words of appreciation that are specific to the person involved.

Quality Time means giving someone your undivided attention, and doing something that has meaning for them.

Receiving Gifts: Gifts are visual symbols of love, and are more important to some people than to others. A gift is something you can hold in your hand, and know that someone was both thinking of you, and actually implemented the thought by getting the gift and giving it to you.

Acts of Service involve doing things the other person would like you to do, and expressing your love by doing those things.

Physical Touch is a powerful vehicle for expressing love. Human and animal babies need touch in order to thrive. When we arrive and leave, and stand and greet each other here at Community of Light, we hug each other as one way to express love.

These are things you can think about as you interact with people in your life. If someone believes that showering you with gifts is the most effective way to express love, when what you want is to be complimented and told you are loved, the gifts will not be as welcomed as the giver intended, and neither person may feel loved and appreciated. By paying attention to each other's primary "love language," communication can happen far more effectively and constructively. Both parties benefit from this.

All of us express the need for love in our lives in one way or another. If we are looking for love in our lives, the best way to find it is to notice where it is already present. Pay attention to your "love language," and that of those close to you. Pay attention to the ways in which you are asking for love, and whether or not they are working effectively for you. Pay attention to those around you who may be seeking love in unconventional ways, and look for ways to pass on love and attention in constructive ways. Be your most authentic self in each moment. Stay in the consciousness of love and abundance whenever possible. Know that with love, all things are possible. And be kind and gentle and loving with yourself in the process. Because "learning to love yourself is the greatest love of all."

HOPE

5/10/15

Our topic for this month is Hope. Hope is defined as a combination of the desire for something and the expectation of receiving it. How often do we use or hear the expression, "Hope for the best?" One way to look at "hoping for the best" is that it's like sending out a ray of light ahead of us, lighting the way, and creating the energy of what the desired outcome is. It doesn't mean that we only "hope" and neglect all the other aspects of creating. It just means that we create a positive energy that we can follow to our goal.

In the dictionary, trust is a synonym for both faith and hope. We can choose to define the word Hope as "optimistic knowing." It is knowing that all things operate perfectly in Divine Order. And that means everything, all the time. Order operates perfectly in our lives every moment of every day. It's not some nebulous concept that exists in the stratosphere, but rather it's exactly how the universe works, perfectly, even when it doesn't seem that way to our impatient selves. It is knowing that things unfold for our highest and best good. It is knowing that the effects that we experience in our lives are caused by our thoughts, words, and actions. We choose and create all of our experiences.

Being defined as a combination of the desire for something and the expectation of receiving it, Hope can be a powerful force. In doing improv comedy, we are taught to "choose to know." In any given scene, when we come out on stage, we choose to know how the characters know each other, and what their relationship is, and how they feel about whatever is happening in the scene. In activating Hope, we can trust ourselves, and "choose to optimistically know" what is awaiting us around the next bend on our path.

In contemplating Hope, it looks like a spark at the core of my being. Sometimes, this spark is tiny and flickering. Sometimes, it is powerful and expansive. For me, Hope is what sustains me in the darkest of times. There is always a spark, no matter how small, that I know I can count on, no matter what may be happening. When we trust ourselves, and do all the things that we know are beneficial to our growth process, the spark grows and ignites the surrounding area. When we move forward in the ways that we know work best, the spark becomes a flame, and the glow from within us shines very brightly, lighting our way to the next step on our path.

Many of us are familiar with the story of Pandora's Box, and the notion that the box is opened, and all kinds of evils are released. What may be less commonly known is that after all the evils are released, Hope is what remained. In the midst of pestilence and worry and ills, Hope remains – sometimes small, but ever present and stalwart – a beacon for us to use as a guide, a spark that is always ignited.

Sometimes, that spark is really challenged. In her book, "Five to Fifteen: A Woman, A Prison, A Redemption," my friend Denise Sassoon writes about her experiences with addiction, prison, and ultimately recovery. She talks about the depths to which she sank in battling her addiction. Recovery was a long and complicated process for her, that took a number of twists and turns. She finally succeeded in finding her way out of her darkness. She writes, "In recovery, as in life, there are 'moments' of clarity. That relapse was one of those. The nature of the beast of addiction is that it is the purest form of selfishness. I didn't stay put and face the consequences of my actions for any selfish gain…" She continues, "After years of treatment, therapy, and attempts to get clean, I figured that it would never happen for me, that I was a hope-to-die junkie..." And, finally, "In spite of myself, my cynicism, my hopelessness, my paranoia of the cult-like feeling there, I had changed." Despite the hardships that she endured, and caused for herself, hope remained, and she was able to see herself through to a positive conclusion.

In our darkest moments, sometimes having a small flash of hope is what sustains us, and allows us to move toward the light that is always present within us. Sometimes, we just have to wait a moment for things to change, because things will always change. As the song from "Annie" says, "The sun'll come out tomorrow, so ya gotta hang on till tomorrow, come what may." When we trust in Divine Order, and create for our highest and best good, all things come to us in the proper sequence and in the proper time. Sometimes we have to be patient in order to allow the seeds that we've planted to come to fruition.

Operating from a place of Hope, which is a combination of the desire for something and the expectation of receiving it, there are definite steps that we can take to achieve our goals. The more we trust in ourselves, and in natural law, the more beneficial the results that we achieve. And, "hoping for the best," in conjunction with taking all the appropriate steps, adds a little extra spark to the mix.

Knowing that the spark of Hope is always present is not an excuse to be lazy, or just "hope for the best." We are always responsible for everything that happens in our lives. We are always creating in each moment. Hope can be a tool in our tool box. When we notice the feeling of being hopeful, it can be a signal to us to do all the things we know how to do to create the highest and best outcome for ourselves. We take that spark and use it to ignite whatever it is we are wanting to create. If we hope to get a particular job, we can use that hope to visualize ourselves working in that environment, coming home at the end of the day very satisfied, and seeing our name on an abundant paycheck. The wiser we allow ourselves to be, the more reality-based our hopefulness is. We don't pull hope from nowhere. In our wisdom and knowing, we hope realistically, based on our past experiences. We project into the future, because knowing where we've been allows us to have a vision of where we're going.

If we project thoughts of lack, that is what we draw to us. The universe is perfectly abundant. There is plenty for everyone. This is a YES universe. If we want a different harvest, we have to plant different seeds. If we hold thoughts of prosperity, we draw happiness, health, and wealth to us. That is how abundance works. If we are experiencing feelings of lack, the best thing to do is to start giving something to others. It may not always be money – it may be time, energy, love, words – whatever fits in that moment. The important thing is to open the flow by giving. And to keep optimistically knowing that everything works out for the best.

If we are wanting more of something in our lives, it is useful notice where it already exists. If we are wanting more prosperity and abundance, notice where it already exists. If we are wanting more love in our lives, notice where it already exists. Whatever we desire more of, and hope for, we can trust ourselves to create. Abundance is all around us. The key is allowing it to flow easily to us, and not getting in our own way. When we allow our good to flow to us, we affirm our worthiness. When we trust in ourselves, we create the highest and best for ourselves.

In closing, we can't just sit around, "hope for the best," and not do any of the things that we know are beneficial for us. We can, however, trust ourselves, "hope for the best" in each moment, and send that positive energy out with each breath we take, while we continue to utilize the thoughts, words and actions that create our highest and best good.

RETHINKING MISTAKES AND PERFECTION

6/21/15

How often do we hear someone say - well, nothing's perfect or nobody's perfect? These are pretty common expressions. As metaphysicians, we know that everything is perfect. Always. We are always creating, and we are always creating perfectly. If there is something in our lives that we wish to change, we can make a change in ourselves. As we understand that, we empower ourselves in knowing that we are the creators of our own lives and experiences. Our topic for this month is "Realizing Perfection." One of the ways to realize perfection is to look a little differently at the concept of what we call "mistakes."

As we grow up and learn to define words, the experiences that we have related to those words may trigger emotions in us. Mistakes and perfection definitely fall into that category for me.

Growing up in my family, it was not okay to make mistakes. I took piano lessons for many years. I would practice, and then be so excited for my dad to come home from work, so I could show him what I'd learned. I'd play my little piece, and often his response would be: "Do you know how many mistakes you made?" I always felt crushed when he said that. Throughout his life, when I talked to him, he sometimes interrupted me to tell me how many times I used the phrase, *"you know"* in my sentences. I believe that his intentions were to teach me, but the effect was not particularly positive for me.

And I learned very well from my dad. I notice that often my first reaction to something or someone is to immediately find all the faults and "imperfections." As I read through posts on Facebook, my attention is drawn to spelling and grammar errors and "typos." The reality is that when someone makes a "mistake" in what is being typed, we often read it more carefully, than when it is written "correctly." And sometimes, when our phone makes a choice to auto-correct something in a text, it just creates something that is amusing, and ends up lightening our day. We have the choice in each moment to be self-critical or self-compassionate. Which choice serves us better, and is for our highest and best good?

In preparing to be a parent, I decided that I would teach my kids a different way of thinking about things. I told them that mistakes are your friends because you learn from them. I told them it was OK to try things, and that if at first you didn't succeed, it was OK to keep at it. I encourage my children, and others in my life, to give themselves credit for small, incremental steps on the way to learning new things, and making changes. Sometimes "mistakes" can be amazing stepping stones.

When I looked up *"famous mistakes"* online, I came up with some interesting examples:

In 1876, a Western Union internal memo read: "This 'telephone' has too many shortcomings to be seriously considered as a means of communication. The device is inherently of no value to us."

In 1943, the chairman of IBM stated: "I think there is a world market for maybe five computers."

In 1977, the founder of Digital Equipment Corp. said: "There is no reason anyone would want a computer in their home."

A Yale professor responded to a paper proposing

reliable overnight delivery by saying: "The concept is interesting and well-formed, but in order to earn better than a 'C,' the idea must be feasible." The student went on to found FedEx.

The developer of the unique adhesives for "Post-Its" wrote: "If I had thought about it, I wouldn't have done the experiment. The literature was full of examples that said you can't do this."

- Henry Ford forgot to put a reverse gear on his first automobile.

- Albert Einstein's parents were told he might be mentally retarded.

- Napoleon finished near the bottom of his military school class.

- The Beatles were turned down for a recording contract by Decca Records.

Think about how differently the world would look if any of those people simply gave up on their ideas because someone else didn't think very highly of them, or because they didn't think they were perfect right from the start.

Traditionally, the word "perfect" means that no more change is needed. However, we know that change is constant, and conditions don't exist where no more change ever occurs. We are constantly creating. We reap what we sow. Our thoughts, words, and actions create our experiences. We have spiritual, emotional, mental, and physical bodies. We process our experiences at each of these levels. If they do not get resolved at the spiritual, emotional, or mental level, they are expressed physically. When we express things physically, it means that we have gone through an experience, and are releasing it. We are changing, and growing, and moving forward. When we express something physically, we have the choice to say thank you and goodbye, so that we can move forward.

And is someone who picks everything apart a "perfectionist" or an "imperfectionist?" In his book, "A Deep Breath of Life," Alan Cohen talks about "perfectionists." They are the people who constantly find flaws and errors that other people have overlooked. If there are many aspects of a job that are well done, and one that isn't, they will focus on that one. In truth, they are "imperfectionists." If they were "perfectionists," they would find perfection everywhere, instead of finding the "mistakes."

What does the word "perfect" mean to you? Before studying metaphysics, I might have thought that perfect meant that nothing needed to be changed, and that the food or the art or the moment could not possibly be improved on in any way, and should stay exactly the way it was. I think a little differently about the word perfect now. As I prepared for this talk, I read a wonderful quote from Anna Quindlen that said, "The thing that is really hard, and really amazing, is giving up on being perfect and beginning the work of becoming yourself." How can we best "become ourselves?" By paying attention to our thoughts, words, and actions. By being mindful in each moment of who we are, and how we are operating in the world, and what life we want to be creating.

Sometimes, our "mistakes" are the parts of our experiences that make us most truly and uniquely who we are. The important thing is not whatever "mistakes" you make, but how you look at them, and what you do with the knowledge that they ignite in you. As we move forward on our path, it empowers us to know that we are perfectly becoming ourselves in each moment. If there is anything we want to change in our lives, the solution is to change something in ourselves. Realizing perfection means loving and accepting ourselves as we are, then moving forward for our highest and best good, and "becoming ourselves" in each moment.

FREEDOM AND CHANGE

7/12/15

Our topic for this month is Freedom and Change, and it inspired me to think about some of the important ways that we are able to free ourselves. One of the most powerful ways that we can free ourselves is through forgiveness. Each day, I use the following affirmations: "With each breath, I fully and freely forgive myself, and loose myself to my highest and best good. With each breath, I fully and freely forgive everyone and everything, and loose them to their highest and best good. With each breath, everyone and everything fully and freely forgives me, and looses me to my highest and best good." Being forgiving to ourselves and others frees us, and empowers us to move forward on our paths.

Forgiveness is a very powerful way to start each day. When we hold onto any guilt, resentment, or criticism of ourselves or others, it is like carrying a heavy burden. It weighs us down, and interferes with our ability to move forward freely and easily in our lives. In his book, "A Deep Breath of Life," Alan Cohen refers to the movie, The Mission. In it, there is a slave trader who is filled with remorse, and chooses to carry his burden with him in the form of a massive sack full of weapons, in order to punish himself. He climbs to the top of a waterfall, where he encounters the tribe from which he took slaves. When the chief approaches him with a knife, the slave trader expects to be killed, and welcomes death in that moment.

Instead, the chief cuts the rope on the sack, releasing the slave trader from the burden that he has been carrying unnecessarily. Instead of carrying a lifelong burden, he is taught to forgive. Forgiving ourselves frees us to move forward, become most truly who we are, and empowers us in the process.

Forgiving others also frees and empowers ourselves. A quote that really resonates for me is, "Holding resentment is like taking poison, then waiting for the other person to keel over." Holding onto any interactions, frustrations, or resentments related to anyone else binds us irrevocably to them. The opposite of love is not hate, it is indifference. When we loose others to their highest and best good, we free ourselves in the process.

Sometimes, like the man in The Mission, it is useful to free ourselves from an experience that happened in the past. We may choose to change the outcome of the story, and empower ourselves in the process. I had the honor to hear the Female Story Tellers of Tucson the other night. In sharing their stories, these women freed themselves from the shackles of past experiences by owning them, and changing the outcome. By empowering themselves, rather than seeing themselves as victims, they change their stories, and free themselves in the process. Forgiveness played a significant role in many of their stories.

Sometimes we need to free ourselves by moving away from relationships that are, or have become, toxic in some way. As we make changes in ourselves, sometimes the people around us need to change also. In a marriage or significant relationship, people may change, and it may become necessary to dissolve the partnership. This can be done in many different ways. Ideally, it is done with love, compassion, and respect for each other, honoring what has been, and acknowledging the changes that need to happen. Friendships or business relationships may also need to have some fluidity, to account for changes that need to happen, also. When we choose to live in balance, it is sometimes necessary to release people in our lives who choose to only take or to only give. It is important to be forgiving towards ourselves and others in this process of change.

At times when we are feeling stuck in some way, it can be very freeing just to take some kind of action. It can be as simple as changing position, like going from one room to another. We can reach out, and talk to a friend. We can do an activity that we've been wanting to do, but haven't yet gotten around to. We can plan a trip, and buy the tickets. What happens for me at times is that a thought will just bounce around in my head, like a record skipping and repeating over and over. If I just stop, and do whatever it is I'm thinking about, or even write myself a note to do it tomorrow when I wake up, I'm able to let it go, at least for the moment. Making a small change can free us in the moment.

Another way to free ourselves is to affirm that we bear our responsibilities with ease, and release any burdens that do not belong to us. In doing so, we free ourselves and others to be most truly who we are. In the last couple of years, I have really changed the way I operate with one of my daughters. In the past, if there was a problem in her life to be solved, I jumped in and took over, receiving mail, paying bills, and generally taking responsibility for things that should have been hers to manage. The other day, she was scheduled to fly home from visiting her sister. She called to tell me that she'd been notified that her first flight was delayed, and because she had a short connection time, she wasn't sure she would make the second flight, and be able to get home that night. She asked what she should do, and I recommended that she call the airline, and work it out with them. In the past, I would have jumped in, made calls, gotten online, figured out what her options were, and taken care of everything. Instead, I gave her support and encouragement, and allowed her to handle everything herself. That involved some long wait times on hold with the airlines, but eventually, she figured it all out, and got home just fine. I was really proud of the way she handled everything, and also proud of myself for staying out of the way, and letting her. It made my life significantly easier to just get out of the way. I went on about my evening with freedom and ease.

The final freedom and change, as human beings in a physical existence, is the transition from the physical back to the spiritual plane. Whether our physical existence lasts a few minutes or more than a hundred years, whether the transition involves violence, or suffering, or happens peacefully in our sleep, this transition is the ultimate freedom and change. There is often fear associated with this transition, when in fact, it is simply a matter of going home, and returning to our true nature as spiritual beings. In the cases where an individual chooses to leave the earth plane in a way that seems sudden and premature to those around them, it can be even more challenging for us to accept this change as the freeing experience that it truly is. As the ones left behind on the earth plane, we may mourn the loss of loved ones because of the change that it creates in our own lives. We may also choose to celebrate the freedom that this change brings to those we love, knowing that they have moved forward on their paths in the most significant way possible.

We are the creators of our own lives. When we honor that responsibility, and choose our thoughts, words, and actions with care, forgiving ourselves and each other at each step along the way, we have the freedom to be who we truly are, and the ability to change and move forward in each moment in a truly powerful way.

REALITIES AND POSSIBILITIES

8/2/15

Our topic for this month is Realities and Possibilities. On the most basic level, it may be useful to ask ourselves whether we accept a reality filled with limitations or whether we are willing to allow miracles to happen. In his book, "A Deep Breath of Life," author Alan Cohen speaks to the topic of Realities and Possibilities for me. One discussion is about pygmy horses. The breed started out the same size as regular horses. Over time, they are bred to be smaller and smaller, through the breeders' choices and selections. It's the same way with our thoughts. We are created with infinite possibilities. If we choose to think small, we are small, and become smaller and smaller. If we think in terms of limitations and lack, we constrict our world. If we allow ourselves to explore infinite possibilities, then the possibilities are infinite. Some of the ways in which we restrict ourselves, and keep ourselves smaller than what is possible, include every time we think, or tell ourselves, "I can't." Any time we hold resentment towards anyone or anything, we constrict our world. Any negative thoughts cause us to shrink instead of expand. When we allow our inner light to shine, and believe that miracles can happen, we expand our consciousness, and our world of possibilities.

Connecting with our higher self can be a useful tool in the process of expanding the possibilities in our lives. In her meditation series with Deepak Chopra on Manifesting Grace Through

Gratitude, Oprah talks about the rewards of the higher self. She says that we can "seek to access our higher selves where we are able to fully unlock the divinity and grace of the universe, becoming one with the divine order of all," and that begets miracles.

In "A Deep Breath of Life," Alan Cohen also talks about goldfish who are accustomed to living in a small bowl. When they are placed in the much larger bathtub, while their bowl is being cleaned, they continue to swim in the small circle that is the same size as their bowl. When we limit our thinking, we swim in that same small circle. When we refuse to step outside our comfort zone, and meet new people or try new things, we swim in that same small circle. If we live in one place throughout our lives, and never experience other people, other places, and other cultures, we restrict our environment in a way that keeps us swimming in a small circle.

Alan Cohen then talks about how sharks adapt to the size of the space that they are living in. If they are in a small home aquarium, they remain small. If they are in the ocean, they grow to be one of the biggest presences in their environment. It's the same way with our spirit. If our minds remain closed to new ideas or different ways of thinking, we keep ourselves small. In some ways, our Community of Light represents the ways in which we were willing to move beyond what was familiar, and be more expansive. Less than a year ago, many of us were part of another organization that was somewhat limited in the ways in which ideas were presented and accepted. We chose to move beyond those boundaries, and to create a new environment that is much more open to, and accepting of, infinite possibilities.

Sometimes, in order to expand, we just need to be willing to take risks. My nephew recently graduated from college. He is getting ready to move out on his own for the first time, and live in a different state. He's chosen to move to San Francisco, even though he does not yet have a job lined up. He has signed a lease on an apartment with a friend that does have a job. His mom has expressed concern over how confident he sounds and appears. Although I believe that he understands the realities of looking for a job in a competitive market, and the high cost of living in that particular city, he is choosing to believe in the most positive of possibilities – that he will find a job in a reasonable amount of time, and that he will make enough money to support himself.

When I think about my own personal spiritual journey, it is definitely one of realities and possibilities. I remember my first meditation in a class. I believe I fell asleep. When it came time to share, I did as I had been instructed, and simply said that I was grateful to be there. The woman next to me then shared her experience, which included a past life memory with a husband, and children, and a career, and so on. At the time, I wondered if I would ever move beyond where I was at that moment. Here I am, 13 or so years later, standing in front of you, and sharing my experiences. One of the ways in which I have opened up to possibilities is in the way that I lead meditations. I have a number of meditations which I have written, and I used to read and follow the scripts fairly precisely. Over time, I have come to trust in the inspiration that shows up for me, when it's time to lead a meditation. Words and images flow into my mind, when I allow it to open up to new possibilities, and the results are far greater than they were when I restricted myself to reading certain words on a page. One of the most important ways that I have allowed possibilities into my spiritual experience is in the area of messages and readings. At first, I depended on cards to guide me in giving messages. Over time, my trust in my abilities has grown so much. I remain open to the possibilities that are infinite. I allow information to come through me to the person that is receiving the message. It is a pretty amazing experience, that continues to evolve and change all the time. I know that the information comes from a source far greater than myself.

In A Course in Miracles, Marianne Williamson affirms that there are two primary emotions, love and fear. In every situation, we always have the choice to choose one or the other. How are our lives impacted when we choose love instead of fear on a consistent basis? Many of the situations that I have been describing come down to a choice between love and fear. When we choose fear, we restrict ourselves to a certain way of thinking or a small bowl to swim in. When we choose love, we open ourselves to all possibilities.

Recently, after one of our healing and message circles, an older gentleman, who had come for the first time that day, offered to do some additional healing on a young woman, who happened to be in a wheelchair, who had also come for the first time that day. The man's process was somewhat different than others that I have experienced. As he worked on the woman, many sounds came from him, including what sometimes sounded like deep laughter, and other kinds of grunting noises. At first, I wasn't sure whether this was a positive experience, or whether I should step in, and intervene in some way. There was some fear reaction triggered for me, because the situation was unfamiliar. At a certain point, I checked in with the woman to make sure she was OK with what was happening, and she was, so I just let them be. I decided that even though what was happening was outside of what the norm was for me, and unfamiliar, I was willing to accept the possibility that miracles happen, and just be supportive in the moment.

Albert Einstein said, "There are only two ways to live your life. One is as though nothing is a miracle. The other is as though everything is a miracle." In each moment, we get to decide which way we choose to live, and whether we want to accept a small reality or infinite possibilities.

INTENTION

9/13/15

Our topic for this month is Intention. Setting intentions is an important and beneficial part of moving forward on our path of growth and unfoldment, and increasing our understanding of ourselves. It is useful to pay attention to what our actual intention is. This story about judo gives an interesting example. The student says: One day the head teacher, a seventy-year-old eighth Dan judoka, legendary for his insightful teaching called me aside after a randori. "How can you do beautiful Judo if you don't risk falling?" he asked. I was taken aback. I thought the whole idea of a randori was to avoid getting thrown. He continued, "A lot of judokas don't like to fall, so they try to avoid it at all cost. By doing this, they get tense, their techniques become wooden and their Judo lacks zest." Seeing he had piqued my interest, he went on, "Real Judo is like life. The little losses and gains don't count for much. What matters is whether you lived beautifully, with courage and joy. For this, you must learn not to fear falling or failure, and welcome it like a friend. Because only when you learn to love it, then can you really live to your full potential."

What I love about this story is the notion that when the student tries to avoid falling, he is not able to become the best that he can be. In order to live up to his full potential, he has to let go of the fear of falling and failure. His intention is to be the best judoka that he can be. When his actions are about avoiding falling and failing, he is unable to move toward that goal most effectively. In welcoming it like a friend, and learning to love both falling and failure, he is able to move along on his path of growth toward his actual goal. It is the same for us in life, when we set our intention to the highest and best possible outcome, it changes the vibration of any interaction. When we set our intentions, it is important to do it in the most positive way possible. If we allow fear to be the dominant motivation, we cannot move forward effectively.

Setting our intentions paves the way for how our life evolves. A couple that I know sometimes see things from very different points of view. They are contemplating selling their house, which is a large, very beautiful place in the Catalina foothills. On the one hand, he would like to live downtown, and be able to walk many places easily. She, on the other hand, prefers to live close to nature, and away from people, where it's quiet and peaceful. He worries that they'll never find a place that suits both of them. She recommends that they set their intention to find a new home that fits both of their needs perfectly.

When we set our intention, it is like paving our own yellow brick road to follow. It shines the light ahead of us, and points us in the direction that is most beneficial for us to travel. What we intend is where we take ourselves. There is a group called Intenders of the Highest Good. The quotes that they post often resonate for me, and a few have really stood out lately.

"I intend that my thoughts, words, and actions are in complete alignment today." When our thoughts, words, and actions are in complete alignment, we move forward with ease, surety, and balance. We know where we have been, we know where we are, and we know where we are going.

"I intend that fear has no more power in my life." Fear only has power, if we allow it to have power. In each moment, we always have the option to choose love or fear. When fear has power in our lives, we are unsure of ourselves, questioning our thoughts, words, and actions. When we remove fear, we are strong, and vibrant, and full of love.

"I intend that I am seeing my path clearly, and walking it without reservation today." This is a powerful intention to put forward. When we see clearly, and act accordingly, we empower ourselves in each moment. It is an affirmation of our own knowing of what is best for ourselves, and an affirmation of the sureness of our steps.

"I intend that the Love in my heart is all I send out into the world today." I've been sitting with this notion, and pondering it a lot in the last couple of weeks. When we intend that the love in our heart is all we send out into the world, it totally changes how we operate in each moment. Instead of feeling angry or envious or frustrated, we can choose to live in love. When we affirm that the love in our heart is all we send out into the world today, it colors every thought, word, and action. Some people talk about looking at the world through "rose-colored glasses." I like to think about looking at the world through "love-colored glasses." This allows us to see everyone and everything in a different light. Who knows what might be happening behind the scenes in anyone else's life? What benefit is there in judging someone else? Choosing to look through the lens of love colors our vision in a most positive way, and allows us to be more open, understanding, vulnerable, and at peace with ourselves and the world around us.

Intention is one of the first steps, and taking action is another important step. Intention without action gets us nowhere. It's like deciding to work out, and buying sporty clothes and a gym membership, and then never actually going to the gym. Intention without action does not serve us well. We must put into practice that which we have set out for ourselves, and in this way, we align our thoughts, words, and actions.

What are you intending for yourself in the next moment? The

next day? The next year? It is useful to examine what your intentions are, and then to plan out the steps to take in order to reach the goals that you have set for yourself. Sometimes, it is helpful to write these things down, and then have a time frame for evaluation of the progress that has taken place, so that adjustments can be made, if necessary.

In summary, our intentions are powerful. Setting intentions guides us on our path of unfoldment. Once we have set our intentions, it is necessary to follow through with appropriate action. And when we choose love instead of fear, we empower ourselves for our highest and best good.

CONFIDENCE

11/15/15

Our topic for this month is Confidence. In the musical, "The King and I," the young boy sings, "Whenever I feel afraid, I hold my head erect, and whistle a happy tune, so no one will suspect I'm afraid." Sometimes, the first step in building confidence is to act as if we feel a certain way, until we are actually able to feel that way. Later in the song, the boy tells us, "The result of this deception is very strange to tell, for when I fool the people, I fear I fool myself as well!" When we act in a confident manner, it helps us to feel more confident. While convincing others that we know what we're doing, we convince ourselves at the same time. This comes back to natural law – what we think, what we say, and what we do is what we draw more of to ourselves. When we act in a confident manner, we draw more confidence to ourselves. And sometimes, confidence is just a matter of believing that we can do whatever it is that we set out to do.

When you speak with authority, people listen. My daughter had the opportunity to teach partner flips to the Bay Area Roller Derby Girls. After listening to her explanation, I proceeded to coach some of the women in how to execute the moves properly. Although I know almost nothing about partner flips, because I spoke with authority, the women listened to me. And as they listened to me, I became more confident in what I was saying. This is another way of acting as if we are confident on the path to actually becoming more confident.

Recently, I read a quote that really resonated for me. "You

should DEFINITELY have more confidence. And if you saw yourself the way that others see you, you would." Sometimes, the way we see ourselves is not an accurate reflection of who we really are. Sometimes, it can be useful to see ourselves through someone else's eyes as we learn to value ourselves more highly. Sometimes, it is useful to draw on others' strength as we build our own confidence. Seeing the way we look to someone who truly believes in us, supports and assists us in learning to love ourselves. In developing my own self-worth and self-love, I looked around at the friends I had. These were people of very high quality, whom I trusted, loved, and respected deeply. I looked to them for guidance about other things. If they were choosing to be my friends, it seemed logical that I must be worthy of their friendship. Developing self-worth and self-love is another important step in building confidence.

Along the same vein, barriers to confidence often exist primarily in our own minds. Doubt, worry, insecurity, and fear are figments of our imagination. Sometimes the person that you have to prove your confidence to the most is yourself. When I think about confidence, I think about the characters in the Wizard of Oz. Although they each doubted themselves and their abilities, ultimately, the qualities were there all along: the Scarecrow was very wise, the Tin Man was very tender, and the Lion was truly brave. Dorothy learned that she had the power within herself all along. What was lacking in each case was confidence; confidence in themselves and in their abilities. Believing in ourselves is another important step in building confidence.

Acknowledging the power within ourselves is another essential step in our process of growth and development. In the film Willow, a young man wants to become an apprentice to the village shaman. The wizard says, "If you can answer this question correctly, I will teach you the ancient magic." The wizard extends his hand and asks, "In which finger does the power lie?" Willow makes his choice, and it is incorrect. He then goes off to live his life of adventure and romance, and grows over time. Eventually, Willow returns to the village, and the wizard asks him, "What did you want to answer when I gave you the test?"

"I wanted to say, 'The power lies in my own hand.'"

"That was the correct answer," the wizard affirms. "Why did you not say it?"

"I guess I just didn't believe in myself enough," Willow admits.

What the young man was lacking was confidence. When we acknowledge our true selves, our god selves, we can affirm all that we are. The things we tell ourselves are very powerful. If we are consumed with doubts, worry, and other negative self-talk, there is no way that we can be confident. If we replace those thoughts and words with positive affirmations, if we change "I can't" to "I can," and "I'm not" to "I am," we are able to accomplish much more, and to be the best that we can be. And as we act as if we are confident, and believe in ourselves, it's important to put these things into consistent practice. The more we act in a confident manner, the more confident we become.

Another obstacle to confidence may be if we don't believe that we have the capability to do something. We have to believe that even though we don't currently know how to do something, someday, somehow we will be able to accomplish it. Without that belief, it's difficult to be confident.

The talks on Unity and Confidence in the last few weeks have really inspired me. One of the other ministers talked about how challenges in our lives indicate that we are ready to increase our spiritual knowing, ready to take the next step forward on our journey. Given the events of the last month or so,

I am apparently ready for a giant step forward. Another minister's metaphor that we are all pieces of one jigsaw puzzle, and therefore equal in value really resonated for me. One of her recommendations for being in touch with our oneness was: "I can practice seeing myself as a strong, powerful, and loving being, who is an important part of the whole, seeing the sacredness of all." The more we can see ourselves as an integral and interconnected part of a sacred whole, the easier it is for us to feel confident, because we are not alone.

And then another talk reminded us that, "...in metaphysics, there is no other, all is one. God is within each of us and all is in Divine Order. What came to me is that the way for me to move forward is to remember this and realize that there is nothing to fear because there is no "other"...I just need to remember to speak to the "one" in what appears to be the "other"." The more we can remember our connectedness, and that we are speaking to the "one" in what appears to be the "other," the more confident we can be.

So, as we move forward on our paths, we can choose to act as if we are confident, speak with authority, see ourselves as others see us, believe in ourselves and our capabilities, acknowledge our own power, and know that we are all in this together.

EXPANSION

1/10/16

Our topic for this month is Expansion. In thinking about expansion, it is useful to think about what we want to create more of in our lives. We are the creators of our lives and experiences. What we think, what we say, and what we do, is what we draw more of into our lives. It's valuable to pay attention to what we are expanding in our lives.

One of the ways that expansion operates in our lives is in the way we think about things. To paraphrase Star Trek, in order to expand our thinking, we must "boldly go where no one has gone before." To expand our thinking, we must be willing to allow for possibilities. Sometimes things happen that we have little or no explanation for. If we expand our thinking to include things that we may or may not have a logical rationale for, new things are possible. When we open our minds to new possibilities, we may be surprised by the results.

One of the best gifts I got this Christmas was a conversation with my daughter. A friend of ours was asking her about the ways in which she saw herself as like me, and how her perception of that had changed over time. One of the things she said was that I had really taught her to open her mind. That was the best compliment I could imagine. Encouraging someone to have an open mind is one of the highest forms of expansion imaginable.

Interestingly, although our topic for this month is Expansion, when we got the email with the schedule, it said that the topic was Elimination, so I began to ponder that. There are no coincidences, so when I learned that the topic was Expansion, it allowed me to see how much the two go hand in hand. Sometimes, it's necessary to eliminate things that no longer serve us, in order to expand and make room for that which is for our highest and best good. One thing that is useful to eliminate from our lives is thinking small. If we think in terms of lack and limitation, our lives become small and limited. How many times do we hear people complain about the economy going down the tubes or how there is not enough of this or that? If we think in those ways, then the reality we create is limited and focused on lack. If, instead, we know right down to the core of our being, that anything and everything is possible, then that is our reality. When we expand our thinking in areas like prosperity and healing, we create a different reality. Even when others are struggling financially, we are prosperous. Even when others are succumbing to illness and dis-ease, we are healthy. When we expand our consciousness, all things are possible.

One of the biggest barriers to expansion, and something that is useful to eliminate, is fear. Fear can hold us back more strongly than any external bond or cage. If we are afraid that we cannot do something, then we do not take steps to change the situation. And what are we really afraid of? Marianne Williamson has an interesting take on this matter. She says, "Our deepest fear is not that we are inadequate. Our deepest fear is that we are powerful beyond measure. It is our light, not our darkness, that most frightens us. We ask ourselves, Who am I to be brilliant, gorgeous, talented, fabulous? Actually, who are you not to be? You are a child of God. Your playing small does not serve the world. There is nothing enlightened about shrinking so that other people won't feel insecure around you. We are all meant to shine, as children do. We were born to make manifest the glory of God that is within us. It's not just in some of us; it's in everyone. And as we let our own light shine, we unconsciously give other people permission to do the same. As we are liberated from our own fear, our presence automatically liberates others." She encourages expansion in really powerful ways. As we step up to be who we really are by putting fear aside, we move forward, and let our own light shine.

Another interesting aspect of expansion is that the more we expand our thinking, the more we may understand that we are all one. Expansion is actually the path to inclusion. Accepting ourselves is an important part of expanding into inclusion. We must learn to accept all the parts of ourselves that we don't like and are not comfortable being, and also accept all the parts of ourselves that we want to be, in order to be fully and completely ourselves. The more we accept ourselves as we are, the more we are able to accept others as they are. The more we are able to expand our thinking, and embrace the concept that we are all one, the more connected we can allow ourselves to be.

There is a woman in Tucson who has taken this to heart, and has created the Global Art Project for Peace, whose mission is "to joyously create a culture of peace through art." The Project expresses the idea: We Are All One. "The Global Art Project is an International Art Exchange for Peace. Participants create a work of art in any medium, expressing their vision of global peace and goodwill. The art is displayed locally in each participant's community. Global Art Project then organizes an international exchange by matching participants—group-to-group and individual-to-individual. The exchange results in thousands of people sending messages of Peace around the world at one time—visions of unity simultaneously encircle the Earth. The art is sent as a gift of global friendship, and exhibited in the receiving community." In addition to the art projects, anyone who wishes to is invited to send a paper outline of their hand with their name, country, and wish for global peace, love, and friendship. Volunteers in Tucson string the hands together to represent visually the way that when people join their energy together, they create Peace. The exhibition is called "Let's All Join Hands," and is an inspiration for what is possible. This expansion in thinking has the power to change the vibration of the planet.

In addition to expanding our thinking, it is most valuable to expand the love in our hearts. Love is one of the most powerful forces in the universe, and the more we allow love into our hearts, the happier we can be. A wonderful example of this is the Grinch by Dr. Suess. When the Grinch thought in small and limited ways, his life was small and limited. When the Grinch allowed himself to be transformed by the love of the people of Whoville, his heart "grew three sizes." What can we do to encourage our hearts to grow three sizes? One thing that expands love in our lives is focusing on gratitude. The more we are grateful for who and what we are, the more we expand the love in our lives.

What we think, what we say, and what we do is what we create more of in our lives. When we take a moment each day to say, "Let Divine Light Shine," we expand our light, and we raise the vibration of our planet. As we move through our days, it is useful to notice the ways in which we think, and how we want to bring expansion into our thinking. Paying attention to what choices we are making, and what we want to keep and what we want to eliminate, allows us to expand our thinking. Understanding the way fear can get in our way allows us to make different choices in each moment, and to let our light shine more fully. Remembering that we are all connected allows us to expand our view of ourselves and each other in more loving ways. And infusing each moment with love, light, and gratitude raises our own vibration, and raises the vibration of our planet. This is the highest and best use of expansion.

PROSPERITY

4/10/16

Our topic for this month is Prosperity. Prosperity is happiness, health, and wealth, and how we think about these things is very powerful. In considering happiness, it is wise to remember that happiness is always a choice. No matter what is happening in our lives, we have the freedom to choose how we feel about it, and how we respond to it. The other night, a young man came into our blues dance gathering. He looked vaguely familiar to me, and after a while, I realized that he had attended our dances about three years ago, but I hadn't seen him in a long time. He appeared so completely different, that I almost didn't recognize him. I said his name with a huge question in my voice, and he responded positively. Previously, his hair was very long and dyed very black, his clothing was usually black, and his demeanor was dark. His shoulders were hunched. He didn't make much eye contact, and didn't speak much. The person who walked in this week was standing tall, had short light brown hair, and a big smile. He shook my hand, and came and sat next to me. He engaged in conversation with me and others throughout the evening, asked lots of people to dance, and danced with joy. I told him that I hardly recognized him because he had changed so much. His energy felt completely different, also. He smiled, and said he was much happier now. Happiness has the ability to transform us.

No matter what is happening in our lives, the way we choose to think about and respond to it affects us physically, mentally, emotionally, and spiritually. When we choose to be happy, we feel lighter. We are more able to be present in each moment. We are more open to possibilities. We connect with people in a different way. What we think, what we say, and what we do is what we draw more of to ourselves. When we allow ourselves to be happy, it changes our perspective on the world, and everything looks a little brighter. When we affirm our happiness, we ignite Prosperity.

The second aspect of Prosperity is health. I've been going through some interesting challenges for the past few months. I believe that when we express something physically, it is the final step in the process, it is the point of release, and we have the opportunity to say thank you and goodbye to the issues we are dealing with. I have been igniting flexibility in a big way. I keep affirming that I am flexible in all that I think, say, and do. Our thoughts, words, and actions have a lot of power. I noticed that I had been complaining quite a bit about my physical challenges, and consequently, had been feeling discouraged. I decided to change the way I was thinking, feeling, and talking about what was going on, and have felt much happier. One of my friends and teachers has been doing significant meditation on healing recently. In our discussions, she has been sharing the notion that as our god-selves, we are able to heal ourselves in each moment. I believe this completely, and do my best to remain positive as I face the challenges that I have chosen.

I know that when I complain, and feel small and powerless, lack is created. I remind myself that prosperity consciousness is a choice. Instead of complaining, I can choose to say: I am healed and I am whole. When I stop and say those words, I am healed and I am whole, it changes my consciousness, changes my energy, and draws something positive to myself. Sometimes, I have to do it several times a day, and even multiple times in a row. Changing my thoughts, words, and actions really does make a difference. When we affirm our health, we ignite Prosperity.

The third aspect of Prosperity is wealth. Wealth is not defined by the number of dollars in our bank account, but rather by the way we see ourselves, and the way we think about our lives. In the book Spiritual Economics by Eric Butterworth is the affirmation: I am wealthful, prosperous, and affluent. These words really resonate for me. I like thinking of myself in that way. An interesting aspect of wealth is about how it flows to us and from us, and the relationship between giving and receiving.

Early on in my metaphysical studies, one of the classes about prosperity was taught by a local minister. She talked about tithing and what it meant to her. Why do we give 10% of what we earn to the place that promotes our spiritual development? Her talk impacted me so much that I started doing just that. Whatever money I earned, I immediately adjusted the check I wrote each Sunday to reflect a 10% donation. I wondered occasionally what effect this would have on my finances. Would I still have "enough" money to take care of my needs? Interestingly, I found that as I tithed consistently, I had even more abundance.

Affluence is defined as an abundant flow. In the same way that we can put a rheostat on a light switch, and regulate the flow of energy and the amount of light that is shed, our prosperity is all about our consciousness. The electricity, and our affluence, are always there. Our consciousness is what regulates the flow. Giving freely is one way to open the flow of abundance. I find that when I give fully and freely, abundance flows to me more easily. When we give thanks before the Love Offering, we put into effect the law of many fold return to those who give freely and from the heart. That means that whatever you give is returned to you TENFOLD and more! We bless what we give. One of the definitions of the word bless is "to confer prosperity." Blessing everything and giving thanks is one way to open the rheostat of abundance all the way up. When we affirm our wealth, we ignite Prosperity.

In Alan Cohen's book, A Deep Breath of Life, one of the affirmations he uses is, "I leave behind my limits, and step forward to live as large as God." Think about that for a moment. What we think, say, and do is what we draw more of to ourselves. In thinking about Prosperity, the idea of limitless possibilities came to the foreground for me. We are all part of a limitless whole. We are not separate from God, we are all God, and as such are all-knowing and all-powerful. Anything is possible for us. Happiness, health, and wealth are manifestations of Prosperity consciousness. In each moment, we have the choice of how we respond to any situation. Our thoughts, words, and actions are the only things we have control over, and we have the choice in each moment to decide what we are going to do, and how we are going to feel about it. As I thought about Prosperity this week, the words, "Be still and know that you are God" kept coming up for me. On a number of previous occasions, I have referred to Marianne Williamson's statement about our deepest fear being that we are powerful beyond measure, and it fits in this context also. Who are we to think small, and feel powerless? It does not fit with our knowing that we are God.

Gratitude is another important component in abundance and flow. I am in my ninth year of keeping a gratitude journal. Every night, I write down at least five things that I am grateful for. When I pay attention to what I am grateful for, the flow of abundance is strong, and there is no room for thoughts of lack. Prosperity is not about how much money you have, it's about how you think about things. It's about allowing and accepting an abundance of happiness, health and wealth in your life, and then giving thanks for that abundance.

In closing, when we affirm our happiness, health, and wealth, we ignite Prosperity. When we think, speak, and act like the god-self that we know ourselves to be, our possibilities are limitless. "Be still and know that you are God."

GRACE

5/29/16

Our topic for this month is Grace. When I think about the word "grace," I think about fluidity. There are people that I observe who just move through life with grace. My daughter plays volleyball, and there's a man on her team that I love to watch because he moves with such grace. When he serves the ball, his movements are fluid from start to finish, and it is almost poetic to watch. I remember seeing a ballerina a number of years ago, and as I watched her dance, I was struck by the grace with which she moved, especially her arms. It seemed like their were no bones in her arms, because she moved with such fluidity. How can we be more fluid? Do we spend our time bumping up against every obstacle in our lives? Or are we more like water, moving over, under, around, and through the challenges that we choose? How do we walk through life with grace?

Being Sicilian, Sagittarius, and from New York, being graceful sometimes presents challenges, and I have chosen to learn many lessons about being graceful in this lifetime. My tendency is to speak very plainly and directly, sometimes too bluntly for other people's comfort, and I have learned over time to soften my way of communicating. It is so important to consider other people's feelings, as well as their styles of giving and receiving information, in order to communicate most effectively, and with grace.

How do we walk through life with grace? Beginnings and endings of our physical existence are often an interesting manifestation of grace. When my daughter gave birth to her son, she chose to do it at home, in a birthing tub in her living room, surrounded by a group of loving and supportive women friends. Her ability to go with the flow of events allowed her to go through the experience so gracefully. And following her innate wisdom has allowed her to operate very gracefully as a mother from the very beginning.

At the other end of the spectrum, our dear friend Doris made her transition earlier this month. The ending for her was very graceful. She celebrated her 89th birthday surrounded by loving family and friends. Over the next six days, she slipped gracefully out of her physical body, as she went to sleep. She knew that the end of her physical existence was close, and she was at peace with that. She had lived a very full life, and exited with fluidity. As much as I miss her beautiful smile and her sharp wit, I am at peace with her graceful transition.

The same day that I got the news about Doris passing, I learned that a very close friend of mine, who was like a daughter to me, had chosen to end her life. This news was extremely difficult to handle. When someone makes a transition in such a sudden and unexpected way, it is challenging for those around her to deal with. At first, it was difficult to feel graceful in any way about this event. I felt so angry. My whole body kept screaming, "NO!" I did not want this to be true. I wanted to be able to blame someone for this horrible deed. I felt tremendous guilt and responsibility, and wondered what I could have possibly done differently that might have prevented this from happening.

At the same time, I called upon all of my metaphysical beliefs. At the core of my being, I know that we create our experiences, that we choose every aspect of our existence. I truly and deeply believe that although her time in the physical plane seemed short to those around her, that her existence was complete, and that she went home.

But I was not feeling in any way graceful about this, and just kept bumping up against all the emotions I was experiencing. Fortunately, I have good friends and teachers around me. When I shared that I was feeling responsible for the events that led up to her slide into depression, my close friend and teacher told me that everything I was feeling was normal. She encouraged me to know and affirm that, in fact, I had been of tremendous help to her along her path. She also reminded me that I can still talk to her in the same way that I did when she was in the physical existence, and that I can help her to learn what she needs to learn on the spirit plane.

I woke up the next morning feeling at peace for the first time since I learned that she was gone. Getting to this place is allowing me to deal with this experience with more grace. It is allowing me to be fluid, instead of crashing into every emotion that I am feeling. I am so grateful.

In thinking about grace, it was also useful to think about being gracious. Looking up the word "gracious" brought out similar words that included compassionate, kind, forgiving, generous, and benevolent. When we are gracious, we are compassionate, and understand the behaviors and choices that others make. We make allowances for the circumstances that may contribute to others' choices. There is a quote that suggests, "Be kind, for everyone is fighting a battle you know nothing about." When others may act in ways that seem less than graceful, our tendency may be to react in a negative manner. Instead, we may choose to be gracious, give people the benefit of the doubt, and extend loving kindness. One never knows the positive ripple effect of a kind word.

Forgiveness is such an important component of spiritual growth. The most important person to forgive is ourselves. When we forgive ourselves, and loose ourselves to our highest and best good, we are acting in accordance with grace in the most significant way possible. Being kind, loving, and generous with ourselves is such an important growth step. And when we are kind, loving, and generous with ourselves, it is easier to act that way towards others, also. Forgiveness of others is another important step. In the case of my friend that made her transition by her own choice, it was essential for me to first forgive myself, and then give myself the time it took to be able to forgive her for leaving. The more we are able to forgive, the more we are able to move through life with grace.

In thinking about grace on a divine scale, it is useful to remember, and truly embrace, that God is not something that is separate and apart from ourselves. We are all God, and God is in us, and in everyone and everything around us. When we talk about God's love, we are talking about loving ourselves. Grace does not come from outside of ourselves, it is generated from within the most divine place inside ourselves, our god-self. When we flow through our lives with the fluidity of water, accepting the things that we cannot change, and moving over, around, and through other obstacles, we are operating with grace.

UNITY

7/24/16

Our topic for this month is Unity. In the simplest terms, we are all one. The more we remember that, the more we operate for the highest and best good of all. We are all one, even with the people that we strongly disagree with politically or religiously. We are all one, even with the people that push our buttons most strongly. We are all one, even with the drivers who annoy us the most in traffic. We are all one, even with people who look and act the most differently from ourselves. And we are all in this together. Originally, someone else was scheduled to speak today. A few days ago, she let us know that she couldn't be here today. My first reaction was anger that it was such short notice. But as soon as I read the email, this talk started coming together in my head, and I knew I would be the one speaking. I remembered that when I saw the schedule for July, I wished that I was speaking, so I replaced my anger with gratitude for being given this opportunity. We are all in this together, and in Community of Light, we live that actively, by supporting each other always.

When I think about Unity, and how we're all in this together, the notion of what brings us together and what pushes us apart comes up. For me, love and forgiveness are what bring us together, and fear and anger are what push us apart. One of my favorite Ellen Degeneres comedy routines is where she talks about getting in touch with spirituality and meditation, then one thing after another pulls her off center, and she has to keep reminding herself, "and...back to the loving place." What brings us "back to the loving place?" What are some things that connect us? Sometimes shared experiences, overcoming adversity together, and working towards a common goal remind us of our connection. Like when I was a teenager, and I put my desk lamp too close to my desk and burned a spot. I was so worried about getting in trouble with my parents. My brother, who is 15 years older than me, came to visit, and came to my rescue. He got a pencil, and managed to somehow make the burned spot look like it was old and had happened when the desk belonged to him. I was so grateful, and felt so supported.

One aspect of unity is the importance of working together. The image of a seesaw came to mind. The only way to make it work well is for it to be balanced. Each end needs to work with the other, and there needs to be give and take. If one side has too much weight, there is no movement. If one side is left unexpectedly, the other side comes crashing down painfully. Balance, and working together, is the key to optimal effect. In thinking about unity in terms of a relationship, whether that is a marriage or romantic partnership, a friendship, or even a business relationship, the notion of only one person at a time losing their head can be important. If one person can stay centered, focused, and sane, while the other might be lost in fear, anger, or other disturbance in the force, the outcome is very different than if both people come undone at the same time. If one person can keep it together, the partnership can weather the storm, and come out stronger. If both people go off the deep end at the same time, the partnership may not survive. This goes back to the notion of the seesaw. Even if the two sides are balanced, there needs to be cooperation, and working together, in order for it to work properly. The parts have to function as one unified whole.

In contemplating unity, the fact that today is July 24th had great significance for me, because that was the date I was married 43 years ago. Besides uniting as a couple, this was an important unifying event in my family. A year earlier, when my very Italian Catholic parents found out I was living with a man whom I was not married to, they disowned me. We'd had very little contact during that year, and it was quite painful. When I called to tell them I'd gotten married (having eloped in Mexico), they were overjoyed, and all was "forgiven." My father offered to throw a party for us, but I was still pretty angry with them, and was not too excited by that idea. He told me they were having the party "with or without you." Eventually, I was able to get "back to the loving place," and the party ended up being a lot of fun. Many years later, when my father was approaching his 100th birthday, we wanted to throw him a party, and he was not too excited by that idea. I got to tell him that we were having the party "with or without you!" That was another unifying experience, as people came from all over the country to celebrate this man that they loved so much.

What happens when unity feels disrupted? When we feel united with someone, and their physical existence ends, we often feel grief. This has been very present for me lately. Two incredibly valuable members of our spiritual community made their transition in the last year, and I feel their loss very keenly. One of my very close friends chose to end her own life this year, and I feel her loss every day. When I think of these dear friends as gone, sadness sometimes overtakes me, and sometimes overwhelms me. When I am able to remember that we are all one, and that we are still completely connected, it is comforting. When I remember that their transition was just a change, it is comforting. When I reach out to others, and share my experience, it is comforting. When I remember our connection with all that is, I am at peace.

In thinking about our connection with all that is, a meditation about this came to me several years ago. We are all part of a single whole. Everything we do is connected to everyone else, and has an impact on the whole, in the same way that a pebble thrown into a body of water has a ripple effect. Each of us has a ripple effect on the fabric of society. How do we choose to operate in the world? How do we choose to respond to events that unfold around us? Do we descend into fear and anger? Or are we able to remember that we are all in this together, and be there for one another. Can we get "back to the loving place?" As I thought about this, the words: "United we stand, divided we fall...", kept playing through my mind. The more we can stay in the space of light and love, in the face of whatever events unfold, the more we promote unity.

We are all in this together. When we ask ourselves how we can support each other in being the best we can be, we are in touch with our divine selves, and our unity, more fully. The more we can focus on the ways in which we are connected, rather than the differences which keep us apart, the more beneficial it is to ourselves and our world. The more we can focus on what we are grateful for, rather than what we are angry about, the more we are at peace. The more we choose love, instead of fear, the more unity we bring to ourselves and the world. We are all connected. We are all in this together. We are all one. We choose to live in a country that calls itself the United States of America. It's an interesting notion, especially when we think about politics in this election year. It's so valuable to remember that no matter what anyone thinks or says or believes, the more we remember that we are all one, the more we bring forth the highest and best good for all.

LIGHT

8/28/16

Our topic for this month is Light. I always feel honored to speak at our Sunday services. Today feels a little extra special. We are "Community of Light." And we were guided to this name because that is what we have chosen as our mission, to be the light in the world, to acknowledge the light within ourselves, and to let divine light shine, in order to raise the vibration of the planet. I believe the people that are guided to come and experience Community of Light are drawn towards the light energy that is generated here. By shining light, and being transparent in our transactions, we create an atmosphere of openness, trust, and caring that draws like-minded people to us.

As I thought about Light, the lyrics from the theme song of E.T., "turn on your heart light," kept playing in my mind. What are the things that remind us to "turn on our heart light," and what are the things that cause us to forget that we have that power? We may be conditioned to think of light as something that only comes to us from some external source. What is also true is that we are the light, and that the light comes from within us. Our "heart light" is always available, and always inside ourselves. Our "heart light" is the spark at the core of our being that is, always has been, and always will be the essence of who we are.

In the same vein, there is a Hawaiian spiritual tradition that states that we are each born into this world as a "bowl of light" containing the radiance of heaven. Fear, worry, and insecurity are like rocks that we place in our bowl, that hide our true "light" essence. Enlightenment is simply a matter of remembering who we truly are, being who we truly are, and removing any obstacles to our brilliance. Anything that works against the full expression of who and what we are, may be rocks that we need to remove from our bowl, in order to allow us to be the light that we are truly meant to be.

What do we need to do to turn on our heart light? In the movie E.T., love, touch, friendship, and trust are some of the things that turn on our heart light. When we are kind and loving with ourselves and each other, our light is more strongly ignited. Hugging and cuddling, and other forms of physical affection can also help to ignite the light within ourselves. Another way to turn on our heart light is to laugh. Sometimes, in our darkest moments, it is helpful to use humor to remind us of the light. Laughter can dispel the darkest moments, and ignite the light within ourselves. How many times have we heard the expression that someone's smile "lights up a room?" Another way to turn on our heart light is to remember who we truly are. When we remember who we truly are, spiritual beings having a human experience, our light is more strongly ignited. When we experience feelings of hurt, depression, or loneliness, we are more likely to forget the power of the light within ourselves, and feel like our bowl is full of rocks. At the extreme end of this continuum, if we forget the light within ourselves so much, and succumb to the darkness, we extinguish the light, ending our own existence on the earth plane.

Focusing on the light is the only way that we are able to dispel the darkness. Just as the sun provides light on the physical plane, we experience darkness each day as the earth turns away from the sun. In any given moment, we may think that the light is gone, but, in fact, the light only appears to be gone because we have turned away from it. The light is always there, and always within us, we just have to remember it when we feel the darkest. And sometimes that can be the most challenging thing to do, to remember the light when we feel the darkest. When we feel the most alone, it is often the most difficult time for us to reach out and connect with people who could remind us of the light. When we feel the lowest and most depressed, it is the most challenging time to remember to smile or laugh. I read a quote on Oprah's website that is an important phrase to remember in times of difficulty: "The shadow passes, the light remains." Challenging times are but a shadow that passes. We are always the light, and the light is always within us, and available for us. We just have to remember that in order to get through the shadow moments.

Light is necessary for life, and necessary for growth. We observe flowers that turn towards the light throughout the course of each day. In places where there are many cloudy and overcast days, some people are affected by the lack of light, and may experience feelings of depression when deprived of sunlight for days on end.

On the other hand, the darkness that we experience each day allows us to rest, regenerate, and renew ourselves. Without the darkness, we do not appreciate the light in the same way. Both light and darkness are necessary for growth. The key is to have balance. We cannot live in darkness, and having only light does not allow us to restore ourselves properly.

Sometimes, people are afraid of the dark. And how do we dispel our fear? By turning on the light. A Course in Miracles states that the two primary emotions, love and fear, cannot exist in the same space at the same time. By choosing light and love, fear may be banished. Think about what happens when we lift up a rock or fallen tree limb on the forest floor. Anything that existed and flourished in the darkness scatters and runs away when exposed to light. It's the same way in our own lives, when we expose our fears, doubts, and insecurities to light, they can no longer grow and flourish.

In the movie E.T., the message was that we need to "turn on our heart light." Turning on our heart light allows us to raise our own vibration, as well as the vibration of the planet, and make a change that has a positive impact on the world. If you imagine that as an individual you do not have the ability to effect change, notice what happens when the power goes out, and you are in complete darkness. It only takes one match to illuminate your path. To paraphrase the song, "Let there be love on earth, and let it begin with me," I encourage us all to affirm, "Let there be light on earth, and let it begin within me." When we let divine light shine, we change the vibration of the planet for the highest and best good of all.

INTEGRITY

9/25/16

Our topic for this month is Integrity. In looking up the definition of integrity, the first part of the definition was the quality of being honest and having strong moral principles. The second part was the state of being whole and undivided. The way I interpret this, integrity is about being true to myself. It is knowing what is right, and doing what is right. It is acting in accordance with my own beliefs and my own knowing, no matter what anyone else chooses to do in any given moment. It is doing the best we can, and understanding that sometimes we make less than ideal choices, and when we do, it is important and necessary to own up to that, and apologize when appropriate, in order to fully take responsibility for our actions.

The formation of Community of Light was a pretty dramatic expression of integrity for those involved. We had been members, and in many cases board members, of another spiritual organization. When some actions were taken that were so far out of integrity for us, it was no longer possible for us to remain in that space. We made the decision to leave that organization, and to form a new spiritual community. We needed to be part of a group that was in integrity with our own values and beliefs. It was essential for us to be in a space where each person is encouraged to think for themselves, and express their own truth without negative repercussions. In forming our board, we made the choice to be completely transparent in all of our interactions. Anyone may attend our board meetings. All of our financial records are available for anyone to examine. When we count our donations, two people are always present, so that there is constant accountability. We don't always agree on every aspect of issues that arise, but we are always willing to discuss things, and to hear each others' points of view with love. The choice to live in integrity was the reason this community was born.

Probably the most important aspect of integrity for me is about being true to myself. It is acting in accordance with my own beliefs, no matter what anyone else chooses to do in any given moment. There have been a couple of instances in recent years where situations have arisen in which someone has acted in a way that was very hurtful to me. And yet, because of circumstances, I was in a position to continue to have contact with them on a regular basis. No matter what they said or did, I did my best to act in accordance with my own beliefs and values. I chose to respond respectfully and clearly. Each week, I put their name in the healing box, trusting that things would work out for the highest and best good of all. In one case, after a year of difficulties, the other person sincerely apologized to me, and things have been much better between us since that time. Although it was challenging, I believe that continuing to act in integrity with myself was what allowed the situation to be resolved in a productive manner.

Sometimes, acting in integrity comes at a price. It certainly did for civil rights leaders like Martin Luther King. In my own family, my brother is about 15 years older than I am, so I met the woman that he was going to marry when I was 9 years old. I became very close with her, and when they divorced after 10 years of marriage, I chose to maintain my friendship with her. My brother was very angry with me because of this, and we barely had any relationship for the next 20 years. This was extremely painful because he was such an important person in my life. And yet, my sister-in-law was so valuable to me, that in order to be in integrity, I continued to choose my friendship with her at the cost of family harmony. My parents also struggled with this decision. For a while, they cut off contact with my sister-in-law. Then, they decided that in order to live in integrity, they needed to maintain a relationship with this woman who was so dear to them, who was the mother of their grandchildren, and with whom they had never had any negative interactions. It was not an easy choice for anyone at that time. Eventually, my brother came to accept the choice that I had made, and understood that I still loved him very much. We now have a very positive relationship again.

Sometimes when we are out of integrity in some way, we need to face the consequences of our actions. There are times when I feel strongly about something, and my emotions get a little carried away. I am involved in the organization of a dance group, and sometimes have very strong opinions about how things should go. Last year, in expressing those opinions, my actions inadvertently caused one of the other members to withdraw from the group. In thinking about it, I realized that I had made a poor choice in acting the way I had, so I apologized, both to the individual and to the group, and have since backed off in the way I express my opinions in that setting. Although I still feel strongly about things at times, I use my wisdom, discretion, and heart center in choosing the ways in which I express my feelings and opinions.

The way we allow ourselves to be treated is another aspect of integrity. If we allow other people to treat us less than respectfully, we are not taking care of ourselves, and not being true to ourselves. This talk was pretty challenging for me to write because it brought up every instance in my life that felt out of integrity. Although I live in integrity as much as possible, there are definitely times when I have knowingly made less than ideal choices, especially when it comes to interactions with men, and my need for attention and affection. If I am being honest with myself, I have to take a hard look at that, own up to my choices, and decide what I want to do going forward.

In thinking about integrity, and the state of being whole, I thought about alignment, especially alignment of the head, the power center, the heart center, and the wisdom center. Acting in integrity does not mean hurting others in the process. There are times when we know what the right choice to make is, and allowing ourselves to be guided to act with love and wisdom can be invaluable in having an outcome that is for the highest and best good of all. When we take responsibility for our actions, we are whole and in alignment, and we are acting in integrity.

PRAYER

10/23/16

Our topic for this month is Prayer. My own personal understanding of prayer has really evolved over the years. Being raised Catholic, my first impression of prayer was that it was words to be memorized and recited, like the Our Father, Hail Mary, and Act of Contrition. Then there was the Mass, learned first in Latin, then in English. These words had little or no meaning for me, and no connection to what I eventually came to understand, as I developed on a spiritual path. In thinking about my own relationship with prayer, I might have thought that I don't really pray much. As I have grown in my spiritual understanding, the words prayer, affirmation, and meditation are closely connected for me. I realize that the time I spend in meditation each day is a form of prayer. I believe that prayer is our thoughts, as we communicate with whatever we think of as Source, to either express our desires for manifestation, or to express our gratitude in every way possible.

In expanding my thinking about the word prayer, there is a book called "A Deep Breath of Life, Daily Inspirations for Heart Centered Living," by Alan Cohen, that has had a huge impact for me. This book has a page for each day of the year, and I am on my 15th year of reading it every day. The author makes a number of observations about prayer that resonate for me. He talks about the first minutes of each day being the "formative minutes." How do we begin our day? Do we jump up and rush into the busy-ness of life? Or do we take time for meditation and prayer to set the positive intention for each day?

Another observation is about releasing our prayers to God. He makes the analogy that when we mail a letter, we must let go of it in order for it to reach its destination. We don't climb into the mail truck, and sit next to it on the plane, to make sure it is delivered across the country. It is the same way with prayer. We express our intentions clearly, then release it to Source, for the highest and best good of all.

He tells a story about when human beings appeared on the planet, and the gods decided to hide the secret of life. They thought of all manner of places where humans might look, but finally decided to hide it inside each individual, as the one place we would never think to look. This is a reminder that when we pray, we acknowledge who and what we are. When we express our desires, those thoughts are the seeds of our creation. When we give thanks, we are acknowledging the good in ourselves.

The next observation is about when to pray. People often leave prayer until the last resort. Prayer connects us with the power of the universe, which is love. We always have the choice to make prayer our first response. Love and fear are the most powerful forces in the universe, and cannot exist in the same space at the same time. When we choose love, we vanquish fear. Prayer reminds us to choose love.

Another story he shares is about an angel given the task of finding the person on earth whose prayers had the most power to reach heaven. After journeying far and wide, the angel reported hearing the tears of a little boy, who was reciting the alphabet, saying, "Dear God, I do not know how to read, and I cannot recite from the prayer book, but I love you with all my heart. Take these letters and form them into words that are pleasing to you." This is an important reminder that saying words that are memorized, and recited by rote, is not what makes our prayers powerful, but rather it is our intentions that carry the energy of our thoughts into creation of powerful good.

The next observation is an analogy of a deep-sea diver connected to the source of air at the surface. If the air tube becomes blocked or cut off in any way, the diver is unable to function. The choices then are to panic, flail, try to return to the surface, or expire. We are like divers in earth suits. We are spiritual beings having a human experience. Our life-support tube is prayer, meditation, and any other activity that connects us with Source. If we cut ourselves off from Source, we do not live well or long. Pay attention to the activities that feed your soul, and make them a priority in your day and in your life. Begin your day with some form of prayer or meditation, and take time at the end of your day to reflect, be grateful, and connect with Source.

Another reflection is about the Hawaiian colloquial name for Caucasians, Haole, which translates to "without breath." When the missionaries conducted their church services, their practice of prayer differed radically from the Hawaiians'. The missionary services were somber, muttered, said by rote, and in the Hawaiians' eyes, lifeless and breathless. In contrast, the Hawaiians prayed with song, dance, color, and laughter. The word spiritual is about aliveness and spirit. If we are not bringing vitality and joy to our spiritual path, we are missing its essence. When we move with the energy, we let life flow. When we do things that bring us joy and lift our spirits, our life force flows fully and freely. That is why each week, the person who chairs the service at Community of Life chooses the affirmation and song that best reflects their life force. That is why we always encourage people who attend our services to express themselves fully and freely, whether through tears or laughter, to let the life force flow freely. Let your prayers be the same – full of breath and full of life.

And one of my favorite pages, which I incorporate into my

own daily affirmations, is about gratitude. One of the most powerful prayers we can ever say is, "Thank you." There is always something to be grateful for in any situation. What happens to us does not make or break us. How we think about and process any situation is always the deciding factor. We always have the choice to find the positive lesson in any experience that we have. We always have the choice to say, "Thank you for everything. I have no complaint whatsoever."

Being on a path of spiritual development has lead me to a different understanding of prayer. In the simplest terms, prayers are our thoughts. In some ways, they are conversations with God. In other ways, because we are God, and everyone and everything is God, they are our desires, our hopes, our wishes, and our thanks. Prayer is our way of affirming who we are. Prayer is about giving voice to our innermost desires and our deepest gratitude. It is affirming the deepest parts of ourselves. Each breath can be a prayer, acknowledging that we are doing the best we can in each moment, and giving thanks for that.

SURRENDER

12/11/16

Our topic for this month is Surrender. When I first started thinking about the traditional definition of surrender, it seemed to mean giving up, and that had a negative connotation for me. But as I explored more deeply what surrender meant for me, the word "allowing" came up strongly. Those who know me, know that I may have a small tendency to need to be right, in any and all situations. I recognize that I can get attached to a point of view, and argue very vehemently in favor of that idea. In the past, I have noticed that I might "steamroll" other people's thoughts and words, in service of getting my own point across, and having things turn out my way. In recent months, I have worked hard to be aware of these tendencies in myself. In several groups that I participate in, I have made a point to really listen to what other people have to say. To really consider other points of view. To weigh the pros and cons of each idea that is put forth. The more that I allow situations to unfold gradually and gracefully, without putting undue pressure onto them, the more I am able to surrender whatever preconceived notions I may have walked in with, and come to an outcome that is for the highest and best good of all. Invoking wisdom has been helpful in guiding me on this path.

In thinking about surrender, allowing, and wisdom, the Serenity Prayer came into my mind. "God, grant me the serenity to accept the things I cannot change, the courage to change the things I can, and the wisdom to know the difference." If we think of surrender in terms of serenity and peacefulness, the context is much more positive. If we look at things in our lives, and surrender to those that we cannot change, we are at peace. The things that we always have control over are our thoughts, words, and actions. And those are what we always have the ability to change.

When is it beneficial to surrender? When we have exhausted all of our own possibilities, we may choose to surrender to peacefulness, in any given moment. The ultimate surrender is the transition from our physical existence on the earth plane. One of my closest friends was diagnosed with ovarian cancer in 2006. For four years, even after it had metastasized to her brain, she chose an aggressive treatment regimen. Then, at a certain point, she knew that she'd had enough. She made the choice to surrender, and fight no longer. She spent her last few weeks in a beautiful hospice setting, surrounded by her beloved family and friends, and made a very peaceful transition, knowing that she had done everything she could have, and surrendering to her next steps.

Sometimes surrendering can be about something small. Many years ago, I used to travel about 90 miles for graduate school once a week, and stay overnight. I had a Swiss Army knife in my travel bag that belonged to my husband, and one day I couldn't find it. I emptied my bag, searched carefully through everything, and all around the room where I was staying, but there was no sign of the knife. Eventually, I gave up, and just went and bought a new one. When I returned to my room later that day, even though no one else had been in the room, my original knife was sitting on top of my clothes in my bag. Sometimes, when we surrender the illusion of control, the thing that we have been seeking simply shows up for us.

Surrendering can also be very simple. Each night, we surrender to sleep to allow our body, mind, and spirit to refresh and rejuvenate. If we refuse to surrender to sleep, it doesn't take long for our mind to stop functioning properly. In the practice of meditation, we have the choice to surrender to the simplest act of one breath. We can choose to take a moment to surrender our inner chatter, and allow ourselves to be open to whatever divine visions, words, or feelings are available to us.

When we surrender in the most positive way, we allow the highest and best good to come into our lives. In "A Deep Breath of Life," author Alan Cohen talks about being in a room full of people, and having a vision of unlimited blessings raining down upon them. Each was able to receive the blessings only according to whatever vessel they were holding up to catch them in. The question is what are we allowing to come into our life. Are we holding up a thimble? Or are we holding up an enormous vessel capable of collecting all the blessings that the universe has to offer to us. When good wants to come into our lives, how do we respond? Do we think that we are not worthy of such abundance? Or do we allow all the good into our lives? Do we surrender to the positive energy that flows around us always, and is always available to us? Or do we resist because we are not able to accept the good in any given moment? In a conversation with a close friend and fellow minister recently, she talked about having an epiphany. She realized that God didn't say, "Maybe we can have some light or maybe it's just too dark out here." God said, "Let there be light!" Are we willing to claim our own power in the same way when we manifest our heart's desires? Are we willing to let there be light in our own lives?

The Serenity prayer affirms: "God, grant me the serenity to accept the things I cannot change, the courage to change the things I can, and the wisdom to know the difference." Let us move through our days with just the right combination of wisdom, courage, and serenity, knowing when to stand up for ourselves powerfully, and when to surrender with grace.

CLARITY

2/5/17

Our topic for this month is Clarity. Clarity is the ability to see clearly, and, in some ways, is at the heart of all metaphysics. One of our primary goals in navigating this human existence is to know ourselves, and in order to do that, we have to see ourselves clearly. In order to know ourselves, one of the things we can do is to observe our thoughts, words, and actions, and be very honest in our assessment of the choices we are making. One of my personal favorite affirmations is, "I see clearly and act accordingly." We affirm that we see clearly what we are thinking, saying, and doing, and then act accordingly based on our observations. We have to be aware of what we are doing in order to make any changes we desire.

What are some of the ways in which we can learn to see ourselves more clearly? In thinking about clarity, the use of a camera or binoculars came to mind. When bringing an image into focus with a camera or binoculars, two things are important. The first is that we must be still. The second is knowing that a small adjustment can make a big difference in the clarity of the image. In seeing ourselves clearly, it's useful for us to take time each day to be still. If we are constantly in motion, we do not have time to see anything clearly. The second part is that when there is something in our lives that we want to see more clearly, making small adjustments, rather than huge shifts, is often the most effective way to bring it into clarity.

In pondering this talk, I came across a very interesting quote that related to clarity for me. "Attitude is the difference between an ordeal and an adventure." This week brought me a very distinct experience of that as I traveled home on a plane. About 20 minutes into an hour long flight, the captain announced that we had to turn back because of a problem with the left engine. Some people became stressed and anxious, and I did my best to help them remain calm. In that situation, it was very clear to me that there was absolutely nothing we could do to change the outcome, and the calmer we remained, the more positive the experience would be. The pilot did an amazing job of landing us safely and smoothly. I later learned that one engine had caught on fire, and then stopped completely. Fortunately, planes are designed to be able to fly and land, even when one of the engines is severely compromised. As we waited in the airport for a new plane, I had some fun and interesting conversations with fellow passengers, and invited a number of them to come and enjoy improv comedy in Tucson. We were back in the air in less than an hour and a half, and made it home safely. The next day, I received an email from the airline apologizing for the "unsettling experience," and offering a voucher for future travel. I came away from the experience feeling very grateful. For me, it had been an adventure, rather than an ordeal, because of the way that I had chosen to look at it.

How we feel about someone often colors how we think about them. Sometimes, when we meet someone whose energy does not match well with ours, we find ourselves judging them more harshly than we might in other circumstances. I was noticing that I was blaming someone else for every little thing that was happening. When I took the time to see the situation more clearly, I realized that my feelings were clouding my ability to see clearly and act accordingly. I made an adjustment, took responsibility for myself, and things went much more smoothly.

And as we see ourselves more clearly, what do we do with

what we see? Sometimes, we see a habit that we would like to change. What we think, what we say, and what we do is what we draw more of to ourselves. The only way to dispel darkness is by shedding light. If there is a habit that we would like to change, it is valuable to focus on the positive. In his book, "A Deep Breath of Life," author Alan Cohen suggests: "Rather than battling what you don't want, cultivate what you do want. Meditate, pray, read uplifting books, keep supportive company, walk in nature, listen to joyful music – all the things that make you happy...If the habit is not in your best interests, it will fall away in the presence of the light you are generating."

In evaluating my own life, I have been observing my behavior, in order to determine what changes I might like to make. Although my dad has been gone from the earth plane for almost seven years, he is still very much with me, sometimes in more positive ways than others. One of the traits that I seem to have inherited from him is that my initial response to almost every situation is to be critical and judgmental. On the one hand, having a sharp mind that processes information quickly and efficiently is an asset. On the other hand, giving uninvited and unwelcome feedback is often not an ideal choice. I have been keenly aware of this lately, and have been working on making different choices. I have been paying attention to situations where my opinions are not welcomed or invited, and choosing to keep my mouth shut instead of sharing my observations and comments. This is working well for me, and I am finding that I am having much smoother and easier interactions with the people around me. I have chosen to wait until I am asked for my opinion before offering it. I may share my thoughts with a close friend, but not inflict them on someone who is not ready or interested in hearing what I have to say. The clarity I have gained from this experience is really valuable to me. I have been choosing to focus on listening to understand, instead of listening to reply. If my opinion is solicited, I do my best to share insights in a gentle and loving way.

When we "Let Divine Light Shine" each day, we raise our own vibration, and also raise the vibration of the planet. At Community of Light, we encourage ourselves and each other to see clearly and act accordingly. To shed light where there is darkness. To know ourselves. We look at clarity in the simplest way - as the ability to see clearly and act accordingly. The more we know ourselves, the more clarity we have. And we all do the best we can in any given moment.

ALLOW

3/19/17

Our topic for this month is Allow. In each moment, we always have the choice to allow or to resist. When we allow, our lives flow with ease. When we resist, we create obstacles to ease. Interestingly, one of the places in my life where I have most learned to allow is in writing my talks. I feel like my talks show up for me, and come through me, much like the messages that we give at the end of each service. When I am patient, and allow the words to flow to the foreground of my mind, the process is smooth and easy. When I feel anxious and worried, I get in my own way and resist, and the process is obstructed.

We each have inner knowing and our own guidance. When we allow our inner knowing and guidance to operate fully and freely, our lives flow with ease. We might think of it as the "little voice in our heads," that reminds us to pick up that extra item at the store, or wakes us at just the right time, even when our alarm isn't set, or brings someone to mind that might just need to hear our voice at that moment. When we resist our inner knowing, we sometimes make less than ideal choices, even though, deep within, we know better.

In the 70's, there was a well known book called, "Don't Push the River: It Flows by Itself." The premise is that when we allow ourselves to move in the direction of the natural flow of life, our path is easy and graceful. When we struggle against what is best for us, and resist the natural flow, our lives do not work with nearly as much ease.

There are times when we find it easy to express ourselves, and times when it is more challenging. I have had the honor to conduct a number of Celebration of Life services. It is important to allow people the time and space to express their feelings during these types of occasions. Sometimes, it takes a moment for people to be able to stand up, and say what they are feeling. By allowing that time, it facilitates each person being able to express what is important to them in that moment.

When someone has something on their mind, it is valuable to allow the time and space for them to express what they need to share. By listening, we create an environment that is loving and accepting, and allows people to move forward on their path. Sometimes, someone just needs to vent what they are feeling. Allowing them to do that gives them the opportunity to relieve the pressure they might be feeling, and then go about the rest of their day with a clearer mind and heart. If we interfere with this process by either resisting what the other person is saying, or by resisting allowing them the time and space to express themselves, communication does not flow, and neither party is left feeling very satisfied.

Each of us learns things in their own way and in their own time. Allowing people the time and space they need in order to learn something is another gift that we can give. People learn in different ways, too. Some people need to see, some need to hear, and others need to feel and do what it is they are learning. Understanding different types of learning experiences allows us the opportunity to learn in the ways that are most effective for each of us. If we resist this process, and only teach in ways that are most comfortable for ourselves, the outcome is much less effective.

One of the affirmations that I do on a daily basis is: "I allow all the good that is possible to come into my life." Allowing your good to come to you is a necessary component of growth. I have a good friend who is very clear about what he wants. Then, in the next breath, he states all the reasons why he can't have what he wants. In order to manifest the highest and best good in our lives, it is essential to allow that good to come to us. When we place obstacles in our own path, we create resistance to having our heart's desires fulfilled.

All of us grow and change in different ways and at different paces. It is important to allow ourselves and others to change. When we have been accustomed to someone acting in a particular way, we may experience some resistance to allowing them to change. Pay attention to the ways in which people do things differently, allow them to change, accept the new version of who they are, and support them in their growth. Then, we can do the same for ourselves. We can make changes, then allow ourselves to become the new version of the person that we are. Sometimes, we meet resistance in either allowing ourselves to change or accepting changes in others. The more we can notice this, and give ourselves and those around us the time and space to adjust and change, the more we operate in the flow of ease.

In thinking about allowing, how we view time is very impactful. In the Greek language, there are two words for time. Chronos has to do with time of day, and the measurement of hours, minutes, and seconds. Kairos means "in nature's time," "in due time," and in metaphysical terms, in divine order. When we allow for things to happen in kairos, we do not impose our own impatience of when is the right time for an event to unfold, but rather allow things to unfold in the fullness of time. We do not resist divine order, but rather allow for the fulfillment with ease.

How do we make the choice to allow rather than to resist? One of the best ways is simply to breathe. It's valuable to give yourself time and space each day to listen to your inner knowing.

As you move through your life, begin to pay attention to the places in your life, and in your body, where you may feel resistance, and remember to breathe. You may choose to begin to replace resistance with allowing. Know that you can always get through the space of one breath at a time, then you can move on to the next breath. As you form the habit of allowing, you will be more and more able to choose to trust in your own inner knowing to guide you.

ME

4/30/17

Our topic for this month is Me. As metaphysicians, one of our fundamental goals is to know ourselves, so this is a perfect place to start. What are the ways in which we know ourselves? And then, as we know ourselves, how do we move from who we are to who we desire to be? One of the ways we know ourselves is through our thoughts, words, and actions. How do we spend our time? What are we thinking, saying, and doing? How do we present ourselves to the outside world? Take a look at the clothes you choose. Are they brightly colored or primarily dark or black? Do your clothes reveal you or do they hide you? Who are the people, places, and things that you spend time with? What percentage of the time do you spend alone and what percentage with others? I have had some interesting conversations with friends recently about how much social interaction is preferable for them. A couple of people I talked to mentioned social anxiety, and the undesirability of being around very many people for very long. Another friend said that it wasn't that she didn't like being around other people, it was just that she was so happy being by herself, that it just didn't occur to her to go out and find others. That led me to think about myself, and my needs for connection. My need to connect with others is pretty far along one end of the continuum. It's not that I don't enjoy time alone. It's more that I feel best when I am very connected with others.

As we look at ourselves, we know ourselves. Sometimes looking at where we've been allows us to know where we are and where we're going. During a recent meditation series entitled "Hope in Uncertain Times," Oprah made reference to a John Bradshaw exercise designed to heal the Inner Child. "Imagine peering through the window of the house that you grew up in. Look through and find yourself in that house. What do you see? And what do you feel? What's going on with you and your relationships with others in the house? What gifts did you possess? What burdens did you carry? What brought you hope?" She suggests that as we heal the wounds of the past, we have much more hope for the future. Looking at the people and things that affected us as we were growing up allows us to have perspective, to forgive, and to have the freedom to make choices about how we allow those people and things to affect us in the present. Oprah also said one of the most powerful definitions of forgiveness that she ever heard was, "Forgiveness is giving up the hope that the past could have been any different."

Facing our fears, and examining what we believe about ourselves is very powerful. On another day in the meditation series, Oprah talked about overcoming fear with hopefulness. She asked: "What are you afraid of? Do you expect that things won't go your way? Fear is a powerful and convincing emotion. Find out where your fear is coming from. Only then can you let it go. Through meditation, we can connect with openness and trust, and let fear diminish. You become what you believe. You become what you expect in your heart. Let's open our hearts to the positive possibilities of uncertainty." It is useful and valuable for us to look at what we are afraid of. To shine light on the dark places in our lives so that we can move forward. Knowing who we are allows us to accomplish what we want with greater ease.

And as we observe ourselves, do we see ourselves as givers, takers, or people who live in balance? I had a reading done several years ago, and was told that I knew all about giving, but not so much about receiving. Many of the people in my life were people who took and took, and I allowed and encouraged that. The image was of each of these people sticking a straw in me in order to take what they needed. And it was a one way street. I was told that people who live in balance couldn't get anywhere near me because I didn't allow others to give to me. These were very powerful words to hear. I decided to look at the relationships in my life, and eliminate some of them. Moving forward, I chose to maintain the relationships that were reciprocal in some way. Not in the sense of keeping some kind of score card, but just in encouraging balance in the interactions I had with others. I learned to say yes and thank you, instead of always thinking that I could do it myself. One of the most important aspects of knowing ourselves is being able to look at who we are, and then deciding what we would like to change. Then, as one of the ministers talked about last week, we have to have the courage to act on those thoughts, and actually make changes if we want different results in our lives.

Who are we, and who do we desire to be? What changes do we choose to make in order to move forward on our path? Another way that we can know ourselves is through others' reactions to us, and the feedback we may receive. When we receive feedback from others, it is useful to first consider the source. If it is someone we trust and care about, the next step is to try on the feedback, almost as though one might try on new clothes or shoes. How does it fit? How does it affect the way in which we look at ourselves? Is it uncomfortable at first, but then the more we wear it, the more it feels like us? How do we want to change any behavior in reaction to whatever feedback we might receive? Recently, I got some feedback that I come across with an attitude of "I know better." I've been sitting with this for a while, considering how true it is for me, and how it fits in my life. How it serves me, and how it hinders me. And what I might want to do about it. On the one hand, sometimes the amount of life experience that I have had in relation to others means that I might know better. On the other hand, that attitude can get in the way of group interactions moving forward in a productive manner. It can interfere with open and flowing communication, and it can prevent me from trying out new ideas. It is something I am paying close attention to, and deciding what is useful for me to change, in order to have the most positive outcome possible.

In thinking about ourselves, it is always useful to remember that we are not alone, and are always part of a whole, and connected with everyone and everything that is. Recently, I spent time with a nine year old girl, and we had a very in-depth conversation about life and death. Her great-grandfather, whom she had been very close with (and who I knew well), died a year or so ago. She talked about the invisible thread that connects us all, and how we pump love through that thread to each other, no matter whether we're alive or have passed. She said, "Poppy pumps love to me all the time." It moved me very deeply to share that moment with her. As we move through our lives, it is comforting to think about the invisible thread that connects us all, and to feel the love that is pumping through to us at all times. Earlier this month, one of the ministers encouraged us to look into the mirror each day, and affirm: "I am me." As we move through our lives, knowing ourselves better in each moment, it is useful to love and accept ourselves as we are. This frees us to move forward on our path with ease, as we become the most ideal version of ourselves.

IDEAS

5/28/17

Our topic for this month is Ideas. Everything starts with an idea. Everything that exists in our world was once an idea. Every design, every invention, every modern convenience, every product was once an idea. Then, someone took the idea, and brought it to life with action. At one time, we shared the use of a telephone on a party line with our neighbors. Now, most of us hold in our hands a device that is not only a telephone, but a more sophisticated computer than what was used to send the first rocket to the moon. All the result of an idea. We have ideas about where to live, what to do with our time, how we present ourselves to the world, whether or not to be in relationships with others, how to support ourselves, and what we choose to believe.

When I think of ideas, I think of a spark. It is essential to have a spark to start a fire. And you can't maintain a fire with just a spark. You have to have kindling, different sized logs, air, and space in order for a fire to burn well and productively. When you have the spark of an idea, sometimes it's best to keep it to yourself until it is strong enough to burn on its own. Otherwise, someone may stomp it out or douse the flame before it's had a chance to come to fruition. Some sparks can be fanned into a flame that is destructive, and can burn out of control. Our wisdom guides us in choosing which ideas to bring to light, and which ideas to let burn out.

Ideas are the product of imagination. Ideas are not inherently positive or negative. As an idea comes forth for us, we use our wisdom to evaluate whether or not an idea is beneficial for us. If we decide to move forward with an idea, we use our power to bring the idea into reality. And then, we infuse our spark of an idea with love, so that it serves us for our highest and best good. With each idea that we have, we decide whether to cultivate and nurture it, and bring it to fruition. Sometimes if we are unsure, we may allow others to douse the flame of an idea before it can be manifested. Sometimes we decide to abandon an idea before it can cause any negative consequences. We allow our wisdom to guide us in this.

Where do our ideas come from? Some come from our parents, some from teachers, some from friends, some from spiritual advisors. Sometimes we see or hear things in nature, sometimes on television or in movies. Sometimes we read something that resonates for us. As we grow and develop, we evaluate the ideas that come from outside ourselves to see whether they fit for us. Often, the most valuable and important ideas come from within ourselves, from our inner knowing and guidance, from deep in the core of our own souls, from Source. As these ideas arise, we also examine them, and see which ones deserve to grow.

Another way to think about ideas is that they are like seeds in a garden. Ideas, like seeds, are not inherently right or wrong. It depends on where they are planted, how they are nurtured, how they grow, and what you do with them once they have come to fruition. Some plants may be poisonous under certain circumstances, and have healing properties under others. Our wisdom guides us in knowing the difference. Sometimes, the results of an idea can be like weeds. They need to be removed, so that healthy ideas can have the freedom to grow. We are all familiar with the expression, "It seemed like a good idea at the time." Sometimes, the perspective of time, and the viewing of the results of an idea, allow us to know whether it is a choice that we would make again.

Ideas may be influenced by perspective. We may have an idea of the value of something. The idea of value is not right or wrong, but often dependent on external factors. It is useful to keep that in mind, as we evaluate our ideas and the ideas of others.

Everyone has their own ideas. And how do we respond to the ideas of others? Are we open-minded and accepting? Are we critical and judgmental? Do we help others to nurture and develop their ideas, or do we douse their flame? What happens when someone has ideas and beliefs that come into conflict with our own? Because of the public nature of social media, we now have the ability to see where people stand on lots of different issues that might or might not have come up in our interactions in the past. We have the choice to accept or reject others' ideas. It can be a challenge to be loving and accepting of a person, even when we disagree, sometimes vehemently, with some of their ideas. It is important to remember that we are all one, and to be able to be loving towards the essence of another, even when some of our ideas do not match up very well.

There are so many things that we take for granted in our everyday lives that were once thought of as impossible. They are all the result of someone's ideas. Recently, I was watching a movie, and there was a scene with a self-help guru who talked about the word "impossible." He said sometimes we just have to look at things in a different way, and turn "impossible" into "I'm possible!" That really struck me in a deep way. As we move forward on our path, it is useful to examine the ideas that we have with the thought that, "I'm possible!" instead of "impossible." As the sparks of ideas come forth into our consciousness, let us use our wisdom to decide which ones to feed with the kindling of our thoughts, which ones to support with the logs of our power, and which ones to nurture with love in order to grow and develop for our highest and best good.

IMAGE

6/25/17

Our topic for this month is Image. As I thought about this topic, a lot of questions arose for me. What kind of image do we project out into the world? And how does this external image reflect what is happening inside us? How authentically does the inside match the outside? How do we see ourselves? How do others see us? When is it useful to see ourselves through someone else's eyes? How do we present ourselves to the world? What kind of hairstyle, clothing, makeup, and jewelry do we wear? What is our posture, demeanor, facial expression? How do cultural norms affect the way we present ourselves? How do trends affect us? What images stay with us with the greatest impact? How are images stored in our memories? What do we give our attention to? What images uplift us and what images drag us down? Do we present our true selves to the world, or do we hide behind masks and facades? Do we take others at "face value," or are we willing to look deeper within to find the true essence?

Our physical appearance is the first thing that others see, and that we see whenever we meet anyone else. What comprises our external image? What is the first thing you notice about someone when you see them? Is it their smile, their eyes, their size and shape, their clothing, their hairstyle, their makeup? Is is whether they are male or female? Is it the color of their skin? The length of their hair? Is it some outward indication of their belief system? And how does someone's appearance affect the way that we think about them? In the case of someone who is transgender, their outside image does not fit with their inside reality, and can cause serious distress. How does that impact what we see, and what we think about what we see? When someone is undergoing chemotherapy, sometimes they lose all their hair, and that impacts how we see them, and what we think about them. We sometimes make decisions and choices about who we would like to spend more time with, and develop relationships with, based on their image. What are the ways in which we can look beyond the image to get to know the essence of the person inside?

When we observe others, we form opinions about who they might be, what they might think and believe, and how we feel about them based on the image that they present to the world. As humans, we project our ideas and opinions onto others in the same way that a projector projects an image onto a screen. We see what our own filters allow us to see. Everyone sees things differently, based on their own experiences, biases, thoughts, feelings, and history. And sometimes the image we present masks what is truly going in inside ourselves. Our challenge is to see beyond the image to the essence, for ourselves and for others.

How does what's happening inside ourselves impact our image? When we feel happy, we might choose to wear brighter colors, and to take more time with our clothing, hair, and makeup. We might greet those we meet with a smile, and feel open-hearted. How we feel, and whatever is currently happening in our lives, definitely impacts the way we look, and the way others perceive us. In "A Deep Breath of Life," author Alan Cohen relates the following story: "When Rembrandt set out to paint the likenesses of Jesus and the apostles, he walked the streets of Amsterdam to find men who embodied the character of his Biblical subjects. Rembrandt began with a tall, handsome man who bore the stature and purity of the Christ. Then, after setting the images of the disciples to canvas, Rembrandt was ready to paint Judas, and he searched for a man with a tortured soul. After combing Paris, he found a homeless man sitting outside a store. The man was dirty, unkempt, and his eyes spoke of deep sadness. After painting Judas, Rembrandt thanked the man for his assistance. "Don't you remember me?" asked the man. "I don't think so," answered the artist. "I sat for your portrait of Jesus," the man answered." Our experiences color our image for ourselves and for those who observe us.

Sometimes how we see ourselves can be distorted. The media bombards us with images of what is considered attractive and desirable. If those images are different from the way in which we see ourselves, it can affect how we feel about ourselves. People make all different kinds of choices in order to change their image. In some cases, self-esteem can be so affected that people chose destructive extremes like bulimia or anorexia to change their image. In working on learning to love myself, at a certain point, I allowed myself to see my image through someone else's eyes. Someone who I cared about told me that I looked the way he liked a woman to look. Prior to that, because my image didn't fit what society said was the ideal, I had not allowed myself to feel good about the way I looked. Listening to my friend, and seeing myself through his eyes, allowed me to see myself differently. It moved me along the path of loving and accepting myself as I am. It was very powerful.

Because of the power and immediacy of television and the internet, we are constantly bombarded with images. What do we choose to give our attention to? What images uplift us and what images drag us down? What do we allow to impact us most strongly? What do we fill our social media pages with? What image do we present of ourselves?

In addition to the ways in which we see ourselves and others, there are also the images that people create to represent different belief systems. These images and symbols can have a great impact on us. Places of worship choose to present powerful images and symbols. In some cases, there might be a six pointed star, a goddess with many arms, a man with a large belly and a beatific smile, a pentagram, or a person nailed to a cross that is the primary image presented to the people who walk through the door. How do those images impact the people who see them? What choices do people make based on the images presented to them?

As we move through our days, it is valuable to consider some of these kinds of questions. We have the choice whether to present ourselves to the world hiding behind a mask or to expose our true selves in the most genuine way possible. We have the choice to accept someone at "face value," allowing their image to color our opinions. Or we can choose to look beyond an image, to look deep inside, and to get to know others genuinely, in order to connect with their essence in profound and meaningful ways.

THOUGHTS

8/27/17

Our topic for this month is Thoughts. Our thoughts are the seeds that create the garden that is our life. When we plant one seed, such as corn or watermelon, the harvest that comes up is multiplied a thousand-fold. One kernel of corn or one water-melon seed is the source of a plant which grows an abundant harvest of hundreds more kernels or seeds. This is how it is with our thoughts. Each thought is a seed that we plant, and our harvest is multiplied many times from the original seed. What do we spend our time thinking about? What are the thoughts that fill and feed our souls? We have thoughts about ourselves, thoughts about others, thoughts about what goes on inside ourselves, thoughts about the world around us, and thoughts about what is beyond our human experience.

The power of our thoughts can actually be demonstrated scientifically. I watched a talk recently in which Dr. Bruce Lipton was talking about the effects of thoughts on the chemistry of our bodies. He referenced the Buddhist saying, "What we think, we become." Expanding on that with scientific evidence, he said that defective proteins (which is one aspect of the cause of dis-ease) only account for about 1% of the reasons for dis-ease in the human body. In contrast, the chemical signals produced by our thoughts are largely responsible for creating dis-ease in our bodies. For instance, if we perceive ourselves to be threatened, our bodies respond with chemical signals that activate our internal defenses against threat. Which is all well and good if a lion is, in fact, chasing us. However, if we are just reacting to the stress in our lives in a magnified and exaggerated way, the same chemicals are produced, and the same reaction is triggered in our bodies, which leads to dis-ease.

Take a moment and think about holding a lemon...Smell the lemon...Now, cut the lemon in half, and smell the cut lemon-...Now, put the lemon on your tongue and lick it...Notice your reaction. Realize that you created that entire experience with your thoughts.

To understand the power of our thoughts, we can look at our lives. Do we think of abundance or lack? Our bank balance may be one reflection of our thoughts. Do we think of ease or dis-ease? Whatever is happening in our bodies may be one reflection of our thoughts.

Our thoughts are what create every aspect of our lives. I've been paying attention to the kinds of thoughts I've been having lately. I notice the preponderance of critical and judgmental thoughts that pass through my mind on a daily basis. I was flying the other day, and observing the other passengers as they boarded the plane. There was an empty seat beside me, and a woman came up and just pointed to it, so I got up and let her sit down. I overheard her talking, and for a moment wasn't sure whether she was on the phone, or having a very elaborate (and perhaps mentally challenged) conversation with herself. The only thing we have control over in our lives are our thoughts, words, and actions, and in each moment, we get to choose which ones we nurture and allow to grow. I noticed the way in which I was judging her with my thoughts, and then made a conscious choice to change what I was thinking and doing. I started a friendly conversation with her, and ended up learning interesting things about her, including the fact that she's a screenwriter who divides her time between LA and New York. I was truly grateful that I interrupted the train that my thoughts were taking, in order to share a moment of being present with a stranger.

One of the most powerful ways to influence our thoughts is to focus on gratitude. Focusing for just a few minutes a day on things you are grateful for can dramatically boost your happiness and well-being. Last month, I began my 10th year of writing in my gratitude journal each night. When I take the time to focus my thoughts on what I am grateful for, instead of what aggravated or irritated me, or what might have been unpleasant in my day, I notice the feeling of peace and calm that comes over me. I notice myself smiling and feeling happier when I focus on what I am grateful for, instead of what could or should have been. If you like, take a moment, and think about something you're grateful for today, or something that might have happened, but didn't, and wasn't as bad as it could have been.

We can use our thoughts to shower ourselves with light, or to drown ourselves in negativity. The difference between optimism and pessimism resides in our thoughts. In the book, "A Deep Breath of Life," author Alan Cohen talks about one child being in a room full of shiny, new toys, who looks at everything, then complains about being bored. Conversely, another child is placed in a room full of manure, and is delighted. When asked why, he replies, "There must be a pony around here somewhere!" On the TV show Saturday Night Live, there is a character called Debbie Downer. No matter what anyone else says, Debbie Downer finds the most negative, unpleasant, and depressing aspect about it. If someone gets a raise, she reminds them of the tax consequences. If someone goes on vacation, she talks about all the accidents that have happened at that location. We have the choice in each moment of what thoughts to promote and what thoughts to discard.

And how do we nurture positive and healthy thoughts? One step is by paying attention to our thoughts, and making choices about the people, places, and things that we focus on in our lives. There is a Cherokee legend about a man teaching his grandson about life. "A fight is going on inside me," he said to the boy. "It is a terrible fight, and it is between two wolves. One is anger, envy, sorrow, regret, greed, arrogance, self-pity, guilt, resentment, inferiority, lies, false pride, superiority, and ego. The other is joy, peace, love, hope, serenity, humility, kindness, benevolence, empathy, generosity, truth, compassion, and faith. The same fight is going on inside you - and inside every other person, too." The grandson thought about it for a minute, and then asked his grandfather, "Which wolf will win?"

The old Cherokee simply replied, "The one you feed."

In each moment, we have the choice to decide which wolf we feed. We have the choice to decide which seeds we plant and nurture, and which weeds we discard. In each moment, we can choose the thoughts that promote the kind of life we want for ourselves. We are in charge of our own lives, and we get to choose our thoughts, words, and actions for our highest and best good, as we move forward on our paths.

SERVICE

9/10/17

Our topic for this month is Service. As I pondered this, some questions came up for me. How do we serve ourselves, serve others, and serve the greater good? What is the difference between helping and serving? What does it mean to be of service? And why is it important to be of service?

Interestingly enough, in thinking about Service, it is important to put ourselves first. We must serve ourselves, for our highest and best good, in order to be able to serve others. One of the ways in which we serve ourselves is when we allow our essence to create opportunities for ourselves. We serve ourselves when we follow our own guidance and intuition, instead of allowing restrictions from others to create a box that limits us. As parents, we are most effective when we allow our children to discover their own greatness, and then are there for them when we are called upon. Source operates the same way with us, allowing us to discover our own greatness, as we move forward on our paths. Source does not interfere in our choices, but observes, and is available when called upon for guidance.

We serve ourselves when we take care of our body, mind, and spirit. Making healthy choices with food, exercise, and rest takes care of our body. Making healthy choices about what we watch, read, and think takes care of our mind. Connecting with Source in whatever way resonates for us takes care of our spirit.

How do we serve others? There is an immense difference between helping and serving. When we "help" someone, there is an assumption that they are less than, and in need of our assistance in order to function as well as possible. There is an idea of reaching down to someone who is unable to do something for themselves, and a presumption of unequal status. When we serve someone, we are there in support of their greatness. We make their well-being a priority for the highest and best good of all. Sometimes, the simplest way to serve others is to listen and hold space for them for whatever they may be experiencing in that moment.

Sometimes, we are called upon to serve others. Recently, I was at a dance convention, and noticed a young woman sitting with her foot up as her friend rubbed it. I felt called upon to serve her by offering energy work. I felt a little awkward and uncomfortable approaching a stranger in the middle of a dance event, so I did nothing at first. I watched her dance for a little while longer, then when she sat down again, I responded to the inner call and approached her. I explained a little about energy work, which she was not familiar with, and asked if she would like me to share that with her. She was very receptive, so we moved to a quiet place, and I did Reiki on her, and gave her a mini-reading. She was genuinely appreciative, and said that these kinds of connections are part of what dance events are about. I was glad that I had listened to my intuition, and followed my guidance, in order to serve her.

Sometimes people choose their profession from a service-oriented perspective. Being in service to others was an important part of my daughter's motivation in becoming a chiropractor. The basic philosophy of chiropractic is that the body's innate state is health. The job of the practitioner is to adjust the body, in order to remove any obstacles, and return the body to its innate state of health. My daughter believes that setting an intention before working on patients is of utmost importance. Part of her intention is to be a clear channel conduit for God to be connected to the patient through her.

The way we think about things has power. Even in a restaurant, there is a difference in thinking about a waiter vs. a server. Someone who waits might be impatiently tapping a foot. Someone who serves is there to take care of others. When we serve the greater good, it is for the benefit of all. Any time we put our ego aside, and come from a place of love in our hearts, we are serving the greater good.

The use of the word serve or service has a number of contexts. When someone is in the military, it is referred to as being in the service. The motto of the police is to serve and protect. We take our cars to a service station. All these contexts have to do with looking out for the well-being of others. At Community of Light, when we take a moment each day to Let Divine Light Shine, we raise the vibration of the planet, and serve the greater good. As a spiritual community, we refer to our gathering as a service. How does a gathering like this serve the greater good? Our intention is to create a meeting place for like minded people. We offer a healing meditation to allow people some quiet time to get in touch with their higher selves. We offer energy work to open a channel for balance and healing. We do inspirational talks on a wide variety of topics to share thoughts and wisdom, and give people the opportunity to think about these topics in ways that they might not have considered before. We give messages that come from Source for the highest and best good of all. (And we have snacks to serve the physical body, too.)

Why is it important to be of service? As spiritual beings having a human existence, we are unable to exist alone. When we are of service, we remind ourselves of our connection with all that is, remind ourselves that we are all one, and all in this together. We go beyond the limitations of our single existence, and connect with what is best in all of us. When we are of service to ourselves, to others, and to the greater good, I believe that we channel divine unconditional love for our highest and best good, and the highest and best good of all others. When we are of service, we raise the vibration of the planet, and allow divine light to shine.

In Kahlil Gibran's words: "I slept and I dreamed that life is all joy. I woke and I saw that life is all service. I served and I saw that service is joy."

PATIENCE

11/12/17

Our topic for this month is Patience. I wondered who had chosen the topic for this month, and when I checked, it was me. No surprise. It's often the case that we choose to speak about that which is most present for us to learn for ourselves. It seems that learning about patience is an ongoing task that I have chosen in this lifetime. For me, patience is connected to how we think about and manage time. When we understand that time is unlimited, we have prosperity consciousness, and patience. If we believe that time is a limited commodity, we have lack consciousness, and impatience.

I've been following Oprah and Deepak Chopra's meditation series called "Making Every Moment Matter." Each day has addressed some aspect of our relationship with time, and many of them have been inspiring to me. They talked about our ability to use our time well. This can come down to how fulfilled we might feel in the present moment. When we feel content and centered inside, everything we do is more effective, efficient, and satisfying. Our experience of time is affected by our beliefs, attitudes, and behaviors. When we are focused on the seconds ticking by on the clock, time can seem to crawl. When we shift away from "clock time," we can be in the timelessness of the present moment. When we are in the present moment, there is only patience.

They discussed the saying that time heals all wounds. This is one aspect of patience, to allow time to be a healing force in our lives. As we gain some distance from any particular situation, we are often able to look at it from a different perspective. Acute pain often is lessened as time passes. The way in which we choose to spend our time determines if our old hurts are healed or held onto. When we experience "inward time," it can be one of the most powerful ways to help us mend. Another way to make time a healer in our lives is in our constructive use of sleep time, play time, down time, and quiet time.

How do we come into balance with patience in our lives? One of the ways we do this is by being in the present moment. When we allow ourselves to be fully present in each moment, each moment is perfect. We are not consumed with worry or anxiety about the future. We are not preoccupied with regret or guilt about the past. One of the ways in which we are able to heal the past is by noticing our reactions to triggering situations without judging or condemning ourselves. When we allow ourselves to be fully present in each moment, we begin to heal our old wounds. We are not concerned with whether or not we are enough, because in any given moment, we are enough. When we are in the present moment, there is only patience.

How do we become fully present in each moment? One way is to pay attention to our senses. How are we in contact with the earth and whatever surface our body is touching? How does it feel? What are we seeing in this moment? What sounds might we be hearing? Are there any smells that we are aware of? Are we tasting anything right now? When we are fully present with another person, we are attending to what is happening in this moment. We look into the other person's eyes. We listen to not only the words that are being said, but the feeling that is being conveyed. We are not spending time worrying about how we look, or what the next piece of information is that we want to convey, or where we have to be next. We are engaged in the present moment, and giving it our full attention. Deepak says, "When we know our true self as present awareness, we transform our beliefs about time. We realize that time is not a fixed thing outside of us that measures our life, but a malleable experience we create from within our awareness."

Another way to allow ourselves to be present is to breathe, and to focus on our breath. When we are going through challenging times, it can be valuable to remember that we only have to get through one breath at a time. As we allow ourselves to get through one breath, being fully present, we can move forward on our path for our highest and best good.

When we are worried about arriving at a destination, we can feel impatient instead of being present for the journey. I notice when I am tapping my foot, checking the time, sighing, and using colorful language to those around me that I perceive to be "in my way." When we remember to breathe, and become fully present in any given moment, our body relaxes, our awareness of our surroundings increases, and we are able to enjoy what is happening right now. When we are in the present moment, there is only patience.

In the Greek language, there are two words for time. Chronos has to do with time of day, and the measurement of hours, minutes, and seconds. In Chronos, we may feel impatience. Kairos means "in nature's time," "in due time," and in metaphysical terms, in divine order. When we allow for things to happen in Kairos, we do not impose our own impatience of when is the right time for an event to unfold, but rather allow things to unfold in the fullness of time. We do not resist divine order, but rather are patient with ourselves and those around us, as we allow for the fulfillment with ease.

As spiritual beings having a human existence, it is often important for us to remember to be patient with ourselves. Part of our journey in this lifetime is to remember who we truly are. Occasionally, we stumble on our path. It is valuable to be patient with ourselves, in the same way that we are patient with a toddler who is just learning to walk. We try things out. We stumble. We fall. We pick ourselves up, and do it again, as we strive towards mastery. As we move forward on our path, being patient with ourselves and others, and remembering to be fully present in each moment, time becomes our ally instead of our enemy, and we allow ourselves to enjoy each moment to the fullest for our highest and best good.

BALANCE

1/14/18

Our topic for this month is Balance. What happens when we try to balance too many things all at once? Living alone, I am aware of the usual sounds in my house. The other day, there was a loud unexpected sound emanating from my kitchen. When I checked, I had attempted to balance too many dishes and containers of varying shapes and sizes in the sink. Each was filled with water. Like an elaborate Rube Goldberg creation, the balance point was reached, and then exceeded, and the entire structure collapsed and crashed down. Fortunately, it all stayed within the confines of the sink. When we try to balance too much in our lives, at some point, it can all come crashing down around us. Finding the right balance between too little, too much, or just right is a fine art. My mother used to have an expression for when she had too much going on at once. She said she felt like a "one-armed wallpaper hanger with hives!"

When we watch a child learning to ride a bicycle, we have an immediate visual reference to the importance of balance. Tip too far in either direction, and down they go. Accomplish balance, and they are in for a smooth and fun ride, getting places with more ease than they would have otherwise. Consider the seesaw (or teeter totter), which can only operate when it is in balance, otherwise someone may be stuck on the ground or someone may be bounced off the other side. As a dancer, balance is of paramount importance. Although the partnership of the dance matters tremendously, each partner must be responsible for their own body and their own balance. If one partner does not pay attention to balance, they can not only hurt themselves, but can drag their partner down with them.

Young mothers (and fathers) sometimes have real challenges with balance. I watch my daughter as she juggles taking care of an active and inquisitive four year old, with growing a successful business, with nurturing a primary relationship, with maintaining a newly purchased house, and exercising and cleaning up after two energetic dogs. What I observe is that sometimes taking care of and finding time for herself gets the short end of the stick. It's a constant balancing act.

In thinking about balance, it is useful to consider the balance between ourselves and others, and the balance within ourselves. In thinking about ourselves and others, we can look at how we maintain the balance between giving and receiving. A number of years ago, I had a reading that was really impactful in my life. The medium told me that my life was out of balance. She said I knew all about giving, but was not allowing myself to receive. I began to recognize all the times I said, "I've got it," "No, thanks, I don't need any help," "You don't have to," and "What can I do for you?" She said my energy looked like everyone in my life had a straw stuck into it and were sucking the life force out of me. She told me that the behavior was self-reinforcing, because I was only attracting people who were interested in taking. She said that people who live in balance couldn't get anywhere near me because my energy didn't allow it.

If we are out of balance, and only are adept at giving, we may end up feeling drained because of the one way flow in our lives. Following that reading, I made some adjustments in my relationships. I gradually learned to say, "Yes, thank you," and "It would be great if you would do that." It was a little challenging at first, because I grew up in the time of women being encouraged to be strong and independent and to do everything for themselves. I believed that asking for and accepting help could be construed as weakness, and was a betrayal of all things feminist. I grew to realize that accepting help can both help us live in balance, and is also a gift to the giver in allowing them to feel useful and needed. Going forward, I began to pay attention to whether or not the relationships in my life were reciprocal. Not in the sense of keeping score, but more in being aware that there was give and take, and some sense of balance.

In thinking about the balance within ourselves, we have physical, mental, emotional, and spiritual bodies, and it is important to pay attention to balance in each of these aspects of ourselves. If we are completely sedentary, we may be out of balance in the physical area. It is useful to pay attention to what kinds of exercise work for our bodies, and how we feel when we move in ways that make sense for our bodies. What we choose to eat and drink has a major effect on our physical bodies. Are we getting enough rest to allow ourselves to regenerate and renew our physical energy? Do we pay attention to the balance between work and play in our lives?

Some people, including my mother, experience a lot of challenges in the mental area. My mother was labeled "manic-depressive," which was later relabeled as "bi-polar," as her mental energy and moods swung in wide arcs that caused her to feel very unbalanced at times. What we read, watch, listen to, and feed our brains with affects our mental balance.

Taking care of ourselves and having balance emotionally, means having outlets for our feelings, making sure to have someone to listen to us when we have something to share, and being able to connect in real and meaningful ways. When our emotions are out of balance, we might find ourselves spiraling into depression, unable to stop crying, and sometimes going to the extreme of choosing to end our own lives. Some people may shut off emotionally, refusing to allow feelings to surface in any discernible way, which is equally detrimental.

Being spiritually balanced can mean giving ourselves quiet time to connect with Source. I spend time each morning doing meditation and affirmations to set the tone for my day. I do Reiki on myself each day. Reiki is a balancing energy, and when our energy is in balance, we are much more able to heal ourselves. Finding the ways in which we feel spiritually balanced makes a difference in our ability to function optimally in our human forms.

It can be useful to think about some of the other ways that balance may operate in our lives. There is the balance between quiet and noise, rest and activity, work and play, being with others and being alone, taking care of others and taking care of ourselves. As we move through our lives, it is valuable to pay attention to balance in the physical, mental, emotional, and spiritual realms in order to accomplish our journey as gracefully as possible, and reach our highest and best potential.

CONSCIOUSNESS

3/11/18

We had the choice of Abundance and Intention for our topics this month. In my mind, they are intertwined, and the underlying premise is our consciousness. Consciousness is the lens or filter through which we view everything in our lives. It affects how we go about our lives. One way I sometimes think about consciousness is that it is our inner light. We have the ability to raise our consciousness, and make our inner light glow more brightly, with each breath we take.

In the book, "A Deep Breath of Life," author Alan Cohen has some pertinent things to say about consciousness. He cites a woman going through a divorce whose husband wants the very nice car she is driving. She says that because she brought the car into the marriage, at first she argued with him. Then she realized that it was her consciousness that drew the car to her, and that it didn't matter if he took that car, because she had the ability to draw a dozen cars like that to her. Cohen says, "What we have is not a result of luck or circumstance, but thought and attitude...The life we live is not cast upon us like a net, it is magnetized by our attitude...The most powerful way to improve your circumstances is by upgrading your attitude."

What we think, what we say, and what we do is what we draw more of into our lives – law of attraction, law of creation. What are we creating with our consciousness? Lack or abundance. Happiness or unhappiness. Wealth or poverty. Health or dis-ease. Love or loneliness.

How do we raise our consciousness, and cause our inner light to glow more brightly? Our thoughts, words, and actions, and the people, places, and things we surround ourselves with, are what contribute to our consciousness. Just as the food we feed our bodies comprises our physical makeup, what we read, watch, and listen to, and with whom and where we spend our time feeds our spirit. One of the most powerful things that affects our consciousness is what we tell ourselves. That small voice inside our head can be our most powerful ally or our worst enemy. Our self-worth and self-esteem greatly affect the way we see ourselves, and the way we operate in the world.

Things that may be ingrained in us from childhood can be very powerful, also. A few years ago, one of my daughters described me as a "judgmental Italian mother." Having had one of those myself, I immediately took offense. But because I respect my daughters, and listen to what they have to say, I have been examining the parts of that description that fit for me, and deciding what I want to do about it. I know that I am a work in progress, and am willing to give myself credit for learning and growing as I move forward on my path. It comes back to consciousness. I have talked in the past about the issues I have had with being impatient, intolerant, and entitled, and I think this relates. I had to learn to love and accept the "judgmental Italian mother" part of me, in order to change my consciousness about it.

One of the places I was noticing it rearing its head was in the improv troupe that I perform with. I found myself picking apart everything that I and my fellow troupe members were doing. After each show, when we would gather to discuss the show, even when others thought the show had gone well, I would be rolling my eyes, and offering my opinions about each flaw that I had observed. As you might imagine, this was not well received. I realized that, first of all, others were not necessarily interested in my opinions. Secondly, we are all volunteers, and the primary goal of doing improv is to have fun. I had lost sight of that for myself. In the last few months, I have gotten back to having fun. I have changed my consciousness about doing improv. These days, I show up, I do my best. After the shows, I listen respectfully, and if I have comments to make, they are always compliments about the things people have done well that night. It feels so much better. I have changed the way I think, the things I say, and what I'm doing, and it has shifted my consciousness.

In considering abundance consciousness, it is useful to consider its opposite, which is lack. Whenever we think "not enough," whether it is attendees at an event, money in the bank, or time, that is an example of lack consciousness. There is always plenty for everyone. When we think and intend that there is plenty, there is always enough. At the improv theater where I perform, some of the players are concerned with how many people are in the audience. How many are enough? For me, it is always my intention to do the best that I possibly can whether there are a handful of people in the audience or a sold out house. Do we perform for the people who are there or the people who are not?

Some things make our consciousness glow more brightly, and some things may dim our light, and challenge us to maintain a higher level of consciousness. I've been going through a bit of a challenging time in recovering from a partial knee replacement in the last month. Having a physical limitation, even when it's temporary, has had an effect on my consciousness. I can't do many of the things I'm accustomed to doing with ease. I do a little, then need to rest a lot. I sometimes feel isolated, and have had moments of feeling very emotional. It does not feel like my inner light is glowing very brightly at times. Having a hip replacement seven years ago was a particularly dark time for me. I learned a lot about asking for and accepting help. Going through this more recent experience has been an interesting growth marker for me. Knowing some of the challenges that can accompany recovery, I am able to see some of the ways in which my consciousness has changed, particularly in the area of asking for and accepting help. I have been reaching out to friends and family, and saying "yes" and "thank you" on a daily basis. Although this recovery is still challenging, I notice a huge difference from seven years ago. One of the areas that I'm still working on is being patient with myself and the process of recovery. This change in consciousness remains a challenge for me.

One of the most important ways to raise your consciousness is to be in touch with your godself. Take a moment and close your eyes, and breathe. Consider the thought: Be still and know that you are God... Be still and know that you are God... Be still and know that you are God. Are you willing to be the Source, the knowing, the power, the love? This can be your greatest gift to yourself, to embrace your godself, expand your consciousness, allow your inner light to glow brightly, and know that all things are possible.

PURPOSE

5/6/18

Our topic for this month is Purpose. What is our life's purpose? Picasso said, "The meaning of life is to find your gift. The purpose of life is to give it away." As metaphysicians, we understand that one of our primary goals is to know ourselves. In knowing ourselves, our life's purpose becomes clear to us.

Recently, I read a blog a friend wrote which inspired me to think of how developing our life's purpose can be likened to a tree. A tree has roots which are akin to the things we learn as we are growing up. The roots are our foundation. If they are strong and well-developed, they reach deep into the earth, and form an extensive network that supports us as we grow, and allows us to stand strong, even in harsh conditions. Our family, our community, our values, our spiritual beliefs are some of the things which comprise our roots. Our roots anchor and ground and support us, allowing us flexibility as we grow. Our ancestors, our genetics, and even our past lives are also part of our roots. Many factors contribute to how we grow and develop, and how we grow and develop influences what our life's purpose becomes.

A tree needs water, air, and light to live and grow. These are some of the things that nourish us on a daily basis, the ways in which we take care of ourselves. Some of the things we need include love, friendship, and a daily practice of connection with Source. We need space and freedom to grow and develop. We need light in the form of the ideas that we surround ourselves with, what we read, what we watch and listen to, the people, places, and things with which we surround ourselves. At times, we need to prune the thoughts and ideas and choices that may have served us at one time, but may no longer serve us, in order to make room for new ideas to grow and develop.

In Picasso's words, when we discover our gift, our purpose is to give it away. Think about how many different kinds of trees exist. Some trunks are slim and flexible. Some are massive and solid. Some are deciduous, going through cycles of losing their leaves and regenerating each year, while others retain their foliage throughout the year. Some are made to withstand harsh, cold climates, and others ideal for the tropics. Some trees are cultivated simply for their beauty, others are more functional. Some trees are homes to animals and birds. Some provide shade and shelter. Some bear fruit for nourishment. Even when a tree is cut down, it may be used for lumber to provide homes or for fuel to build fires to provide warmth and the ability to cook food to sustain life. Like the fruit from a tree, when we discover our gift, our purpose is to give it away.

A tree's purpose, as well as our own, may evolve over time. When a farmer plants a tree in a field, the sapling may have a fence around it to protect it from being trampled by the cows. As the tree grows large and strong, it may provide shade and a place to scratch the backs of those same cows. Later in life, after having had some kind of career, and perhaps having raised a family, one may reevaluate one's purpose in life, and choose yet another expression of purpose.

As spiritual beings having a human existence and learning all we can from it, each of us has a purpose to this existence. How do we discover what our life's purpose is, and how do we go about giving it away? In the last few months, I have had a number of conversations with people about their life's purpose. This question can be approached differently at various times in a person's life. A person may come to understand that their life's purpose is to serve. How they choose to explore that can look very different from one person to another. One person may experience a religious calling and enter the priesthood or become a nun, and choose to serve in that way. Another may become a doctor or nurse, and choose to serve the physical needs of people around them. Some may be called to teach in one form or another, and serve others in that way. Some people choose to serve their country by enlisting in the military. Some people choose to feed the physical body, others choose to feed the soul. The consistent thread, no matter what path we choose, is that it is fulfilling. A useful question to ask ourselves is how can we contribute.

How do we determine our life's purpose? One way is by listening to our inner guidance, and paying attention to the experiences that resonate most strongly for us. My mother's diagnosis of manic-depression when I was 14 years old began a role reversal where I was the one taking care of her that continued for the rest of her life. Our relationship was challenging, but definitely contributed to my understanding of my life's purpose. Shortly before she passed, my mother told me that no one could or would have taken better care of her than I had. She said that she and my dad had always worried because I didn't have a regular full time job, but that now she understood what my life's work was, and that she was very proud of me. Taking care of others in a whole variety of ways has been a significant part of my life's purpose. The path to developing as a Reiki Master Teacher and Metaphysical Minister has been one of becoming more and more of who I am, rather than what I do. In terms of life's purpose, I know that the ability to listen, hold space, and act in the capacity of mother figure to my own children and others has been very important for me.

If we are on the path that is for our highest and best good, it will bring us joy and lift our spirit. We are not meant to drudge through life in pain and misery. We are meant to soar, as we become more and more of who we truly are. And each of us is unique. Finding your life's purpose is an individual journey. If we do what others tell us to do, or what society demands, or what we think we "should" do, it may not fulfill us. Our task is to forge our own path in the best way we can. As Dr. Suess put it so succinctly, "Today you are You, that is truer than true. There is no one alive who is Youer than You."

As we move through life, continuing to determine what our life's purpose is, we can pay attention to the things that bring us joy, lift our spirit, and make our hearts sing. Moving in the direction that is for our highest and best good serves ourselves as we serve others. Like a tree, we put down roots, take in water, light, and air, and bloom in the way that is just right for us. Like a tree, we find our gift, then give it away.

COMPASSION AND FORGIVENESS

6/10/18

This year, Community of Light speakers have the choice of two topics each month. I wasn't sure whether I was going to speak this month, then I read the topics: Compassion and Forgiveness. And I knew that I needed to write and speak about these topics for my own personal growth. I have been noticing how "judge-y" I can be for a while now. There is a song from the musical South Pacific called, "You've Got To Be Carefully Taught." It's about prejudice, and learning to hate and fear anyone who is different from you. And that we're not born this way, but learn it from those around us. My parents were both very critical and judgmental, and I was carefully taught. I notice how often I do that now with others. I notice other people's weight, and judge. I see how they dance, and judge. I look at how they parent their children, and judge. I watch how they perform improv, and judge. I see their spelling and grammar, and judge. I notice how they drive, and judge. And as these thoughts come through my mind, my inner knowing responds with, "Send only love." I do my best to listen to my inner knowing, and change the patterns I learned...sometimes with more success than others.

As I notice the times when I judge, I am reminded of the quote: "Be kind, for everyone you meet is fighting a hard battle." This resonates very strongly for me. As we remember that we often don't know what's happening behind the scenes of those around us, it is important to be compassionate, and make allowances for whatever may be happening to others. In the book, "A Deep Breath of Life," author Alan Cohen talks about a religious man who lived across the street from a prostitute. Every time a customer left her house, the man placed a stone in a little pile, symbolizing the extent of her sins. Years later, they died within a short time of each other. When shown to his heavenly place, he was shocked to find a pile of stones like the mound he had built to mark the prostitute's wrongdoings. Then, he noticed the magnificent estate where the prostitute strolled. He was sure there was some mistake. He was a religious man, and she was a prostitute. A voice answered that there was no mistake. It said that the woman did the only thing she could to support her young daughter, and with each customer, she prayed to God to get out of her situation. The voice said that the man was only fascinated with her sins. She was talking to God, and he was talking to rocks. At the end, each got what they prayed for. This story reminds us that things are not always what they seem. Making the choice to be compassionate, rather than to judge, is for the highest and best good of each of us.

On our path of spiritual growth and development, there are many tools that we can use. One of the tools I use is writing with soap on my bathroom mirror. I use this technique to remind myself of the things I need to work on or focus on. Because soap stands out well, but also washes off easily, I find this to be an effective technique. One of the words I have used on more than one occasion is Compassion. This was especially true during the last several months of my mother's life. My relationship with my mother was quite challenging for many reasons. She passed almost eight years ago, and I still find myself working on my relationship with her. While my mother was alive, I had to dig deep to find compassion for her within myself. I didn't always understand her. I frequently disagreed with her. I felt like some of the choices that she made were very limiting. I chose to parent very differently than she did. My mother only worked for a few years in her life, then got married, and chose to place her husband's needs and wishes ahead of her own much of the time. She had serious challenges with mental health, beginning when I was in my early teens, and to a great extent, our roles were reversed from then on. Some years after she passed, she came to me in meditation, and told me that she had chosen the life and challenges that she went through, so that I could learn what I needed to learn, and become the person that I have become. That impacted me very strongly, and I had far more appreciation and compassion for her after that.

What happens when we feel compassion, and when we experience compassion from others towards ourselves? When we feel compassion, we are reminded of our humanity. We are reminded that we are all in this together. We are reminded that we are all connected, and what happens to one of us, happens to all of us. It increases our understanding of each other. When we experience compassion from others, it can soothe us. We feel supported. It brings us closer to one another. The more we understand one another, the more we are able to know that we are all in this together, and do not have to do everything alone.

Compassion and Forgiveness are inextricably tied together for me. In understanding compassion, it is essential to be forgiving...forgiving of others, and even more importantly, forgiving of ourselves. In a talk I did several years ago, I had listened to one of the other minister's talks and was inspired by it. She said it had been some time since she'd spoken at the spiritual community, so she'd asked God what she should speak about, and she specified that she wanted it to be new and different and spectacular. She said the answer came back as, "Forgiveness." She said she told God that wasn't new or different, and God answered, "It's crucial." I have to agree with her and God. Forgiveness is crucial. It is especially important to begin with forgiving ourselves. As I notice myself judging, it is essential for me to forgive myself, in order to move forward. I have to forgive myself for not always being the person I aspire to be. I have to forgive myself for being impatient, and short-tempered, and less kind than I would like. I have to forgive myself for trying to control events and situations. I have to forgive myself and others, and loose myself and others to the highest and best good. I had to forgive myself for the way I acted with my mom. I came to understand that she was doing the best that she could, and forgave her, too. Forgiving ourselves and others is crucial because it frees us from the past, and allows us to move forward with ease.

In a meditation series, Oprah said that one of the most powerful definitions of forgiveness she ever heard was, "Forgiveness is giving up the hope that the past could have been any different." We all do the best we can at any given moment. As we move through our lives, it is useful for us to operate with as much compassion as we possibly can, knowing that everyone we meet is fighting a hard battle. It is useful for us to forgive ourselves and others, in order to move forward with grace and ease, making space for us to be the best selves that we are capable of being.

ONENESS AND SEPARATION

9/23/18

"We are all in this together," is a phrase I often use. In thinking about Oneness and Separation for this month, it seems particularly appropriate. We are part of a whole. What happens to one of us affects each of us. We are connected at the deepest level of our souls. If we conceive of God as everyone and everything, there is no separation between us and God. There is no separation between us and each other. And there is no separation between us and all that is. Sometimes remembering that is easier than at other times.

Connection is a basic human need. How do we connect with others, and experience oneness? In this day and age, technology provides us with so many options like texting, instant messaging, Skype, Face Time, What's App, cell phone calls, landline calls. It's amazing to be able to reach out to someone anywhere in the world at a moment's notice. When I spent a couple of months in Mexico in 1973, it wasn't even possible to send a letter that would have arrived before I got home. It's useful to be able to connect in all the ways that technology allows for, and it's important to remember the value of actual human contact, and not let technology replace that.

When we connect with someone physically, it might be a small touch, a handshake, a hug, or a more intimate connection. One of my dance teachers told me I was a "connection junkie." I really enjoy connecting with others in many different ways, dance being an important one for me. Hugs can be a way to connect with others, and definitely make a difference in my day. Family therapist Virginia Satir once said, "We need 4 hugs a day for survival. We need 8 hugs a day for maintenance. We need 12 hugs a day for growth." Hugs can actually affect your physical well-being. I read that "hugging increases levels of the "love hormone" oxytocin. ... A 20-second hug, along with 10 minutes of hand-holding, also reduces the harmful physical effects of stress, including its impact on your blood pressure and heart rate."

What are some other ways we connect with others? Sometimes, just making eye contact with someone serves as connection. When we have a conversation with someone, we might experience varying levels of connection from "this is enjoyable" to "this person really understands and gets me on a deep and personal level." The more we connect with another, the more sense of oneness we feel. When we feel happy, loving, grateful, and relaxed, we may feel a sense of oneness and connection. There are sometimes people we meet and have the sense we have known them forever, and feel oneness. And others that we instinctively want nothing whatsoever to do with, and feel separation. Sometimes acknowledging our oneness is as simple as holding the door open for a stranger, and other times it's as deep as holding someone's hand, and being completely present for them, as they prepare for their transition from the earth plane.

We might be aware of spiritual connection. How often are you thinking about someone, and soon after get a call or text from them? There can also be connection between the earth plane and the spirit plane, with people who have either not yet arrived physically or have made their transition. If we open ourselves to these kinds of experiences, we may notice different ways of connecting.

When someone close to us makes the transition from the

physical plane, we often feel the separation as pain and loss. We may believe we are unable to communicate with them anymore. Although it may not be possible to pick up the phone and talk to them, we are still able to communicate in other ways. Sometimes there will be a sound, a feeling, a thought, or even a smell that reminds us of their presence. When someone leaves suddenly and abruptly, especially if they are young, and make the choice to end their physical existence, it can be jarring to those close to them. When we remember that we are all connected, all one, it can be comforting to us.

Recently, I experienced the loss of three people within 24 hours. The first was the younger brother of a very close friend. He was 23 years old, and chose to end his own life. Although I deeply believe that some people just need to go home, I also feel a unique kind of sorrow for someone who ends their life before they've had a chance to really live it. The other two were women in their 70's that I had been very close to, one for 41 years and one for 16 years. Their transitions were both sudden due to unexpected medical issues. In both cases, I can't believe they're gone. I'm going through a grieving process in the wake of their passings. I notice memories that come to the surface of my mind, and I feel connected to them. Sometimes, the feelings of missing them cause me to feel sad, and I allow the grief to wash through me, because that is my human reaction to the situation. It has been a bit of a challenge to remember all the things I know and believe, in the wake of the feelings of grief. I am grateful for being able to reach out to friends and family to ask for help, and to connect with them as I mourn. Death is a part of life, and the way we choose to deal with it can either promote oneness or separation.

What causes us to feel separation from each other or from whatever we conceive of as God? When we focus on our differences we feel separate. When we look at things like religious or political beliefs, size and shape, cultural attributes, language, or skin color, and focus on the differences, we feel separate. When we experience feelings of anger, hatred, insecurity, or disrespect, we feel separate.

When we feel love, we are one. When we feel anger, we are separate. When we honor each other, we are one. When we disrespect each other, we are separate. When we trust, we are one. When we doubt, we are separate. When we take care of each other, we are one. When we turn away, we are separate. When we focus on connection, and the things we may have in common, including our humanity and the fact that we are spiritual beings having a human existence, we are one. When we remember that we are all in this together, we are one.

CHOICES

10/14/18

Our topic for this month is Choices. The good news is that with each breath we take, no matter what choices we have made in the past, we have the opportunity to make a choice that is for our highest and best good. Sometimes we hear people say, "I had no choice." This is simply not true. We always have a choice. Because at the very least, we have the choice in how to respond to any given situation. We always have a choice about our thoughts, words, and actions. We have choices about our attitudes, our expectations, and our perspective. We have choices about what we say to ourselves and what we say to others. And then we have choices about what we do or choose not to do. When we talk to my four and a half year old grandson, we often use the phrase, "Make a different choice." It's empowering to know and acknowledge that we can always make different choices, and the power to be able to make choices is huge, no matter how they turn out.

In improv, we talk about choices in every scene we do. There are no wrong choices. There are only choices that are stronger, that advance the scene, support our partners, and allow the characters and relationships to develop with ease. It's the same in our lives. Choices in themselves are not right or wrong. We make choices, and then there are positive or negative consequences. If we choose to see ourselves as victims, we may feel helpless and powerless. If we feel like life "just happens" to us, we may feel helpless and powerless. If we feel like things are just "bad luck", we may feel helpless and powerless. If we take responsibility for our choices, including the consequences we manifest in our own bodies, we feel powerful. Louise Hay's book, "Heal Your Body," lists many physical conditions, along with the root cause, and the affirmation to change our views. If we hold on to things like grief and resentment, we may develop dis-ease in our bodies. We can empower ourselves to own our choices and the consequences, and move forward for our highest and best good.

It may be useful to think about the kinds of choices we make during the course of a day. We choose whether or not to wake up to an alarm clock, and whether or not to hit the ground running. We choose what to feed our body, and in some cases, whether or not to feed our body. We choose how to feed our spirit, and whether or not to take time for daily contemplation and meditation. We choose who we spend time with. We choose what we watch or read, and how we react to it. We choose whether or not to work at a job that is fulfilling, and choose whether or not we affirm prosperity in our lives. We choose how we speak to others, and how we listen. We choose how deeply we breathe with each breath we take.

It can be useful to think about the kinds of choices we make during the course of a week. Do we balance work and play? Do we balance rest and activity? Do we balance time with others and time alone? Then there are the choices we make during the course of a month or a year, and even through the course of a lifetime. We decide what to do about vacations and free time. We may choose to do what is best for ourselves or what is best for those around us. We choose whether or not to listen to our inner guidance. We choose where we want to live, both in terms of what kind of dwelling we live in, as well as the location. We choose the kinds of relationships we have. We choose whether or not to partner with someone on a long term basis, and whether or not we have children. We have the ability to choose abundance and prosperity. We choose whether or not to treat ourselves and others with loving kindness. We choose how we celebrate both the small and large events in our lives. Do we take time to acknowledge events that have significance or just let them pass by? On a soul level, it may be useful to think about the way we choose our family of origin, and all the experiences we create in the course of our lifetime(s).

When we face losses in our lives, we have many choices in how we deal with them. Dealing with the grief and loss of several people that were close to me in a very short period of time was challenging. One of the things I chose to do to help me deal with that grief and loss was to get some body work done. The experiences that we have get processed through our bodies, and it can be useful to support ourselves in that way by releasing through body work. After the practitioner worked on me, he gave me some words to use in processing the grief I have been feeling. He suggested that I say to those who have passed: "I love you. I loved the time we had together. I lovingly let you go." It's been very helpful to me to be able to say those words when the grief rises to the surface. It's been helpful to choose to let go, rather than to allow the grief to overwhelm me.

As we examine the choices we are making in our lives, we have the ability to look at both the choices and the consequences, and then decide if we want to continue on the same path, or make different choices, and go down a different path. In his poem, The Road Not Taken, Robert Frost writes, "Two roads diverged in a wood and I – I took the one less traveled by, and that has made all the difference." In another spiritual community that I was part of, there was an affirmation at the beginning of each service that included the words, "our choices belong to us, and are the seeds that create our lives." It can be useful to think about how the choices that we make create our lives, and how the path we choose makes all the difference.

It may be useful to examine the choices we make, and the consequences of those choices. The choices we make impact both our physical health and our spiritual health. There is a big difference in choosing to be upset or angry vs. choosing to communicate in order to resolve differences. And it works in reverse, too. We may look at what's happening in our lives or our bodies, and see what choices we made to lead to those outcomes. Then, we have the option to make different choices once again.

Recently, I was talking to someone who was describing the difference she perceived between the things we choose and the things that just happen to us, such as losing a job or health issues. In my personal belief system, I believe we choose and create everything that happens in our lives from a hangnail to a catastrophe. When we acknowledge that everything in our lives is a choice, we empower ourselves, because if it's a choice, then in the next moment, we have the power to make a different choice, and we have the power to change our lives.

LIGHT AND LOVE

1/27/19

Recently, I was in San Diego, staying in a high rise apartment overlooking the bay. When I woke up, the sky was completely overcast. As I sat and watched over the course of the next few hours, the cloud cover kept changing. At first, there were just shades of gray, then gradually some areas lightened. A little patch of blue appeared. Then a ray of sunlight. The clouds kept moving and changing, and more and more blue sky showed through, and more and more sunlight shone. As the clouds changed, and the light changed, the water also changed. Eventually, most of the clouds had disappeared, and the sun was shining brightly, and the water reflected many colors. Then over time, the clouds slowly crept back, covering more and more of the blue sky, and concealing more and more of the light, until it was completely overcast again. I found this to be an interesting metaphor for the light that we are. Our choice of topics for this month are Light and Love, which are very connected for me. Our light is always shining brightly and completely. Sometimes there are choices that we make and things in our path that obscure our ability to shine, or our ability to see our own light, or allow others to see it, but our light is always present. What conceals our light and what allows us to shine brightly?

Do you notice that your light feels diminished by anger or being critical and judgmental? How do physical illness, pain, depression, and loss obscure your light? When you feel fear or anxiety, do you notice the impact on your light? When you have thoughts of lack, loneliness, or being left out or excluded, does it feel like your light shines less brightly? It can be useful to notice what affects our ability to shine, so that we can allow the clouds to part, and experience the brightness of our light.

What are some of the things that allow us to experience our light more fully? In honoring Dr. Martin Luther King, Jr. this week, I saw a quote from him that applies very directly to this: "Darkness cannot drive out darkness. Only light can do that. Hate cannot drive out hate. Only love can do that." When we are kind, and do what we can for others, our light shines more brightly. When we listen to our inner guidance in meditation, our light shines more brightly. When we promote peace in ourselves and in our world, our light shines more brightly. When we are present and genuine, and loving with ourselves and each other, our light shines more brightly.

Which leads me to the second topic: Love. In the book, "The Five Love Languages," author Gary Chapman describes the primary ways in which people choose to express and receive love. They are Words of Affirmation, Acts of Service, Receiving Gifts, Quality Time, and Physical Touch. It can be useful to pay attention to the ways in which you both express love and prefer to receive it. Because if we are offering love, and it is not being well received and appreciated, or if we are wanting love, and aren't able to see that it is being offered, our light may feel like it is obscured.

"A Course in Miracles" states that love and fear are the most powerful emotions, and they cannot exist in the same space at the same time. When we choose love, we allow our light to shine more brightly. It's interesting to pay attention to where we find love in our lives. Some people find it easy to say, "I love you..." to friends, family members, romantic partners, etc. Some people find it very challenging. It's interesting to see what kind of salutation people use when signing emails and letters. Who do you feel like you love, and how do you express it?

Interacting with family can impact love and light. I got to spend time with my siblings recently, and felt like I learned some things about love in the process. We don't see each other as often as we did when my parents were alive. When I got together with my sister and my brother, I recognized an old pattern, where it feels like they gang up on me and tease me. It triggered old feelings of hurt. I did my best to respond differently, by not reacting in a negative way, and not returning hurtful remarks. I experienced my sister as being mean and sharp with me, and it was unpleasant. The next morning, I was feeling sad, and thinking that maybe I just didn't want to spend time with my family any more. Then, my sister came back from a walk, sat down, looked me in the eyes, and apologized for how she had treated me. We acknowledged the old patterns, and the fact that both of us have changed and grown, and decided we wanted to make different choices in how we treat each other going forward. For the rest of the visit, we did our best to be present and conscious with each other. Her ability to be present and genuine allowed her light to shine more brightly. The effect was that I felt closer to her than ever before. I always love my sister, and I feel like I love her a little bit more after this experience. The more loving we are, the more we allow our light to shine.

Our light is always present. I'd like you to take a moment and close your eyes. Imagine a spark at the core of your being that is, always has been, always will be your light. Feel it emanating from your heart center, and moving gently throughout your entire body. Then, feel it expand 360 degrees around you. With each beat of your heart, allow your light and love to expand just a little bit more. This is who you truly are...an infinite being of light and love. As you allow your Divine light to shine, you raise your own vibration, and the vibration of the planet. Breathe with ease and gently come back to this physical time and space, and when you are ready open your eyes, and be greeted by my love.

In moments of stress and challenge, the more you can remember your light, the better you feel, and the more able you are to cope with whatever happens in your life. Our light is always present. The choices we make with our thoughts, words, and actions affect our perception of our own light and others' ability to see our light. When we choose love, our light shines more brightly.

UNDERSTANDING, COMMUNICATION, & RECIPROCITY

3/17/19

There were three topics to choose from this month, Understanding, Communication, and Reciprocity. Once again, they felt very connected to me. Any one of them could have been enough for a whole talk, and it was exciting for me to see how they could be woven together. The topic Understanding was the subject of my very first talk over ten years ago, and it was interesting to see how my take on this has evolved over time. The words: "I understand" can be a very powerful way to connect with someone, a way to describe the sharing of a common experience. There are different levels of understanding. We might say, "I see," and understand on some level. Or we might really "get it," understanding it completely – physically, psychologically, emotionally, experientially – as fully as a human being can comprehend something, as Robert Heinlein describes in his book, "Stranger in a Strange Land," to "grok" it.

Understanding may evolve over time. When I was learning to dance, my understanding developed gradually. I knew about feeling the way music inspired my body to move, and I knew how to move my body. Over time, I learned the steps and footwork. What grew particularly was my understanding of connection, and how to follow. When I was learning to do Reiki and healing, I learned to open myself up to the energy. When I first felt the flow of energy, it unnerved me a little. Over time, my understanding of energy flow, and what happens in my body and in the other person's body, grew and developed, and I was able to allow the energy to flow easily and freely. As I work on someone, sometimes information comes up for me to share with them. My understanding of this grows as my abilities grow. Understanding increases my comfort level.

Metaphysically, understanding is represented by the feet. Here are a few examples of common expressions that are related to understanding. Think about taking a step back so that you can see something more clearly, see the bigger picture. When you only look at one piece of a puzzle, you can only see that piece. When you step back, you can see the whole picture, and then the single piece makes sense in a whole different way. Think about stepping into the unknown as we take on new challenges. When we get "tripped up," how do we right ourselves? Sometimes we understand the importance of taking baby steps, and other times are willing to take a leap of faith. There are many different ways of taking steps on our path of growth and development, and in our understanding of ourselves and each other.

As we look at where we've been, we have a better understanding of where we are, and where we're going. As we understand ourselves, we have a better understanding of each other, and the world around us. One of the ways we increase our understanding of each other is through our next topic, Communication. There are so many different kinds of communication, and the ways in which we can communicate change as technology advances. Where we once used phones just for phone calls, we can now video chat or send email, texts, snaps, and tweets. We can communicate with our words. We can use symbols or emojis. With so many ways to communicate, it's even more important to be clear in our communication with each other. When we communicate through digital means, we miss the non-verbal nuances that are such an important component of communication. We always communicate with a look, a touch, a gesture, a tone of voice, a body position. Giving a gift is a form of communication. We can give or withhold affection, and that is definitely a type of communication. What we say and what we don't say is all part of communication. Dance is another kind of communication, and it's important to be able to listen as we move our bodies together to create a flow that works well for both partners.

There is also the kind of communication that comes to us in other ways. In my experience, the messages that we give come through us. I feel like my talks show up for me. Have you ever had the experience of thinking of someone, and then they call or show up? There are the types of communication that seem straightforward and direct, and the types that are less easily explained. One of my friends finds feathers unexpectedly, and feels it's her mother communicating from the other side. Sometimes a song will run through our head, or we will see an interesting message on a billboard, and we understand that this is a type of communication. As we allow ourselves to be open to possibilities, we may find ourselves learning new ways to communicate, and we may understand different types of communication that come to us.

One of the things that enhances our communication with each other is our third topic, Reciprocity. I had a reading done in 2002 that was very impactful in my life. The woman told me that I knew all about giving and not much about receiving. She said that people who live in balance couldn't get anywhere near me because I didn't give them the opportunity to give to me. She said that I was depleted because I had no source, and just allowed people to take from me. As a result of that reading, there were some relationships that I changed immediately. Since then, I pay attention to reciprocity in relationships. It doesn't mean that I keep some kind of scorecard. It means I am aware of balance. I have come to understand the importance of being able to ask for help when I need it, and to say thank you, and accept help when it is offered. When we offer something to someone else, it is important that some type of exchange be available, in order to live in balance. This is one of the basic premises in Reiki. When we offer energy work to someone, or offer to teach them, there needs to be an opportunity for exchange of some kind. People feel in balance when there is an exchange component to their inter-actions, and relationships are more balanced when there is re-ciprocity. There is a power dynamic that may not be healthy that operates when only one person is doing the giving. In dan-cing, the give and take between the partners is what makes the connection special.

In communicating with each other in a reciprocal way, it's important to hold space for each other for whatever each of us might be needing in any given moment. As we understand ourselves and each other, and communicate as effectively as possible, we become the best version of ourselves. As we be-come the best version of ourselves, we contribute to raising the vibration of our planet, knowing that we are all in this to-gether, and making it a better place for all.

PATIENCE AND TIMING

6/9/19

The topics I chose for this month are Patience and Timing. As an improv comedian, I am very aware of the importance of timing. It can make or break a scene. It can mean the difference between a huge laugh and falling flat on your face. We commonly use expressions about timing. "Timing is everything." "His timing was just a little off." "He had the worst timing." "Two timing." "Being in the right place at the right time." The same amount of time might feel like a split second or feel like it takes hours. Time can fly or crawl. Our experience of time can slow down or speed up depending on what we're feeling. Patience can play an important role in timing, because if we are impatient, we may not be able to wait for the optimal time to do something for our best advantage.

When we think about events in our lives, timing can be a crucial factor. When is the most beneficial time to ask for a raise, to ask someone out on a date, to have an important conversation, to plan a celebration? When we listen to our inner guidance, we are often directed one way or another. There are times when my finger is poised to dial the phone, and my guidance tells me to wait. Timing certainly operated in interesting ways in my dad's life. My dad lived through the stock market crash of 1929, and the Depression. In 1938, he moved from New York to California because he couldn't find work and support his family. When his father became gravely ill, my dad took his three year old son on the train back to New York. My brother became ill on the trip, and they had to stop in Chicago to see a doctor. By the time they reached New York, my grandfather had already passed. Several months later, my father bought new furniture from Sears, and it was delivered on December 6th, 1941. The bombing of Pearl Harbor happened the next day. Because there were so few men living in California at that time, even though he was 35 years old with a wife and child, my father was drafted into the Army to serve in World War II. Timing is everything.

As humans, we often choose interesting lessons in patience. In our lives, things happen in the proper sequence and in the proper time, even though it doesn't always feel that way to our impatient, human selves. I'm sure most of us are familiar with the passage: "To everything there is a season, and a time to every purpose under heaven." Divine Order always operates perfectly in our lives. Sometimes we just need to be reminded of that. This week, some crystal clear examples of patience and timing showed up in my life. I had a bunch of errands to do, and had just finished the last one, when I realized I had a flat tire. Although I had just been driving all over the place, when I got the flat, I was safely in a parking lot. Perfect timing. Roadside assistance came after a reasonable amount of time and changed the tire. Patience paid off. When I tried to start the car, the battery was dead. Although the technician was still nearby, he said he couldn't jump start the car because he had another call to respond to, and that I needed to initiate a new service call. Patience activated again. I had an appointment that I needed to get to, so I called a Lyft and went to my appointment. I called Roadside Assistance again, and after my appointment, met the same person back at my car to jump start the battery. Perfect timing. Then I drove to Auto Zone, and had the battery tested and replaced, which only took a few minutes, and didn't cost anything because of the warranty. Perfect timing. Then I drove to Walmart to get the tire fixed, and ended up sitting there for two hours because they were short handed. Patience. I got finished just in time to make it to the movie that I had purchased tickets for in the morning. Perfect timing.

As I thought about Patience and Timing, the words "this too shall pass" kept coming to mind. Sometimes, we get very caught up in whatever moment we are experiencing. It can be useful to remember that "this too shall pass." Whether it's turmoil over a relationship, challenges at work, excitement over meeting someone new, or contentment about an accomplishment, this too shall pass. Whether it's the best of times or the worst of times, this too shall pass. As spiritual beings having a human existence, sometimes we can get caught up in any given moment. It can be useful to keep perspective on the fleeting nature of our existence, and remember that in each moment, we are doing the best we can, and "this too shall pass."

When we are caught up in any given moment, it can be challenging to remember the bigger picture. In the Greek language, there are two words for time. Chronos has to do with time of day, and the measurement of hours, minutes, and seconds. In Chronos, we may feel impatience. Kairos means "in nature's time," "in due time," and in metaphysical terms, in divine order. When we allow for things to happen in Kairos, we do not impose our own impatience of when is the right time for an event to unfold, but rather allow things to unfold in the fullness of time. We do not resist divine order, but rather are patient with ourselves and those around us, as we allow for fulfillment with ease.

As spiritual beings having a human existence, it is so valuable for us to remember to be patient with ourselves. As we move through our lives, when we remember to breathe, we are more able to listen to our inner guidance about timing. It doesn't always feel like we get it right, but we do. We create and choose the experiences that are for our highest and best good in any given moment. In the same way we might be patient with a small child who is learning something new, it is optimal when we give ourselves time to become our best selves, offering encouragement and support, and loving kindness along the way. As we move forward on our path, being patient with ourselves and others, and remembering to be fully present in each moment, time becomes our ally instead of our enemy, and we allow ourselves to enjoy each moment to the fullest for our highest and best good.

In closing, let's remember that "to everything there is a season, and a time to every purpose under heaven." Let's sing it together: "To everything, turn, turn, turn...there is a season, turn, turn, turn...and a time to every purpose under heaven."

CHANGE & FREQUENCY

8/25/19

The topics for this month are Change and Frequency. When I first looked at the topics, I was pretty clear about what Change meant to me. I wondered what Frequency (or how often someone does something) had to do with metaphysics. Then I realized that it was not about Frequency as an occurrence, it was about Frequency as our *vibration*, and that was an AHA moment for me. I was talking to my daughter about this, and she said that how often and how consistently we do something can have a big effect on our ability to change, so that gave me something more to think about. Some of the questions I asked myself are: how do we change, and how does our vibration affect our ability to change, and our changes affect our vibration? In a recent discussion, my nephew was sharing information from a book he had read about changing habits, that involved cues and routines, and how to create lasting change in your life. How does how often we implement a thought or an action facilitate both our intention and our ability to change? And how do we evaluate whether or not we have made lasting changes?

How do we change? Sometimes we change just by living our lives. Our skin and our hair may look different as time goes by. Our joints may not function as optimally as they once did. Our energy may vary. Some people change their names, either because they want to change their vibration in the world, or by choosing to take someone else's name in marriage. What we are called on a daily basis affects our vibration, so names matter. Some people are called a variety of nicknames, and that affects our vibration, too. Sometimes we notice habits that we decide to change. One of the most publicized times of change is at the beginning of each year. We hear about "New Year's Resolutions." Gym memberships increase. Diets may be initiated. Habits are evaluated, and changes may be implemented. Smoking is one habit that people give a lot of attention to, one way or another. In order to make lasting changes, it is useful to look at the cues that exist in our lives, and the routines that we follow. In order to make changes, we begin with intention, then follow through with action.

One of the habits that I continually work on is my behavior while driving. I notice that I am very critical and judgmental about other people's driving choices, and am often very vocal in expressing my opinions. I have experimented with many different solutions over the years. Recently, as I notice my irritation being activated, I say to myself: I am safe, I am happy, I am comfortable, I am grateful. Using these words changes my vibration, and redirects my attention. Gratitude is always transformative for me, and paying attention to what I am grateful for raises my vibration.

Another change I have been working on is in my relationship with my grandson. I may have some issues with control... When my five year old grandson is defiant or doesn't listen, it triggers a reaction in me. I would feel myself getting angry, and sometimes would yell at him. This caused a very unpleasant response in him. He would get upset, and not want to be around me, and we would both end up feeling distressed. On my most recent visit, as soon as I started noticing myself getting worked up, I would stop. I would say something like: "My intention is that we have a pleasant time, that we talk to each other nicely, and listen and cooperate and have fun. What would you like to do?" This would change the vibration and energy of our interaction immediately. We could then both get on the same page, and have a mutual goal that we could work towards together. I was able to be consistent with this throughout my last visit, and it was such a pleasant change.

I notice that I often have strong reactions and opinions to many things that happen around me, whether or not they affect me directly. A couple of months ago, I was having lunch with a close friend, and in the course of our discussion, she said the words, "I don't have to have an opinion about that." Those words stopped me in my tracks. Being Italian, that was an option I had never considered. I have heard and used the expression: "not my circus, not my monkeys," which is helpful. But this took it to a whole different level for me. I have been implementing this change in my life. As I notice that I begin to get worked up about something, I remind myself, "I don't have to have an opinion about that." It changes my energy and vibration immediately, and settles me down. One of the requests that my daughter has made in the last several months is that I not comment negatively on whatever is happening, because apparently whatever I was thinking and feeling was falling straight out of my mouth! I've been actively working on this from the inside out. When I remind myself that I don't have to have an opinion about something, it changes my vibration, and in consequence, changes my external behavior also. During this recent visit, my daughter complimented me on the ways in which I'd changed. She said that she and her sister know me very well, and can tell when I'm being genuine and when I'm faking it. She said that whatever I'd been doing, it was working. When I asked her to elaborate, she said that I was actually being the person that I've said I wanted to be. I took this to mean that I had integrated the changes beyond just talking the talk.

In order to change, we first notice the behavior or habits that we wish to change, then set our intention. We pay attention to the choices that we make, and increase the rate at which we make the more positive choices. We then begin to feel the changes in our vibration, and the more positively we feel, the more rewarding the changes become, and the more able we are to maintain them consistently. With each breath, we gently and lovingly remind ourselves that in any given moment, we are doing the best we can. We affirm that we see clearly and act accordingly. We remember that our behavior changes our vibration and our vibration changes our behavior. And we move forward with the goal of being the best self that we can be.

REFERENCES

Cohen, A. (1996). *A Deep Breath of Life – Daily Inspirations for Heart Centered Living*. Carlsbad, CA: Hay House